Making Money

Paul Clitheroe is a founding director of IPAC Securities Ltd, one of Australia and New Zealand's best known research and investment houses, and has been involved in the investment industry since he graduated from the University of NSW in the late 1970s. He has completed the two-year post-graduate course offered by the Securities Institute and is an associate of that professional body. He was a board member of the Financial Planning Association of Australia between 1992 and 1994; in 1993 he was elected the Vice President and in 1994, the President.

Since June 1993 he has been hosting the prime-time Channel 9 program 'Money'. He has been a media commentator and conference speaker for over ten years and is regarded as a leading expert in the field of personal investment strategies and advice. Paul lives in Sydney with his wife, Vicki, and three young children.

Chris Walker is the director of Barrenjoey Communications, a marketing services consultancy. He has a BA and MBA from Macquarie University. He has wide commercial experience, primarily in property, media and new enterprise development. Chris lives in Sydney with his wife, Roberta, and daughter Grace.

Authors' Note

We want to keep this book as relevant as possible. If you have any ideas regarding financial matters that you think should be included in future editions, please write to Paul Clitheroe, 'Making Money', IPAC Securities Ltd, Locked Bag 15, Grosvenor Place, Sydney, NSW 2000.

D0316827

Making Money

Paul Clitheroe *written in association with Chris Walker*

Viking

Viking
Penguin Books Australia Ltd
487 Maroondah Highway, PO Box 257
Ringwood, Victoria 3134, Australia
Penguin Books Ltd
Harmondsworth, Middlesex, England
Viking Penguin, A Division of Penguin Books USA Inc.
375 Hudson Street, New York, New York 10014, USA
Penguin Books Canada Limited
10 Alcorn Avenue, Toronto, Ontario, Canada M4V 3B2
Penguin Books (N.Z.) Ltd
182–190 Wairau Road, Auckland 10, New Zealand

First published by Penguin Books Australia, 1995
10 9 8 7 6 5 4 3 2 1
Copyright © Clitheroe Communications Pty Ltd, 1995

Typeset in 11/13pt Sabon by Midland Typesetters, Maryborough, Vic. 3465
Made and printed in Australia by Australian Print Group

National Library of Australia
Cataloguing-in-Publication data:

Clitheroe, Paul.
Making money.

Includes index.
0670 86739 X.

1. Finance, Personal–Australia. I. Walker, Chris, 1954–
II. Title

332.02400994

Acknowledgements

Trying to put everything I've ever learnt about money into a book without resorting to jargon or an overdose of statistics has been a challenging task. As it was, it took about a year longer than I thought it would, and it certainly would not have seen the book-shelves for many more years if it was not for the help of my old university friend, Chris Walker.

Working with talented people is always a pleasure, but it is even more so when you have known them for many years. Chris played a vital role in helping me to research and flesh out many chapters in the book. In particular, his professional experience in the residential property market was of great value in setting out practical advice on buying a property.

Many others also provided assistance in helping to make this book as practical as possible. Wendy Oakes spent many months researching a whole range of issues for me, the IPAC research team also provided a number of graphs on their research conclusions to help reinforce some important money issues.

Thanks also to Martin Schoeddert, Professor Graeme Newell and Peter Wills from the Faculty of Management, University of Western Sydney.

I would also like to thank my personal assistant at IPAC Securities, Karen Schmitz. This book was written in between commitments to my Channel 9 'Money' program, IPAC, as well as to the birth of our third child! Without Karen to organise my business affairs, this book would have been an impossible task.

Finally, thanks also to the thousands of 'Money' show viewers who have written to me about their money experiences over the last three years. Much of this book reflects those experiences which you have shared with me.

Paul Clitheroe

Contents

Introduction

This book is about building wealth and investing your money wisely. It draws on all the experience that I have gathered in a decade and a half of listening to people's money concerns and giving them advice on how to best achieve their goals.

It is not a textbook full of dry academic theory. Nor does it provide 'hot tips' or 'get rich quick' schemes. It will provide you with a practical commonsense guide – in plain English – on how to 'get rich slow', and on how to best invest the money that you have.

I realised many years ago, that my clients and people I know rarely became financially comfortable due to a spectacular business success, a 'get rich quick' scheme, gambling or even luck. The huge majority of Australians who are financially comfortable, have got there by spending less than they earn year after year, and using their savings to build wealth.

Sounds simple, but I know it isn't easy to do. That's why this book opens with my ten essential steps to growing and protecting your wealth.

For those of you working to improve your financial position, I promise you that by following these steps you can 'get rich slow'. It's not difficult, it just requires some planning. Many people become depressed that it is just too hard to put some money aside on a 'normal' salary. Well, this book is for everyone – not just those earning a high income. I'll show how, for example, saving $1 a day can be turned into over $500,000. No miracles here, just a regular savings strategy, time, and the power of compounding returns.

For those who already have some money to invest – savings, an inheritance or retirement money – this book demystifies the world of investment. It explains in a practical fashion how and where to invest, managing investment risks and maximising the return on your money.

I have really enjoyed writing this book – with much help from my old friend, Chris Walker. It contains pretty much all I know about the essentials of investment.

My experience as a financial adviser has shown me that money alone does not bring happiness or health. In fact, I've seen all too often the destructive side of money. What money does is give you options about the type of life you, and those you love, want to lead.

This book will help you to take control of your money – and, therefore, take more control of your life.

CHAPTER ONE
Taking Control

Money. It seems to be a major issue for all of us in one way or another. During my school days I did odd jobs and picked oranges to give me a bit of pocket-money. During my uni days I was a part-time bartender at the Regent Hotel in Kensington near the University of New South Wales. The long summer holidays were usually spent in my home town of Griffith, again working as a bartender but this time at the Griffith Leagues Club. I'd rather like to pretend that I had a sophisticated plan for the money I earned, but I didn't. It was used to pay – in the main – for activities outside my studies. Things at the time that seemed vital, like golf balls, a couple of cheap, backpacking holidays or a six-pack of beer for a party or football game.

No, I didn't save a cent. My only defence (with the benefit of hindsight) is that I was investing in my own education. As I recall, at the time I was simply enjoying my early adult years – and thank heavens I did! One of my central philosophies when it comes to money, is to always remember that life is short.

I've now been working in the money business for around 16 years. Four years were as an employee of a major financial advisory company and then, in 1983, with four partners, I started up a company – IPAC Securities – where we specialise in investment research and advice for our clients. So, for over a decade and a half, I've been privileged to meet with a wide range of people to talk about their lives, hopes and fears, and how money relates to all of this.

Without any doubt, meeting with thousands of people, listening and advising, has taught me more about money and real life than anything I ever learnt at university. I've seen first-hand how money can cause real heartache but I've also seen how it can allow people to live the lives they want to lead and provide security and contentment. My goal with this book is to help you achieve the latter.

Wealth Builders and Wealth Protectors

Now, I know that the readers of this book will basically fall into two categories – 'wealth builders' and 'wealth protectors':

- Wealth builders. You are about to start working or you are like me, still working and trying to build up your wealth. You may have absolutely nothing, or you may be well on your way to having an amount of money that will support you without having to work. You'll be wondering how best to create wealth – buy a house, pay off the mortgage, top up super, or start your own business.
- Wealth protectors. You are like my dad or my clients who are using the wealth they have built to provide a satisfying lifestyle. You are concerned about your money not lasting for long enough, having enough income each year, helping or leaving money to the kids, volatile investment markets, confusing legislation and so on.

If you're a wealth builder, follow my 10 steps to financial security and you'll have the knowledge to get to where you want to go. If you're a wealth protector, most of my 10 steps will apply to your situation but you should also read my keys to successful investment in Chapter Eleven.

My 10 Steps to Financial Security

My real life money experience has taught me that there are 10 commonsense steps that will really work when it comes to your life and your money.

Step 1. Have a plan

It sounds sensible but the problem is: what is a plan and what should it look like? Now this is where personality comes into it. Some people have a very clear idea of where they want to be, others don't – but we all have *some* goals.

Before you can plan you must have objectives which may depend on your age. Here are some examples:

For a young person

- I am planning to complete my education by doing a three-year apprenticeship. During this time, I will earn little money as I am investing in my skills to allow me to earn a better income when I have completed my apprenticeship. This is my main objective.
- During the three years I will live at home, I plan to save $50 a week and I am going to use this to travel to Europe at the end of my apprenticeship. I will reassess my plan at that time as I may use the money to buy a car, or continue to save for a deposit on a home.
- My employer's contributions to super will form a base for my future.

Now while this may seem pretty vague remember that youth always requires flexibility. It isn't really possible to have a plan at age 18 or 20, that says at age 65 I will:

- have been happily married for 40 years
- have three children and six grandchildren
- own my home
- have an investment property
- be retired.

Life isn't that certain. The older you get, the more settled your life tends to become, so your plans firm up.

For a married couple with young children

- We will continue additional mortgage repayments to pay off the family home in nine years.
- At that stage, we will buy an investment property, start an investment plan or top up super.
- We will have sufficient insurance if one of us is injured, sick or dies.
- We will educate our children as well as we are able.
- We will continue to monitor our employers' super and to top this up if our budget allows us to do so. Our target is a 10% contribution each.
- We plan to be financially independent by age 65.

For a retiree

■ We wish to leave at least the value of our family home to our children. We have a will lodged with our solicitor.

■ We have $250,000 investment money. We plan to use that to give us $20,000 p.a. in income after tax. If doing this reduces the capital that is left to our children then that is acceptable.

■ We will apply for any pension benefits available to us.

■ Our investment plan will be one of security first. We will avoid high-return/high-risk investments.

■ We wish to stay in our home as long as possible. If, for health reasons, we cannot stay at home we will consider living in an environment where help is available.

⚷ KEY THOUGHT

Setting objectives is central to a plan. After all, there's not much point in having a plan if you have nothing to aim for!

Once you have set your objectives you have a good reason to do a plan – and a reason to stick to it. I'm sure our young apprentice is much better able to stick to his plan to save $50 a week by thinking about the end objective – the trip, car or home. Trying to save $50 a week for no particular reason does not work for long in my experience.

Now you can start to build your plan – which is how you achieve your objectives. You can get very sophisticated with your planning but in my experience, commonsense plans work best. Certainly a financial adviser can help you (but you will still need to be able to tell the adviser your objectives). Here's an example of a simple plan:

Objective	Plan
I want to save $50 a week.	Do a budget. Have $50 taken from your pay and transferred to a separate, low-fee savings account without ATM card access.

I want to pay off my mortgage in nine years.	Get your bank to work out how much your repayments need to be. Will your budget allow for this? Arrange to have your repayments increased.
I want to lead a comfortable life in my retirement.	Use your budget to plan how much you need to spend each year. Write down your assets, and what income your assets can generate and for how long. Can you get a pension? What level of risk are you comfortable with? You may find a financial adviser can help you here.

What Your Plan Should Contain

Your objectives.	Be as specific as you can. Set short- (this year), medium- (1 to 5 years) and long-term (5 years plus) objectives.
Your budget.	This is a 'must do' – 99.99% of us won't win Lotto or inherit $1 million. You will only achieve most of your objectives by spending less than you earn.
Your current financial position.	I own the following assets:

Home value: $180,000
Car value: $ 7,000
Bank account: $ 2,000
                      $189,000 (A)

I have the following debts:

Mortgage: $110,000
Credit cards: $ 1,000
                      $111,000 (B)

I have already built up assets with a net value of:
$78,000 (A−B)

Important facts.	My assets and my life are/ are not insured properly. I have a will that reflects my wishes.

Making Money

By working through these four items you have taken the first *key step* to controlling your money.

You understand where you are now. Your objectives tell you where you want to be. Your plan should take you from where you are today, to *where you want to be*.

> **0—⊤ Key thought**
> You will only achieve your objectives by spending less than you earn.

Step 2. Take control of your money

Chapter Two, 'Your Budget', gives practical details on how to budget and what to do if your budget doesn't work – which, believe me, happens all too often! But, before we go into that, I want to convince you that you *must take control of your money*, and budgeting, leading to saving, is a vital part of the process.

Now, it drives me absolutely nuts when I think that if you are on the average income of around $35,000 p.a., in your working life you will earn around $1.7 million in today's dollars. If inflation averages 3% this becomes $3.6 million. But how much are you likely to save? If you are like most people, not much, unless you do something about it!

I know life is expensive. And I reckon that you think if you earned an extra few thousand dollars, you'd be okay. But you know what? You wouldn't.

Let me explain. I have clients who earn as little as $20,000 and as much as $1.5 million a year. Guess what? They *all* have a problem saving money.

'That's ridiculous', I hear you saying. How could anyone earn so much money and not have some left over? Well, life is like that – our expectations and our expenditures grow in line with what we earn. We rapidly learn to spend the extra we make. Maybe my own situation is typical.

Back in my beer-pulling days at the Regent Hotel in 1974-6, I used to earn around $33 for two night shifts (let me remind you a large glass of beer cost 33 cents in 1974). My family paid my education fees and board at Baxter College at the University of New South Wales so the $33 was spending money – and, in those years, I always had some cash in my pocket. Nowadays, I earn a lot more than that but I rarely have spare cash.

Why? Well, there's the mortgage, three young kids, two cars, better clothes, eating out occasionally, taking holidays and so on. In 1974, my only possessions were jeans, T-shirts and a $120 pushbike. If it was too far for the bike, the bus was fine. My expectations have changed and my basic cost of living has soared.

Believe me, we tend to spend all we earn – and to justify it. But take note that many of us are living well beyond the basics (food, shelter, clothes) and are spending money on things we want (a selection of clothes, cars, holidays, movies, eating out) rather than on what we need.

θ━ Key thought

It's not what you earn that matters – it's how much you spend.

I have financially comfortable clients who have never earned above the basic wage. I also have clients who are nearly broke who earned 20 times the basic wage. What is the single difference? It's simple – my comfortably off clients consistently spent less than they earned and they saved the rest. They paid off their home, didn't build up credit card debt, and paid cash for cars, holidays and household goods.

θ━ Key thought

Make a commitment to the concept – if you can't afford it, you can't afford it.

I want you to take control of your money because life will be a lot happier if you do. But I don't want you to think you can't afford to have fun along the way. That's silly. I want you to do a budget that includes fun things in it. I want your budget to allow you to enjoy your money but still enable you to save.

And saving is critical, because if you can save on a regular basis you will become financially comfortable. If you can't, you won't.

Look, I realise budgeting for regular saving is pretty boring, but, it's 'getting rich slowly' and it's the only way I know how to *guarantee* that you will actually get there.

Now, if you have already tried a budget and found it doesn't work, don't despair. There is another way of achieving your goals without a budget to help you save. Read about it in Chapter Two – 'The damn budget doesn't work!'

Step 3. Save little, save often

I am told on a regular basis, 'the stuff you talk about makes sense, but it's all too hard'. But what many people don't realise is that you don't need to save a fortune every week. I'll talk more about this in Chapter Three, 'Savings', but let me entice you with a thought that, on the face of it, may sound preposterous.

If you save $1 a day during your working life, how much will you have at age 65? Well, if you can average 10% on your savings (which is quite possible), $1 a day saved from age 18 to age 65 should be worth around $500,000 after you pay tax on the 10% you earned each year. Two dollars a day is 1 million, $5 a day is $2.5 million. No miracles, no magic or silly numbers – just a sensible savings strategy and compound interest.

Hang on though – you (like me!) may not be 18. So how does it work for us? Well, when you're older, hopefully you can save more than $1 a day. Let's say you save $5 a day. In 25 years time, it should be worth over $200,000; $10 a day should be worth over $400,000. Even with only five years to save, $10 a day should be worth around $25,000.

Save more if you can and, as you read the rest of this book, I'll answer your questions about where to save – the mortgage, investment property, shares or super – and I'll give you lots of practical savings ideas. The point I want to make here is that, while the amount you save is important, it's a *commitment to regular savings* that makes the difference.

Step 4. Avoid punting and silly risks

If there is one thing experience has shown me, it is that risk equals return. Now, low-cost punts like Lotto, a lottery ticket, or a bet on the Melbourne Cup don't worry me at all. These are small things and can be good fun. I lose my money cheerfully, because we don't have a statement in our plan that says 'we plan to become comfortable by winning Lotto'. Incidentally, do you know what your chances are of winning Lotto? Well, it's around 7,059,052 to 1. I wouldn't count on it!

Humans seem to instinctively want to find an easy way to make money and one that involves little work, like the 'get rich quick' schemes you often see advertised in the papers. The ads use the words 'easy',' simple', 'no capital required', 'high returns', and 'get rich'. Clearly, the operators of these schemes understand human psychology.

Think about it, though. They want you to pay them to access *their* 'get rich quick' scheme. If it works so well, why don't they use their own scheme to get rich themselves? It's painfully obvious isn't it? The schemes don't work.

Here I'll take one bet I know I will win. I'll bet you the scheme operator uses your money to do what you should be doing – paying off a mortgage, buying shares or investing in property.

The only way I can see to make money out of 'get rich quick' schemes is to sell them to some mug or, preferably, lots of mugs which, I'm pleased to say, is not in my plan – and I hope it is not in yours.

As an investor you must also be careful when it comes to higher returns than you would normally expect. Do you remember the Estate Mortgage advertisements in 1990? They ran television and print ads claiming very high returns and that they were better than a bank or a building society.

Simple research would have shown you that their returns were up to 5% higher than equivalent investments. This is because they were lending money on high-risk projects. After all, if they were paying investors 17% (given their annual fee was around 2%), then they must have been lending money out at 19%.

Now, if you could borrow from a bank in 1990 at 15%, what sort of people borrowed from Estate Mortgage? As was soon discovered when Estate Mortgage collapsed in 1991, anyone prepared to pay 19% were borrowers who the banks wouldn't touch – and with good reason as it turned out. They were high-risk borrowers whose high failure rate ultimately brought Estate Mortgage down. The result was that hundreds of thousands of Estate Mortgage investors lost part or, in some cases, all of their life savings.

The message here is simple. If something offers a higher return it will have a higher risk. Don't get me wrong, though, I'm not anti risk. If you take no risk you must expect a low return. Just don't let anyone fool you into thinking you can get high return with low risk.

Investors should manage risk, not avoid it. As I demonstrate in Chapter Thirteen for instance, shares make a terrific long-term investment, although they are riskier than cash. Over 10 years, they typically earn you around 5% p.a. more on your investment than leaving it in a bank. With cash in a bank, however, your chances of losing money in any one year is zero, while with shares you have a 28% chance of losing money in any one year.

⊖━ Key thoughts
- Risk equals return.
- If it looks too good to be true, it is.
- Don't plan to be financially comfortable by punting.

Step 5. Don't plan to save cash

So, if you don't save cash what are you meant to save – sea shells? Not really – unless you live in a tribal community who uses shells as money.

Look at your budget for the *past* year. It may show that you should have saved $2,000 – but where is the money? It's most unlikely to be in your pocket or your standard savings account because, in my experience, Australians can't save cash.

The only way you can save is to put your savings away *before* you spend the cash. So, if you have planned to save around $2,000 a year, based on how you are paid you must plan to save either $38.50 a week, $77.00 a fortnight or $167.00 a month.

It's vital this amount is taken away from you *before* you spend it and that way you won't really notice its absence. So, either have your paymaster transfer it to a separate bank account or increase your mortgage repayments or your super contributions. This way you will 'get rich slow'.

☗━ Key thought

Have your savings automatically taken away *before you spend them.*

Step 6. Plan to own a home debt-free

Now, you don't need any convincing here do you? This is conventional wisdom. Yes, I know renting can be shown to be more cost-effective than home ownership in the short-term – but in the long-term home ownership comes out in front.

I also know negative gearing can be a very tax-effective way of buying a property in which you might one day live but, as a general rule, owning your own home and eliminating the debt against it as quickly as possible is a key wealth creation strategy.

We'll look at this in far more detail in Chapter Six, 'Owning a Home', but let me say again that first and foremost, plan to own a home.

Step 7. Super is good – invest in it!

It may take some work on my part to win you over to the line that super is good. You no doubt see it as confusing, ever-changing, overly complex, too restrictive, and loaded with fees. And, you are right.

Believe it or not, though, the government is on the right track with a compulsory super system. Australians are not good voluntary savers which is why many people own nothing at retirement except perhaps their home. And the only reason they own that is because the bank would have taken it away if they had not kept up their repayments.

I believe compulsory saving via super is good for us and it has so many elements that fit with my 10 key steps. It is regular saving; it's tax-efficient (really, it is!); it's generally invested in good quality long-term assets (shares, property and fixed interest); and the fact that (like your house) you really can't get your hands on the cash is also a huge plus. As *a part* of your long-term plan, super makes sense.

Step 8. Minimise tax

I am always amused when people complain about paying too much tax. On a global scale, we are at the low end of the tax take compared to societies that have a similar standard of living. More importantly, it seems to me that people who pay a lot of tax earn a lot of money. Investors who pay a lot of tax, have a lot of investment income.

An easy way to pay less tax is to earn less money. But who wants to do that? Overall, it rather pleases me when my tax bill goes up each year – it means I'm doing better.

Despite this somewhat arcane way of thinking, I believe you should still plan to legally minimise your tax. In other words, I want you to *legally avoid* tax, but *not illegally evade* tax. In Chapter Ten on 'Tax', I cover the basic as well as more complex ways of reducing your tax bill.

The key point is that while you should always try to minimise tax, you should never let tax minimisation strategies drive your investment decisions. For instance, if it is appropriate for you to borrow money for a good investment, go ahead and do it. And if this investment gives you tax advantages along the way, fine, treat that as a bonus, not as the main attraction. If you find yourself or an adviser saying, 'let's negatively gear (borrow money) for an investment to reduce tax', stop. Take a deep breath and think hard.

Don't let me give you the impression that borrowing money to invest is not legitimate, it is, but if the investment is not fundamentally sound you will *lose money you do not own*, outweighing any tax benefits you could ever hope to receive.

> ⚿ **Key thought**
> Focus on investment returns rather than on tax benefits. Tax should not drive your decisions.

Step 9. Protect assets

Now, I'm sure you already understand that you need to insure your home, contents, car and other valuables. This type of insurance is cheap and a 'must have'. However obvious it is, though, I estimate that over 50% of Australians either do not insure assets, or are underinsured.

The other asset you need to protect is *you*. What happens if you get sick, have an accident or, at the extreme end of it all, die? I am a very firm believer in buying as little insurance as you need but, at certain stages of your life, you really need quite a lot. Chapter Eight, 'Insurance' will provide you with the details you need.

Step 10. Take advice if you need it

You'll have to forgive my bias when I talk about the advantages of having a good adviser. I know there are plenty of shonks out there who want to separate you from your money, but there are also a growing number of excellent advisers who are not simply trying to flog you product for commission.

In Chapter Nineteen, 'Choosing an Adviser', I go into plenty of detail, but let me say here that you can plan to build and protect your wealth by yourself and you don't need to be Einstein to do it either. Simply following my 10 steps and reading this book will give you most of what you need to know – it's just that most of us find it more efficient to do what we do best and to consult others for assistance when we need it.

Even if you do choose to see an adviser you should still work through these 10 steps. The best way to use an adviser is not to be totally dependent on their skills but to develop a relationship where you both have an understanding of your plan. Then the adviser can be of great assistance in selecting and monitoring your investments, tax, and insurance.

Live the life you want to lead

Let me add one final point. It concerns me that a few people I know have reached their financial goals but have developed such squirrel-like habits that they hate spending money on anything. Remember, I believe the value of money is to give you options – *you must plan to have fun along the way*.

I would also hope that one day when you do stop work, that you recognise that part of your hard work was to give you freedom later in life. Unless you have accumulated millions you will then start to eat into your capital. But that's okay – that's what it's for!

From my perspective, an ideal financial situation for my and my wife's lifetimes is as follows:

My ideal financial situation for my lifetime

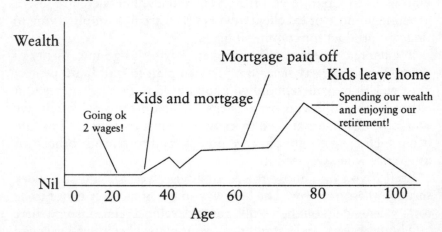

Here I'm assuming we die at 100 which is pretty optimistic despite my attempts to exercise and eat rice, fish and vegetables. So, realistically, the kids will inherit something because the odds say we will die in our late 70s to 80s. As you can see, we plan to spend our accumulated money to have a standard of living that we have planned for.

⚷ Key thought

It's quite amazing how a little commonsense and planning combine to make you rich – slowly!

So, there you have my 10 steps. It's not hard to sit down and use these steps to build your own plan. And, I hope you can see how important it is to have one, no matter how basic.

My 10 steps

1 Have a plan.
2 Take control of your money.
3 Save little, save often.
4 Avoid punting and silly risks.
5 Don't plan to save cash.
6 Plan to own a home debt-free.
7 Super is good – invest in it!
8 Minimise tax.
9 Protect assets.
10 Take advice if you need it.

Making Money

Key thoughts

- People tend to spend 110% of what they earn.
- You can't save cash.
- Being the richest person in the graveyard isn't very clever.
- People don't plan to fail, they fail to plan.

CHAPTER TWO
Your Budget

Budgeting! The very mention of it makes us wince. Why? Well, I think it's because budgeting confronts us with just how much money slips through our fingers – and with how little we have to show for it. But that's one of its purposes – getting that jolt is good for us.

Budgeting encourages us to take a disciplined approach to spending and saving, enabling us to reach short-, medium- and long-term goals which otherwise might prove unattainable. It helps us find extra money to put into investments, or to pay for a holiday. Budgeting is the most important and effective tool for getting our finances under control.

These are big claims I know, but have you ever heard of a successful business that doesn't have any plans? I'm sure you haven't, because businesses without plans don't last very long. And in business, at the heart of every plan is a budget.

A business' budget is designed to maintain financial control and to prevent money being wasted. These are the same as your goals so you have to treat yourself like a business. After all, you generate some pretty big figures too. (I mentioned previously that the current average Australian wage of around $35,000 per year multiplied by a working life of 47 years (from 18 to 65) works out at a hefty $1.7 million.) Yet, there are many Australians who, after a lifetime of work, end up with little more than the home they are living in – if they are lucky. Having a budget is the first step towards ensuring this doesn't happen to you.

Even people earning very good money never seem to have any. That's because they, like all of us, have a tendency to spend about 10% more than they earn, no matter what their income levels are. I have some very well-paid clients who say the solution to their lack of funds is to earn even more than they presently do. That's wrong. Chances are they will overspend any increased income they receive. In fact, some people who know they will be receiving a pay rise in December start spending more in July just to get used to the feeling of it!

What do I say to these people? I tell them to do a budget, find out where all the money is going and then cut back on the least necessary areas to the point where not only does their income not exceed expenditure, but there's actually something left over to save. This is what budgeting is all about.

θ━☞ Key thought

A budget tells you where your money is going, where you can cut back, and where you can save.

Whatever you do, don't convert your unspent income into cash and put it in your pocket – because you'll spend it! Saving cash is virtually impossible.

The important thing is to control your own life which means controlling your money and a budget is a very important part of the process of making it happen. Here are some aspects to consider:

The discipline has rewards

Most people don't like the discipline of a budget – but it does have its benefits. Without the discipline of a mortgage you would never pay your home off and without the discipline of a budget you would never save. There's a big stick hanging over you with your mortgage – if you don't pay it the bank takes the house – but if you don't save there's every chance you will retire poor.

Budget for fun

People say that they find the whole idea of a personal budget too restrictive, too ordered, and that it takes all the fun out of life. Well, this is only true if you don't budget for fun – and many people don't. A budget that doesn't allow you to enjoy yourself is completely unrealistic and will be ignored. That doesn't mean all budgets are useless, just that bad budgets are.

Be realistic

Putting together a sensible, real-life family budget that doesn't specify everything down to the last grain of rice (a guaranteed waste of time) is not difficult. In fact, I've made it very easy for you by including a budget guide in the end of this chapter. All you have to do is allocate a couple of hours to work through it. Sit down by yourself or with the family, fill it out as accurately as you can and please, be realistic.

Be flexible

A budget should be flexible so don't despair if your circumstances change, rendering your budget inappropriate. You may change jobs, have a baby, receive a rise, or move house. It's not a problem. Just do another budget. Businesses, after all, fine-tune their budgets frequently. Even if there are no major changes in your life I recommend you review your budget every six months.

⊙━┳ Key thought

A budget is not a rigid document designed to make your life miserable. It's a flexible tool designed to make your life better.

The damn budget doesn't work!

How often have I heard that a budget doesn't work? In fact, if I had $1 for every time someone has told me that their budget is a disaster, I wouldn't need to do one myself – the money would be pouring in!

Making Money

I know for some people that a budget just doesn't work and the main reasons I hear are:

- I just can't stick to it.
- Unexpected expenses keep cropping up.
- It's boring.
- My life keeps changing.
- It's just too depressing.
- I'm too tired, or too busy.

If you've tried to budget and it didn't work, ask yourself if the budget was realistic in the first place. If not have another go at it. Let's face it, for a large number of people, for all sorts of reasons, budgets have not worked and will not work.

So what do you do? You stop flogging a dead horse and switch to the pretty simple plan of 'paying yourself first'.

Paying yourself first

With this strategy you only have to make one budgeting decision, which is what proportion of your income can you save? If you reckon you can save 5% of your income, as soon as you get paid and before you do anything else with it, have it put into your selected savings vehicle. You see, once you pocket it it's as good as spent.

Now, you can take your other 95% and spend it any way you like but *don't touch the 5%*. That money is your future.

I promise you that after a few months, unless you are on a very tight budget, you won't miss it. If a pay rise comes along add 1% or 2% to the 5% before you learn how to spend the money.

Before long, you can build up a very healthy savings habit without a budget. But remember, you cannot spend more than 95% (or whatever your chosen percentage is). No abusing credit cards, personal loans or other forms of debt.

⊶ Key thought

A budget is the best option but if it doesn't work for you, use the simple principle of paying yourself first and spending the rest.

Budget planner

The planner's purpose is to show you just how much you are spending, on what, and where opportunities exist to make savings. You might be amazed, for instance, at how much you spend on magazines, tobacco or alcohol. If you cut back on these items you could probably save yourself hundred of dollars. Or maybe you could save by not going to the hairdresser's so often.

The planner will tell you if you have earned more than you spent, or if you have spent more than you earned. If you have spent more than you earned you will either have to reduce your spending – and now you will have a better idea how to – or you will have to generate more income. On the other hand, if you have earned more than you spent, do something sensible with these savings by putting them into, say, shares, property, managed funds, superannuation, a savings account with no card access, or your mortgage. It's important to get rid of unspent money this way before you learn how to spend it – which never takes long.

Making Money

Money Budget Planner

HOME	Week	Year
Mortgage Repayments		
Rent		
Local Council Rates		
Water Rates		
Electricity		
Gas		
Telephone		
Maintenance – Repairs		
Furniture		
Appliances		
Hire Purchase		
Rentals		
Other		
MOTOR VEHICLE		
Registration		
Petrol		
Repairs . . . Maintenance		
Lease or Loan Payments		
Other		
FOOD		
Groceries . . . Milk, Bread		
Meat		
Alcohol		
Cigarettes/Tobacco		
Eating Out . . . Restaurants		
TOTAL		

INSURANCE	Week	Year
House		
Health Insurance		
Home Contents		
Motor Vehicle		
Income Protection		
Death Cover		
Other		
FAMILY EXPENSES		
School Fees		
Child Care		
Pets		
Sporting Activities		
Subscriptions/Memberships		
Public Transport		
Newspapers and Magazines		
Clothing		
Personal Care		
School Costs		
Gifts		
Hairdresser . . . Barber		
Holidays . . . Travel		
Other		
TOTAL		

Making Money

HEALTH	Week	Year
Medical Bills		
Dental Bills		
Medicines		
Other		
OTHER FINANCE		
Loan Repayments		
Store Cards . . . Lay-bys		
Superannuation		
Credit Cards		
Professional Fees		
Donations		
Other		
TOTAL		

INCOME

Your After Tax Income	
Spouse's After Tax Income	
After Tax Income From Savings Accounts	
Other	
TOTAL INCOME	
LESS YOUR EXPENSES	
YOUR SAVINGS	

CHAPTER THREE
Savings

When Frank Sinatra, surrounded by expensive silverware in the film *High Society*, crooned 'Who Wants to be a Millionaire? – I Don't!', he wasn't ringing too many true notes with the audience. Most of them would have been humming 'I do!'

Of course, Frank could afford to feign such disinterest in money – he was being paid a packet. Because of his great voice he was already a millionaire when he made the movie and he's probably even richer now. But most of us aren't blessed with such a wonderful – and bankable – gift.

Winning the lottery, picking a string of 100 TO 1 winners, earning a six-figure salary or pulling off a great business deal – there's no denying any of these would give your current finances a terrific boost. But, alone, they won't guarantee you'll end up wealthy. And, let's face it, for many people the chance of achieving any of them is low.

The bedrock of wealth

As I have said, I have financially comfortable clients who have never earned more than the basic wage and, at the same time, I have clients who have enjoyed enormous incomes during their working lives and yet have retired virtually broke. The basic difference between the two is simple: one lot saved, the others spent. Saving is the absolute bedrock of accumulating wealth.

> ⚷ **Key thought**
> No other factor is as important in becoming financially secure as saving. It's even more important than investment.

27

Making Money

If you are a bit surprised by this let me clarify what I mean by 'savings'. It's not just the money that goes into your passbook savings account, it's any money that's not spent now on everyday consumption but put aside for future use in the following month, year, decade or for use in retirement. It's any money that goes into your mortgage over and above the interest charge, into your super, into a sound investment, into a savings plan or bank deposit or into a separate account for some special purpose.

Why is saving so important to the creation of wealth? Well, if you put nothing aside into a savings vehicle during your working life, by the time you stop working you will have nothing material, regardless of what your income was. It's that simple.

Saving little, saving often

The trouble with saving is that it's not much fun – certainly not as much fun as spending. It requires discipline and commitment, which don't come naturally to most people. So the secret is to find ways of making saving a relatively easy and painless process. Try this simple method on for size.

When you come home from work or the shops go straight to the piggy bank or moneybox and put the loose change from your pocket or your purse into it. When the moneybox is full, bank it into your savings account, pay it into a managed fund, or put it towards your mortgage. Just don't dip into it while it's at home.

You might think I'm joking, but I'm not. This very basic savings technique can generate enormous figures over time.

For instance, if you saved just $1 per day from age 18 you would accumulate around $500,000 after tax by age 65 (assuming 10% annual earnings). If you or saved just $2 per day the figure would be $1 million, $5 per day would be $2.5 million.

This method of accumulating a large sum of money couldn't be easier or less painful, and it illustrates dramatically how powerful a long-term, regular savings regimen can be.

Now, while I reckon that most of us can put aside a few dollars a day without even noticing the absence, I also reckon that many of you reading this book aren't 18. Those of you who are older may be thinking you've left your run a bit late. Well, you haven't! It's never too late to save, and there is no time like the present to start.

When you are older, and presumably earning a significantly higher income than when you were 18, saving more than $1 or $2 per day shouldn't be all that hard. So, say you are 40 and you save $5 per day, by retirement at 65 you should have accumulated over $200,000. And, if you could save $10 per day it should be worth more than $400,000 by then.

Some of you will be saying that your budget is so tight you can't spare a single dollar to save. Okay, I know that almost everyone goes through some very difficult periods, particularly when there's only one income, kids and a mortgage to contend with. But for most people the tough times don't last forever. As soon as they stop you really should grab the opportunity to save.

Let's put our potential to save in perspective. If you were 30 years old on $30,000 p.a. and you expected your income to increase by 7% p.a., by 65 years of age *you would have earned $4.1 million.* If you were 40 years old on $40,000 p.a., given the same growth, you would have earned $2.5 million by retirement. These are huge figures generated from average earnings. Even a small percentage of this saved would produce a very significant sum by the time you stop working. In the light of this, it makes me despair to think how much money passes through people's hands during their lifetimes and how little of it they retain.

The 'power' of compound interest

Let's look again at the $1 or $2 a day saving schedule. The reason that savings (and debts) can accumulate so dramatically over longer periods is due to the 'power' of compound interest (which is the method of interest calculation applied to most savings vehicles and applied to most debts).

Compounding is where interest not only accrues against the principal but also against any previously accrued interest. It is, therefore, interest on (principal and) interest. Simple interest is where interest is paid on the principal only.

Over time the difference in the impact of the two methods of calculating interest becomes quite astonishing, as the following table demonstrates:

Making Money

Compound interest

Year	Principal	Compound interest	Balance at end of year
1	$1,000	$1,000 x 10% = $100	$ 1,100
2	$1,100	$1,100 x 10% = $110	$ 1,210
3	$1,210	$1,210 x 10% = $121	$ 1,331
10	$2,358	$2,358 x 10% = $236	$ 2,594
20	$6,116	$6,116 x 10% = $612	$ 6,728
30	$15,863	$15,863 x 10% = $1,586	$17,449
40	$41,144	$41,144 x 10% = $4,114	**$45,258**

Simple interest

Year	Principal	Simple interest	Balance at end of year
1	$1,000	$1,000 x 10% = $100	$1,100
2	$1,000	$1,000 x 10% = $100	$1,200
3	$1,000	$1,000 x 10% = $100	$1,300
10	$1,000	$1,000 x 10% = $100	$2,000
20	$1,000	$1,000 x 10% = $100	$3,000
30	$1,000	$1,000 x 10% = $100	$4,000
40	$1,000	$1,000 x 10% = $100	**$5,000**

Apart from the enormous difference in the final amounts, note how the impact of compound interest accelerates as time goes by – between Years 20 and 30 the compound interest balance grew by $10,721, whereas between Years 30 and 40 it grew by $27,809, almost three times as much.

Here's another example. Let's say Mary decided to put an annual lump sum into a managed fund earning a real 3.5% p.a. (after fees, tax and inflation). Let's assume her initial deposit was $3,000 and that this was increased annually by 4% p.a. for inflation. Let's also assume that all earnings were reinvested.

If Mary began this regimen at age 21 and continued it for 15 years, by the time she reached 36, and by which point her final annual contribution had grown to $5,403, she would have accumulated a total of $106,695.

Now, if at age 36 she left this total amount in the fund,

contributing nothing more to it, by the time she was 65 it would have compounded to $868,942.

As a comparison, let's say John *began* the same type of regimen as this (under the same set of assumptions) at the age of 36, at the time Mary stopped. Let's also say his initial annual deposit was $5,403, the same as Mary's final deposit. Significantly, even after making contributions every year until he reached the age of 65 – by which time his final annual contribution would have grown to $16,202 – John would still not have reached as great an accumulated amount as Mary (who had ceased annual contributions at $5,403, 30 years prior). John's total accumulation at age 65 would have been $833,977.

⊶ Key thought

Because it takes time for the power of compounding to really kick in, the moral is: the earlier you start saving, the better.

Tips to help you save

Whatever your overall saving strategy, there are plenty of ways you can reduce your regular level of spending and save without having to live like a monk. Try these:

- Only buy items you need when you need them, that is, don't treat shopping as a hobby or a leisure activity.
- Don't buy something unless you have the money to do so. Just remember the old maxim – if you can't afford it, you can't afford it!
- Pay with cash, not with your credit cards. Credit cards make buying too easy and can be a real debt trap for unwary or compulsive shoppers.
- Don't buy the first thing you see – shopping around is very important.
- Ask for discounts on items like whitegoods, furniture, and even clothes. You'll be amazed how many shops are prepared to

bargain and all you have to do is ask – they can only say 'no', and many won't.

- Wait for end-of-year and end-of-season sales before buying.
- Buy next year's Christmas presents at the beginning of the year during the January sales.
- Take advantage of bulk discounts, for example, carton prices on wine and beer.
- Take your lunch to work.
- Buying generic (unbranded or in-house supermarket brand) products. The quality may not be as high as some branded products but for staples like flour, sugar and butter I can't pick the difference.
- Shop in supermarkets rather than more expensive corner stores.
- Be prepared to buy second-hand rather than new goods.
- If you are a smoker, give up. Not only will it save you around $50 per week (based on a packet a day), you'll feel better and so will everyone around you. Put that $50 you save into your super – you'll need to build it up because you'll probably live longer!

⚿ Key thoughts

- Saving is the bedrock of wealth.
- Even a small amount saved regularly will build up over time into something significant due to the power of compounding.
- You can't save the cash that stays in your pocket, so don't plan to.
- You should direct a portion of your income straight into savings before you get your hands on it – which means before you spend it.
- You won't miss what you've never had.
- Establish part of your savings in areas difficult to dip into like superannuation, your mortgage, or at least a separate savings account with no card access.
- Saving requires commitment and discipline but choosing the right savings strategy can make the process a lot easier and relatively painless.

CHAPTER FOUR

Buying Things

Let me lay my cards straight down on the table (and I don't mean my credit cards). If you want to buy something, try to pay cash. And if you don't have the cash, think again whether you really need to make the purchase. This is a very simple, straightforward philosophy, and, while there are big ticket circumstances where it's obviously not practicable – such as buying a house, funding an investment or establishing a business – if you stick to it wherever possible you shouldn't get into too much trouble with money.

The reasons to pay cash and avoid debt are clear enough – interest is yet another cost to bear, and entering into debt puts you under a legal obligation to the creditor which can have serious consequences if you can't meet repayments. Namely, the creditor might take your purchase back or, worse still, might take other assets too.

Credit cards

I'll explain how credit cards work for the benefit of the 60% of Australians who don't have any. They are a vehicle for providing instant debt financing up to a predetermined limit which is set either by you or the credit card issuer (a bank, a building society, or a credit union). The whole idea of a credit card is to enable you to buy things at shops and businesses without the need to have the ready cash, or to enable you to receive a cash advance against the card through a bank, a money changer, or an automatic teller machine (ATM).

Whenever you make a purchase or take a cash advance against your card you incur an immediate or deferred interest charge on that transaction. And the way the interest is accrued normally places the card into one of two camps – where interest is charged immediately, or, where you have up to 55 days interest-free before any interest charges kick in. (In the case of cash advances interest always accrues immediately.)

Whether you have a card with up to 55 interest-free days on purchases or one that accrues immediate interest depends upon the policy of the card's issuer and some will offer customers a choice between the two. When you opt for a card with an interest-free period you are more likely to be charged a higher interest rate. Also, the cards with interest-free periods are more likely to attract an annual fee – ranging from around $15 to $50 – than immediate-interest cards on which there is normally no annual fee. Some cards also have nominal transaction fees.

As a card-holder you are sent a monthly statement detailing all purchases and cash advances and any interest that has accrued over the period. You then have the option of paying the account in full or just repaying as little as a specified minimum monthly amount by a nominated date.

Clearly it is better to pay the account in full to minimise interest charges but many people just pay the monthly minimum, rolling over the bulk of the account into the next billing period which is highly inadvisable. The compounding interest makes buying things on credit very expensive and if you continue to make further purchases with the card you can find yourself in the grip of serious debt.

Now, it's at billing time you want to pay particular attention to the issuers' policies on interest-free periods. (These can be quite rigorous and, as they vary from one issuer to another, it's a good idea to shop around for the card with the best conditions and rates – though they can be changed at any time.)

When you receive your statement you normally have 25 days (although it may be only 14) to pay your bill. If you have up to 55 days interest-free, this period attracts no interest charges (assuming it started from a $0 balance). If you don't pay the statement out in full some cards charge interest on the outstanding amount taken back to the items' *purchase dates*, not to the end of the interest-free period. What's more, if you buy more on your credit card before you've totally paid the amount already owing you may be charged interest from the date of the new purchases – in other words, no more interest-free period. Your interest-free period on any new purchases may not be reinstated until you have paid fully for all previous purchases.

Most issuers offer their customers a choice of credit cards – Visa, MasterCard and Bankcard. There is really no significant difference between them except that Bankcard is not accepted internationally.

My last word on credit cards is they can be very convenient, they are safer than cash in the event of loss or theft, and they are very useful if you are travelling overseas, particularly in America where sometimes only credit cards (not cash) are accepted. The trouble is they make buying too easy, eroding your savings and in many cases encumbering you with excessive debt. You must exercise control over your credit cards, rather than the other way around and you must certainly never delude yourself that having a credit card is the same as having the cash in your pocket!

Charge or debit cards

Charge cards are a variation on the credit card theme and, in Australia, the two best known are American Express and Diners Club. Where they differ from credit cards is that when you receive your monthly bill you are expected to pay it in full.

Charge cards have no interest charges – unless you don't fully pay your bill each month in which case you will incur very high interest indeed. In the case of American Express, in September 1995, the monthly interest charge against unpaid billings was 1.9%. Amex also charges a joining fee and an annual subscription fee ($30 and $60 respectively in March 1995).

Charge cards may cause less personal indebtedness than credit cards because you can't carry debt over from one month to another, however, 'up-market' cards like American Express have no preset spending limit – you set your own. So, if self-control isn't your strong suit you could find a charge card even more dangerous than a credit card!

Making Money

Store cards

Store cards are a form of credit card issued by retailers like Myer/ Grace Bros, Target, David Jones and Katies. More than 600 different retailers in Australia issue store cards which are only for use in their own stores.

The good news about store cards is that they attract no annual fees and have a good interest-free period – normally a maximum of either 55 or 60 days. The bad news about store cards is that they usually incur higher interest rate charges than credit cards. A difference of around 5% is not uncommon and it can be as much as 10%. Another negative is the way interest is calculated. Generally, if you don't pay your account in full there are no more interest-free days until you do.

Also, shoppers are sometimes invited to use their cards to buy big ticket items where they are given, say, six months to pay, interest-free. What's often not pointed out is that if the item is not paid for in full during that period, then interest may be charged on the total price of the item, backdated to the date of purchase and regardless of how much has been paid off.

Let's say, for example, you use your card (or enter into some other type of in-house financing arrangement) to buy a $2,000 lounge suite on the basis of it being interest-free for 12 months. After 12 months you only manage to pay off $1,000. Under many of these 'interest-free' arrangements you could then find that interest has been added to your bill. Twelve months interest in fact, starting at the date of purchase – and on the full $2,000, not on the $1,000 outstanding. To make matters worse, the interest rate would probably be very high – much higher than the average credit card or personal loan rate.

In this example, if the interest rate was 24% p.a. (rates as high as 30% are not unheard of) at the end of 12 months you would owe $1,480 (being the outstanding $1,000 plus 12 months interest of $480 on the original purchase price of $2,000). And now you would have interest at 24% compounding on this new amount of $1,480 to contend with. Get the picture?

0— **Key thought**

If you go into debt to buy anything that has an interest-free period, pay the debt out within the interest-free period – even if it means borrowing the money from somewhere else to do it!

Tips on using credit cards

Look, I know that relatively easy access to personal loans and credit cards can be very helpful at times when money is (temporarily) tight or you find yourself in an emergency where you need funds on the spot. But you mustn't let the ease with which you can get access to debt undo you.

Credit cards are particularly hazardous for those who, by their own description, are 'born to shop'. 'Born to stay broke' is more like it. My recommendation to anyone who fits this description is to throw your credit cards away, *now*.

For those of you who do want the convenience of a card:

- Shop around for the best card – there *are* differences between them.
- Only keep a minimum number of cards – preferably one.
- Try not to carry any debt from one billing period to another.
- Carry a card that is readily acceptable overseas.
- Try not to use your card, that is, try to pay cash!

Lay-by

Lay-by is an old-fashioned but perfectly acceptable way of buying. It doesn't encourage wild and impulsive consumption – the sort that puts you in the poorhouse – and, if you stick to the rules, you'll pay no interest.

When you lay-by you pay a deposit and the store keeps the item while you pay off the rest of the money in instalments. There's a good incentive for you to pay off your debt because you don't get your purchase until it's paid for!

Making Money

Terms and conditions vary from store to store but generally you need a deposit of 10% to 12%. You're then given two to three months to pay the balance although it can be longer on more expensive items. If you run into financial difficulties most stores will extend the lay-by period by another month or two, but you do need to check the store's policy if you can't or don't want to complete your payments. Some stores will keep up to 25% of the cost of the item.

Personal loans

Of the literally thousands of letters I receive, approximately one third are from people suffering from problems with personal loans. Whenever you contemplate taking out a personal loan, think very carefully why you are doing it because most purchases financed through personal loans leave you with no real asset, only a debt. If, however, after coolly thinking it through, you decide you must have the item go ahead and take the loan, but make sure you shop around – interest rates and conditions on personal loans vary considerably.

Always try getting finance from a bank or credit union first as their rates should be significantly lower than from a finance company, sometimes dramatically so. In mid-1995, for instance, unsecured personal loans interest rates ranged from the low teens (bank) to almost 30% p.a. (finance company). Secured loans started at just over 10%. (See below for more on secured and unsecured loans.)

Also note if the interest rate quoted to you is a flat rate or a reducible rate. Most loans are reducible but you can't assume this. A flat rate of 8% from a finance company may look better than a reducible rate of 11% from a credit union – until you realise that an 8% flat rate may be equivalent to a 15% reducible rate in terms of total interest paid over the life of the loan.

The rate of interest offered to you, no matter who the lender is, depends on the lender's perception of the risk of the loan application. The riskier it is perceived to be, the higher the interest rate offered – if, indeed, a loan is offered at all. The factors that go into the lender's estimation of the loan's risk include an appraisal of you the applicant, and of the item you wish to purchase. Loans for second-hand cars, for instance, often attract higher rates than loans for new cars.

The personal information the lender may want will pertain to your employment record, your income, your age, whether you own a home or rent one, what assets you have and so on. The information required about the intended purchase can vary from being quite detailed to none at all.

Personal loans are normally repayable over three to five years, though it can be longer. They can be variable or fixed rate and can be secured or unsecured.

Secured vs unsecured loans

A secured loan is one where the lender takes additional security over another of your assets – one worth more than the value of the loan. An unsecured loan is one where the lender takes no security other than the item you are buying. Because of the relatively high risk to the lender, unsecured loans are offered at higher interest rates.

In the event you default on a secured loan the lender has the right to take possession of the secured asset and sell it to recoup the debt. If you default on an unsecured loan the lender can take back the unsecured item (if it still exists) and sell it but, if this doesn't cover the outstanding debt, you may be obliged to sell other assets to make good the debt. However, the unsecured lender can't take possession of your assets willy-nilly and sell them from under you. Well, not without bankrupting you first! (See Chapter Eighteen for more on bankruptcy.)

Borrowing on the house

There is another way of structuring a personal loan, and that is by having the amount you wish to borrow added to your mortgage, taking advantage of mortgage interest rates which are traditionally the cheapest form of debt. So, if you wanted to borrow $10,000 for a holiday (which is not recommended!) you could 'put it on the house' by increasing your mortgage by $10,000. Hey presto! – here's your low-interest financing. The big problem with this, though, is that the $10,000 holiday could end up costing you a small fortune.

Making Money

Let's say you had a $100,000, 25-year mortgage and you added $10,000 to it at the end of Year 1. Assuming a 10% interest rate throughout the life of the loan and adjustments to the payments to repay the loan in the original term, it would add $16,421 in interest repayments to your mortgage over the remaining 24 years. It would certainly want to have been a damn good holiday at that price!

Look, if you have to borrow money it's obviously best to do it at the lowest interest rate possible. But don't fool yourself by borrowing money to buy things like a holiday (which is worth nothing the moment you get back), a stereo, clothes or furniture (which are practically worthless after three to five years). Unless you are very disciplined, using your home loan to buy consumer items is crazy – you may still be paying a fortune for the items 25 years later and long after they have turned to dust.

Cash is king

No matter what type of loan you use it's important to realise there's a big price penalty you pay for debt financing. A hi-fi system priced at $5,000 bought with a personal loan at a reducible 30% p.a. over five years would end up costing you $9,762 ($4,762 in interest), and at 15% p.a. would cost you $7,137 ($2,137 in interest). With cash, on the other hand, it would cost $5,000 at most, probably even less with the discount cash can often attract.

When you take out a personal loan

Avoid taking out a personal loan to finance consumption if at all possible. But if you must, make sure you can comfortably answer the following questions before you sign up:
- What is the interest rate?
- How long will it take to pay the loan off?
- What will be the total cost of the loan?
- Can I afford the weekly repayments?
- If I get a wage rise can I pay the loan off faster?
- Are there any penalties if I fall behind with my repayments?
- Do I really need this item?

Seeking help

If you find yourself in trouble with personal debts, the following organisations are a great place to start to seek help:
NSW – Financial Counsellor Association of NSW, c/- Credit Line (02) 951 5544, 008 467941
VIC – Consumer Advocacy and Financial Counselling Association of Victoria. (03) 9650 5422
QLD – Financial Counsellors Association of Queensland (07) 3257 1957
WA – Consumer Credit Legal Centre (09) 481 7662 or Credit Care (09) 321 9711
SA – South Australian Financial Counsellors Association, c/- Norwood Community Legal Service (08) 362 1199
ACT – Care Financial Counselling Service (06) 257 1788
TAS – Anglicare Financial Counselling Service (002) 34 8457

Key thought
If you want to buy something try to pay cash.

CHAPTER FIVE
The Job Market

I know that some readers of this book will have a secure job (whatever that means), some will be approaching retirement and others will be retired already. So you may be wondering why a chapter on the job market has relevance for you personally.

Well, from a purely vocational perspective it may not. However, from an investment point of view you could find it of value – by identifying the expanding and contracting areas of the economy.

For most of us, our ability to earn an income is easily our most valuable asset and the absence of it would make life look very different indeed. It is important to remember, though, that the job market of today won't be the job market of tomorrow.

Pretty obviously, our population is getting older. We are having less children (1.9 per female on average), living longer (average age for women is 80.86 years and men is 74.9 years) and retiring earlier. This, to me, is a fascinating indicator to where future employment will be. Into the next century, the growth areas for employment and, therefore, the ones that I am focussing on as an investor are based on what I believe our aging population will need.

Tourism

Australia will benefit strongly from local and international tourists. As many Australians retire earlier, are more financially comfortable, and in better health, they will travel. This also applies to our wealthy Asian neighbours. There is no doubt in my mind that the travel industry will grow dramatically.

Health

Sadly, as we get older, our demand for medical support expands rapidly. I believe that private and public health services will represent a bigger and bigger part of the employment market. Added to this there will be huge growth in health-related jobs such as in retirement villages and in a whole range of household help services for the hundreds of thousands of aged Australians who will continue to live at home.

Environment

Environment-related employment will also prosper. As a society, it is inevitable that we will direct more and more resources into protecting our environment.

Financial services

There is no doubt that the success of 'Money' on Channel 9, financial supplements in our papers, and the popularity of investment radio talkback indicate the importance we now place on managing our money properly. The range of investment products and services will grow and will create a large number of jobs for those with skills in economics, business, investment, law and computer technology. My own business, IPAC, has grown from five employees in 1984 to more than 100 in 1995 – that's a lot of new jobs from just one small, privately-owned company.

Household services

Household services is an area that really fascinates me. Phil Ruthven of IBIS describes job growth in this area very well. He talks of the 'out-sourcing' of today's domestic chores such as cleaning, gardening, childminding and even cooking. I'm sure he's right. One of Phil's examples is how, in the last century, we used to make our own clothes and furniture but now a huge manufacturing sector does this for us. He reckons that household services will be the biggest source of new jobs in the next century.

Recent industrial and employment trends

To get a better feel for where the job market is moving, let's look at changes and trends in recent years. One of the most significant industrial changes in the past two decades has been a dramatic decline in employment in the manufacturing sector.

Between 1971 and 1994 the percentage of the total workforce employed in manufacturing fell from 24% to 16%. This was due to a number of factors including the growing use of automation and computer-based technologies, the reduction of tariff barriers exposing Australian manufacturing to the heat of international competition (bringing about closures and/or 'downsizing') and the greater tendency to source material from and relocate manufacturing to low-cost countries, particularly in Asia.

The proportion of the workforce employed in agriculture and mining also fell between 1971 and 1994, respectively from 8% to 5% and from 1.5% to 1.1%. Labour-saving technological innovations and techniques largely explain the falls, plus a trend to large-scale farming, often by large companies.

Now, not all parts of the economy experienced employment losses during this period. The 'services sector' has continued to grow and is now at a point where it employs over 70% of the workforce. This is a sector that includes, for instance, community services*; the wholesale and retail trades; public administration and defence; finance, property and business services; and recreational services† – all of which experienced employment growth in

---

* 'community services' (as defined by the ABS) includes jobs in hospitals and nursing homes, medicine, dentistry, education, community health services, museums and art galleries, welfare and religious institutions, research and scientific institutions, political parties, employment services, police and garbage disposal services.

† 'recreational, personal and other services' (as defined by the ABS) includes jobs in gambling, hotels, motels, clubs, hairdressing, photography, domestic services, film, television and radio production.

the decade to 1994. (*Source: Economic Update 1995*, David Clark, published by the The Financial Review Library, Sydney, 1995.

Industry trends

According to *Where the jobs are 1993*, published by the Institute of Applied Economic and Social Research at the University of Melbourne and based on Australian Bureau of Statistics (ABS) data, the private sector industry areas with the highest employment growth (in percentage terms, not necessarily in sheer numbers) between 1986 and 1992 were community services; finance; property and business; and recreation, personal and other services.*

Small firms with less than 20 employees showed the strongest employment growth, with the biggest increases occurring in Queensland and Western Australia. Job growth in small firms was more pronounced in finance; wholesale and retail trades; property and business services; manufacturing; community services; and construction. In the recreation, personal and other services industries job growth was greatest in large firms.

Over the survey period there was a 10% increase in the number of jobs in small firms with less than 20 employees (having an average size of four persons). At the end of the period (in 1992) there were 1.5 million jobs in small private sector companies – 400,000 more than in 1986. In early 1995 there were 2.6 million jobs in small companies with less than 20 employees.

Employment predictions

In 1991 the Department of Employment, Education and Training (DEET) released a report entitled *Australia's Workforce in the Year 2001* which looked at the anticipated employment demand for 120 different occupations (as classified by the ABS) in 2001. In summary, the DEET report predicted that the occupations

---

* This study did not look at the public sector which accounts for about 30% of jobs in Australia.

which would grow most rapidly in the 1990s are:
- social workers
- psychologists
- economists (anyone who can get it right even some of the time will make a fortune!)
- information science and computing professionals
- vets
- speech pathologists
- welfare and youth workers
- accountants
- pharmacists.

The report also predicted the following occupations would show the greatest decline:
- clergymen
- farmers
- agricultural labourers
- air traffic controllers
- power and chemical plant operators.

What is all this saying?

If the trends that ran through the national, private sector, wage or salaried employment scene between 1986 and 1992 were to continue, and, you wished to find employment in the areas showing the greatest growth (with an eye to job security), you would be advised to look towards the services sector and probably towards a small firm within it. Ideally it would be a small professional firm – the outlook for professionals in terms of both job growth and the ability to ride out tough times is better than any other sector. And the hottest pick of all would be working for a small professional firm situated somewhere in Queensland or Western Australia. (But, of course, the main trends that existed between 1986 and 1992 will not predominate forever and while this survey is instructive, it can only provide pointers to what the future job scene may be like.)

The opinion, though, that the services sector will continue to employ more people at the expense of other industry sectors, appears to be universally accepted. And it's not just the most likely scenario painted for Australia – developed, industrialised countries all over the world are moving towards being service-based economies. Indeed, it has been suggested that, in the not too distant future, only one in 10 of the developed world's workers will be employed in manufacturing. (*Source*: 'Global Agenda Report' by Reginald Dale, *Time*, 13 March 1995.)

Job security follows job satisfaction

So, from the point of view of job security, the service sector is where anyone planning their next career move really ought to look. However, there is more to career choice than job security.

Don't get me wrong – job security *is* important, but it shouldn't be your sole motivator. Finding a vocation you *like* should be top priority. After all, you spend half of your waking life at work so you may as well enjoy it!

And the clincher is that finding a job you like will actually produce its own job security. How? Well, if you genuinely enjoy your work you are more likely to excel at it than someone who doesn't – and that's the best job security you can have. I also believe that people who like their work have a much better than average chance of making good money from it – again, because people who like their work generally do a better job than those who don't.

Personal qualities in employment

I also believe that there are some fundamental personal qualities that will be particularly important in the future employment scene. The more endowed you are with them the greater your chances of success in whatever area of employment you choose.

- Creativity – the fountainhead of success and the one human characteristic that no amount of brilliant technology will ever be able to replace (at least I pray not!).
- Adaptability, being a willingness and an ability to learn new skills and to adapt old skills to new situations.
- The ability to communicate well, and to understand easily.
- Commitment and a willingness to work hard.

Making Money

Coping with rapid change

When thinking about your career, think about your next career too because odds are you will have more than one during your lifetime. Indeed, young Australian university graduates are likely to change career four times and change jobs eight times during their working lives. (*Source*: *Sydney Morning Herald*, 14 January 1995.)

This volatility reflects the time we are living in, which is one of unprecedentedly accelerating change. Extraordinary developments in telecommunications link us instantly and inexpensively to a world reduced to the size of a keyboard, open for business 24 hours a day. These are the early days of the so-called Information Revolution, which many commentators believe will change the world and the way we live as profoundly as the Industrial Revolution changed the world in the 18th century.

Consider Australia's present – there is no longer any real need for many businesses to have a central office which employees travel to every day. Many employees can now just as effectively work wherever they like, be it at home, in a car or in the middle of the desert so long as they have a personal computer, phone, fax and modem.

Engineers in Adelaide can be connected full-time by computer to a team of draughtsmen in Bombay who do the drawings for a fraction of the cost that a similar team of draughtsmen would rack up in the next door offfice. And the drawings can be faxed from India just as rapidly as it would take to walk next door and get them. A team of surgeons in Brisbane can lead another team of surgeons through an intricate operaton in Jakarta so long as both teams are videoed and they have a computer link up . . .

Ten years ago these realities were barely imaginable. And with the power of business and personal computers roughly doubling every two years, coupled with the mesmerising, interactive possibilities of the 'information superhighway' supposedly on our doorstep, who can really tell what things will be like in ten years from now, let alone in twenty or thirty?

The point of all this from an employment point of view is that the only thing you can be certain about in the future is the certainty of change itself. To be successful in the future will entail being able to adapt to the changes going on around you better and faster than your fellow workers.

Education – stick with it

The surest way of maximising your chances of being able to adapt in this changing world is by investing time and energy in your own education – and to continue this process throughout your life. It doesn't much matter if you forget some of the details of what you've learnt or can't use it directly in your work. The point of the exercise is to train you to think, to question, and to come up with solutions to problems.

Also, by completing an educational course you achieve something tangible and have a document to prove it. Not only does this boost your self-esteem and confidence, it demonstrates to an employer that you have the grit and ability to see something you've started through to a successful end, a quality all employers value and seek.

CHAPTER SIX
Owning a Home

During your lifetime you are presented with the opportunity to sink your money into an untold number and variety of investments. And, like most people, you are bound to ignore virtually all of them. This isn't because you necessarily think they aren't any good (although some aren't) but partly because you have plenty of other things to do with your money – like paying the bills – and, if there's anything left over, taking a holiday or simply going out.

Another reason you probably ignore these investment offers is the uneasy feeling they give you – not flowing so much from their merits or lack thereof, but from an uncertainty on your part about their very nature. About how they actually work and, more to the point, about how they make your money grow. Do you want to invest, for instance, in shares, bonds, exotic horticultural crops, or feature films if you don't really understand what makes them tick?

Generally, you pass up such investment opportunities (even if they're worthwhile) because they are just a bit too intangible. They're not as easy to understand as bricks and mortar. When you buy a home you can see, smell and feel it.

There are plenty of good reasons to own your own home, and not all of them are about money. Home ownership gives you a degree of psychological security – even when the mortgage is killing you! It makes you the king or queen of your own domain, and there's no landlord to tell you to get out. When you own your own home you can create the environment you want to live in – you can decorate it any way you like, you can rip out walls, put in a pool or dig up the garden.

Buying a home is definitely an investment that I recommend most Australians make. But this isn't to say that renting doesn't have its benefits – it does, so long as you don't rent forever!

To rent or to buy?

With most of our cities sprawling, residential property close to the city centres is becoming increasingly expensive. Home affordability is spreading outwards and for those who work in the cities and don't want to commute long distances from an out-lying suburb or satellite, or for those who simply like living near the 'action', long-term renting close to a city or town centre will become more common.

Most renters, however, do aspire to owning their own home one day, and with good cause.

Look at it this way. Every dollar you pay in rent goes into someone else's pocket. It temporarily buys you a place to live but gives you little financial benefit in the long-term. If you have to pay to have a roof over your head, you may as well pay the 'rent' to yourself – which is a less painful way of looking at your mortgage.

I know this line of thinking can be criticised (and it is by some economic commentators) because, in the short-term at least, the economics of buying versus renting tend to favour renting. Why? Well, let's say you buy a house today. I'll bet your new mortgage repayments are significantly more than the rent you were paying. On top of this, as a home-owner, you will have the additional expenses of rates, house insurance, maintenance, as well as pur-chase costs like legal fees and stamp duties to meet.

So, the argument goes, because as a tenant you will have more disposable income in your pocket at the end of the week than the harried home-buyer on the same income, you will then have more income to invest in areas with higher historical returns than resi-dential real estate, such as shares. (See comparative investment returns in Chapter Eleven 'Ten Keys to Successful Investing'.) Okay, but who is actually going to do that? Have you ever met anyone who has religiously put away as much as 25% of their weekly income, each week, every week, for up to 20 years or more, into an investment like shares – with only their own self-discipline to make them do it? I certainly haven't, and I doubt I ever will.

And it's not true that the average renter will always have more money than the home-buyer in his or her pocket at the end of the week anyway. Certainly for the first years, the average home-buyer will have relatively less to spend than a tenant on the same income. But while your mortgage repayments might seem a lot now, they won't be looking so frightening in 10 years time. You see, inflation will be working for you. As the cost of almost everything (including rents) increases every year, your mortgage repayments – which *do not* go up with inflation – will begin to look less hefty. (I am not taking into consideration here changes to your mortgage repayments through fluctuations in interest rates which may raise or lower your instalments.)

From a purely financial point of view, the time when renting does turn out to be a better proposition than buying is if you buy and sell a home within too short a time frame. This is because home ownership entails hefty buying costs, hefty repayments and other holding costs, as well as hefty selling costs; and rental payments are normally cheaper than mortgage repayments.

Consider an analysis of the economics of renting versus buying conducted by IPAC. This contrasted the relative financial position of someone buying a home to someone renting the *same* home. The point of the exercise was to find out who would be better off financially over time, the buyer or the renter, how long one would be infront of the other and by how much.

The inputs used in the analysis reflected real and typical market circumstances as well as taking a conservative medium to long-term future outlook.

Property value	$200,000
Deposit	$ 40,000*
Loan	$160,000
Interest rate on loan (fixed)	10.5%
Term of loan	25 years
Inflation	3.5%
Rental income	5% of property value
Annual property price growth	5%
(Rent, Year 1)	$10,000 p.a. (indexed)
Insurances, rates and maintenance Year 1	$4,600 (indexed)

* The analysis included an after-tax calculation of the interest income *foregone* by the buyer on the $40,000 deposit, assuming this money could have been earning 8% in a fixed term investment over the years rather than being sunk into a home.

Purchase costs	$9,271
Return on a fixed interest investment	8% p.a.*
Owner's marginal tax rate	44.5%*

Within these parameters the study found that on a year-by-year basis (non-cumulative), the buyer would be worse off than the renter of the property for the first five years, then just sneaking ahead in the sixth.

More interesting and relevant however was the cumulative result, that is, the total, carried-forward value of the buyer's losses in relation to the renter's gains over the years. Cumulatively, the buyer would be worse off than the renter of the same property for 11 years, just getting ahead in the twelfth.

Here are the actual results from years 1 to 14, with all figures being from the *buyer's* perspective and financial position in relation to the renter's.

Buyer's financial position *vis a vis* renter of the same property

Year	Annual gain+/loss−	Cumulative gain+/loss−
1	−$13,358†	−$13,358†
2	−$ 3,358	−$16,715
3	−$ 2,586	−$19,301
4	−$ 1,765	−$21,066
5	−$ 896	−$21,962
6	+$ 28	−$21,934
7	+$ 1,010	−$20,925
8	+$ 2,054	−$18,870
9	+$ 3,167	−$15,704
10	+$ 4,350	−$11,353
11	+$ 5,613	−$ 5,740
12	+$ 6,959	+$ 1,219
13	+$ 8,397	+$ 9,616
14	+$ 9,933	+$19,548

† The year 1 amount is very high due to the one-off purchase costs of $9,271.

Making Money

This analysis demonstrates two important points. Firstly, a buyer *will* eventually be better off than a renter, but it doesn't happen overnight – indeed it can take a very long time. Secondly, once the buyer is financially in front of the renter, the gap in their respective fortunes widens dramatically in the buyer's favour, as the cumulative results for years 12 to 14 clearly show.

Note that while this scenario is designed to reflect reality as closely as possible at the time of writing, you need to be aware that all analyses of this nature depend on their inputs. Change just one element and the whole picture changes. If, for instance, the loan was not as large as it is here the buyer would pass the tenant earlier. If the property appreciated at a faster rate, the same thing would happen. Conversely, if the rent was lower or the home loan interest rate was higher this would favour the tenant's position. Also note this analysis does not take into account property selling costs which can include fees to agents of more than 2% of the sale price, as well as legal fees and possibly advertising charges, all of which favour a tenant's relative financial position.

⚷ Key thoughts

Plan to buy a property to live in because:

- Buying is economically more beneficial in the long-term than renting.
- Paying off a home is a great way to force you to save. After all, if you don't pay the mortgage the bank will sell the house!
- Yes, there is an argument for renting, but you'll need to be very disciplined about putting aside and investing the money you save in the early years.
- In the long run, well-selected property should continue to increase in value.

Buying the right property

The property you buy to live in should satisfy two criteria – it should suit your own needs and it should have certain physical characteristics which will appeal to future property buyers. I am assuming that at some time you will sell your house and move to another which most people do. Therefore, the house you buy should be like any other major asset you hold – it should be reasonably easy to sell.

For a start, buying a home, like selling one, doesn't happen overnight. In fact, it can take forever if you allow it to. But the way to reduce the time and the inevitable anxiety generated by the whole process is to do your homework properly and to follow a few simple steps:

Look at what's sold

Before you even get in a real estate agent's car for that frequently fruitless inspection of inappropriate properties, get in your own car and drive around the area you are interested in. Look for properties with 'For Sale' signs out the front, with and without 'Sold' stickers on them. Note any properties that interest you and pay particular attention to those that have sold. This is because it's the selling price of properties, not the asking price, that sets the market. Then phone the estate agencies concerned and find out the asking prices of those for sale and, more importantly, the selling price of those that have recently sold.

You won't be able to inspect the sold properties but looking at them from the outside, talking to the selling agent and to neighbouring residents about them will start to give you an idea about the real level of the local market. It will give you a more accurate picture than you'll get from the asking prices.

Check the selling prices

Next, contact the local council chambers to see if they will allow you to inspect their register of property transfers. These list the addresses, prices and transaction dates of all sales in the local area. Some councils will give you free access to this information, some councils will charge you for it and others won't allow you to look at it at all.

Making Money

If you can get access to local council property transfer records, look for the sales in your target price range and locality. Jot down the addresses and then go and look at these properties from the outside. Many of the properties you'll see this time will have had the signs taken down or may not have had a sign to start with.

You can also find out the most recent sale price of any property in your state's land title office. The fees for this service and the procedure vary from state to state but to give you an idea of costs, the South Australian Land Title Office will give you the last sale price of a property if you provide them with an address and $3.60. The procedure is more complicated in Victoria where you can get the last sale price of a property for $18.50, and in Queensland you can find out the last sale price of 10 properties for $20.

Inspecting properties

By now you should have finished your homework and should be ready to do some real inspecting. By this, I mean visiting properties during 'Open for Inspection' times and going over them with a fine-tooth comb, both internally and externally.

It also means going with a number of real estate agents to be shown what's available. If your experience is anything like mine you will be taken to more properties than you really want to see, including some that fall completely outside the guidelines you specified. Don't despair – many people fall in love with a house that's nothing like the one they had in mind. If this happens to you, pause for a moment and coolly establish that the home satisfies your practical needs, that it's sound and that you can afford it. Then think about it some more!

My advice is to look and look and look. Buying a home is as much an emotional decision as it is a rational one, and when the initial rush of blind infatuation with your new love cools you'll start noticing a few shortcomings so I urge you to keep as level a head as possible. Make sure you take your time, inspect plenty of properties, get a good idea of what you really want and of local values before you commit yourself. You are, after all, about to make what will probably be the biggest financial investment of your life – one that will own you more than you own it for a long time!

The buying process

Okay, now you've found your dream home. Before you part with your money, you have to verify that the property is structurally sound and you have to look at the contract to make sure there are no peculiar conditions that apply to the sale.

Sometimes both written building and pest reports are attached to the contract which will save you this outlay. When they aren't and you are serious about the property, I strongly recommend you have them done even though it's at your own expense. These inspections could save you from making a very big and expensive mistake.

There are numerous small companies that do building inspections and pest reports. A written building report will cost you around $300 and a pest report about $100-$150. Look in the *Yellow Pages* under Building Consultants and phone around for quotes – prices do vary.

Negotiating a price

As a general negotiating stance, try to convey the impression that you aren't as keen on the property as you really are. If you are seen to be completely hooked, your protestations about the price being too high will fall on deaf ears.

Having an agent involved in the negotiations will probably work to your advantage. This may surprise you, because an agent is paid by the vendor and is legally and morally obliged to get as high a price as possible for them. While aware of his obligations, the stark reality of a real estate agent's lot is that if he doesn't sell he doesn't eat. The agent's self-interest will mean, in many cases, that he will apply just as much if not more pressure on the vendor to drop the price – known in certain circles as 'crunching the vendor' – as he will apply on you to raise it.

So what sort of money do you offer? As a rough rule of thumb the asking price of a property will be 5% to 10% higher than the vendor is prepared to take. I stress, however, that this is not always the case. If you have done your homework you should know if the asking price is close to the mark or completely ludicrous – which is more likely to be the case where there is no agent involved.

Making Money

If you think the asking price is fairly realistic, offer 15% less. On a house with an asking price of $200,000, for example, this would be an offer of $170,000. If you think the asking price is way over the top, offer 30% less or simply walk away. If you think it's underpriced, try to knock 5% off for luck, but if the vendor won't listen just go ahead and pay it.

Negotiations can go on for days, sometimes weeks, with offers and counter-offers flowing backwards and forwards. If you're dealing direct with the vendor the sale may not be as protracted as through an agent but the principles of negotiation are just the same. Just remember the longer the process takes the greater the danger there is of someone else jumping in and snatching the property from under your nose.

⊙━ Key thoughts

- Work out what you need, want and can afford.
- Do your homework about the market.
- Look at as many properties as you can.
- Have the contract checked, get building and pest reports.
- Closely inspect the property you like on different days and at different times of the day.
- Don't pay more than you can afford.

Maintaining your home

It should be pretty obvious that there isn't much point going out and buying a home if you aren't going to look after it properly. Your home is, after all, probably your most valuable asset: you want to protect its value because when it comes time to sell you'll want to get the best possible price you can. You'll also feel a lot happier living in a home that's well-maintained and where everything works than living in one that's falling down around your ears.

The key thing about maintenance is that you have to carry it out on a regular and disciplined basis. This enables you to catch most small and relatively inexpensive problems before they turn into large and expensive ones. It's the same logic as having your car serviced regularly.

Naturally, the age of your home and its building materials will largely determine how often you should give your home an overhaul. Old timber houses require much more maintenance than new brick houses, for instance, but as a general guide, give your home a good inspection once a year to make sure everything is in good order.

Be particularly on guard for pests, remembering that pest inspection is usually a job for the professionals – they're the ones with the experience and the license to use the chemicals necessary to rid the house of its timber-eating tenants. A pest inspection should be done about once every two years depending on the timber content of your home and the amount of timber, both green and dry, in your locality.

Because maintenance is one of those things you shouldn't cut corners on – because it will cost you dearly in the long run – I recommend you regularly put some money aside into a separate maintenance account to meet those inevitable bills. This is particularly important if you live in an old house and even more so if you live in a timber one which, if nothing else, will need painting on a regular basis.

Maintenance checklist

These are some of the things to look out for – some will entail getting into the roof and under the floor:
- blocked gutters and downpipes
- cracks in the roofing, ceiling, flooring, walls, tiling and paths
- crumbling putty around windows
- damp in ceilings, walls or flooring
- deterioration of wiring
- evidence of animal activity under the house, in the roof or in the walls
- cavities (where possums or rats could get in)
- jammed windows and doors
- leaking taps, pipes and toilet cisterns
- loose tiles and grouting
- mould

- peeling paint
- peeling wallpaper
- rust
- water damage in cupboards around kitchen sink and vanity basin
- water lying in gutters
- watermarks on ceilings or walls
- wood rot.

Moving, renovating and overcapitalising

Let's say you've been living in your home now for five or six years and, while it has been doing the job well enough, the kids have reached an age where it would be better if they had their own bedrooms. Perhaps you wouldn't mind a room to retreat into yourself. Maybe the house needs major repairs or perhaps you simply don't like its look any more. So, what do you do, move or renovate?

Well, you have to consider this with both your head and heart. If you're thoroughly tired of the place you're in and feel like something different, I recommend you listen to your heart and move – even though moving is an exasperating and quite an expensive process. A change of scenery can be revitalising. But if your heart is not really pushing you to move, your head will be saying 'moving's a nightmare! – stay, and fix the place up.'

Moving

By choosing not to move you will be spared some major (and unavoidable) expenses including:
- estate agent selling fees
- stamp duty
- solicitor's fees
- removalists
- building and pest inspections
- searches, surveys
- electricity and phone connections.

The costs of moving

On 'Money' we looked at the set costs involved in selling a two-bedroom house for $160,000 and moving from it to a three-bedroom house bought for $180,000. (1994 figures.)

Estate agent fees (2.5%, negotiable)	$ 4,000
Stamp duty	$ 4,790
Solicitor's fees	$ 1,915
Removalists	$ 1,765
Building and pest inspections	$ 350
Searches, surveys	$ 330
Electricity and phone connections	$ 300
Total	$13,450
To be on the safe side, say	$15,000

Renovating

If you renovate you will be up for some fixed costs as well as any number of variable costs depending on how elaborate the renovations are. The unavoidable fixed costs you'll face are: council fees and the preparation of preliminary plans – and you will need to allow at least $1,000 for these.

Variable costs can entail architect's fees, storage fees, bank fees for extending your mortgage, builder's fees and materials. Of course, building costs vary significantly depending on the design of your home, your choice of materials, site accessibility, method of construction and your own level of involvement – which you should try to maximise. Doing as much work as possible yourself will save a lot of money because paid labour is generally as great a building cost as materials. (I have to admit I'm not really much of a home handyman so I know this advice is easier to give than take!)

Take note that if you intend to do many or all of the renovations yourself that some states require you to get an owner/builder's licence. In NSW and Queensland for instance, you need a licence for any project worth more than $3,000 which requires council approval. This is designed to protect future buyers of your home against unsatisfactory work – and as an owner/builder you are required to take out insurance with the (State) Builders' Licensing Board to cover faulty workmanship.

At the end of 1994, residential building costs averaged around $5,500 per square (approximately 9.3 square metres, exactly 100 square feet), with kitchens and bathrooms being much higher. This figure assumes you do no work yourself and I expect it to be a fair guide for some time.

Average costs of building, November 1994

- It costs between $600 to $850 per square metre to build a non-project home (approximately $5,580 to $7,900 per square).
- To build a project home costs from $475 to $575 per square metre (approximately $4,400 to $5,350 per square).
- Renovations are generally more expensive than building from scratch because of the additional time and costs involved in demolition and reconstruction. Renovations normally range from $800 to $1,100 per square metre or from $7,700 to $10,200 per square.
- Renovating a kitchen normally costs between $9,000 and $15,000, and for a standard bathroom renovation expect to pay between $7,000 and $14,000.

(*Source*: Builders' Advisory Centre, Sydney, 1994.)

Make sure that before you start you get quotes from a number of builders and play them off against each other. Don't be afraid to say to a builder that his quote sounds a bit high and ask him if he could do better. Some builders are prepared to negotiate on price, especially during slow times.

In our example above, moving from a two-bedroom house to a three-bedroom house cost close to $15,000. Ignoring the other qualities of the new house this effectively meant that acquiring an extra bedroom cost about $15,000.

With the set costs of renovating being around $1,000 and the set costs of moving being around $15,000, the home-owner could have spent around $14,000 on renovations to end up with the same level of expenditure. At an average renovation cost of around $8,000 per square, the $15,000 spent on moving could have funded almost two more squares being added to the original house.

To put this into perspective, the size of a bedroom in most new houses is around one square. Therefore, the original two-bedroom house could have been converted into a four-bedroom house for around the same cost as moving to the three-bedroom house. In this example, renovating proves better value than moving – and this is often the case.

When trying to choose between the two options bear in mind that the set costs of moving involve sliding scale fees dependent on the value of the properties you are buying and selling. Also, and most importantly, be aware that the average building cost of around $5,500 and the average renovation cost of around $8,000 are both *very rubbery* figures. The cost of building can range from a rock bottom minimum of around $3,800 per square to, well, the sky's the limit, particularly if you want wall-to-wall Italian marble and gold-plated taps.

Another thing to bear in mind about renovation is that a lot of people renovate their properties just before putting them on the market in the hope it will lead to a much better price and a faster sale. This may not happen. Firstly, unless you renovate sensibly you may not get your costs back, and secondly, there is a significant sector of the market who are actually looking for unrenovated homes. They want a place they can do up themselves and put their own mark on, and hopefully, improve the value of.

Overcapitalising

The big danger with renovating (apart from getting entangled with a dodgy builder – do choose carefully!) is overcapitalising. This occurs when the costs of renovations exceed the market value they add to a property. From this perspective only, you should avoid renovations which represent more than 10% of the property's market value in any one year. And improvements such as a new bathroom, kitchen or additional rooms add much more value to your home than a new roof, wiring, plumbing or expensive fittings. When a modest home is renovated to the point where it becomes the best in the street, odds are it's been overcapitalised and the value of the house will probably rise by only about half the cost of the renovations.

Making Money

If you find you have overcapitalised your options are limited and not very appealing. You can sell and recoup only a part of the cost of the renovations – in other words, take a loss. Or you can hang on to your home and wait for inflation to raise overall market values to a point where they finally catch up with yours. This could take a long time in the low-inflationary times we're living in. Whichever way, overcapitalisation will prove costly.

Also, be aware that the value you add to your home by renovation depends on more than just the cost of the renovations. It depends on how well they are done and how much is done. It also depends on the age and style of the original home, its locality and, most importantly, its position.

If you aren't sure how much value renovations will add to your home and you're worried about overcapitalisation, get advice from one or two real estate agents or from a qualified valuer. Do this before you spend too much money. Certainly do it once preliminary plans have been drawn up and costs estimated and well before you start knocking out walls!

Seeking help

The Housing Industry Association can provide useful information about renovating and buying:

ACT/Southern NSW	(06) 249 6366
NSW	(02) 633 4488
VIC	(03) 9280 8200
QLD	(07) 3846 1298
WA	(09) 244 3222
SA	(08) 346 5091
TAS	(002) 34 8592

If you are planning to build your own home or are wanting to engage a builder, your state's statutory building service can provide information and referrals:

ACT – Department of Environmental Lands
and Planning (06) 207 5111
NSW – Building Services Corporation (02) 9959 1444

VIC – Housing Guarantee Fund (03) 9663 5300
QLD – (07) 3391 8233
WA – (09) 321 6891
SA – (08) 226 8211
TAS – (002) 34 8922

Selling

Selling, like buying a house, takes some time and effort and can be a similarly testing experience. At times you'll probably wonder whether the house is priced realistically, the right method of selling is being used, the agent is on the ball, the market has gone into a freak slump, or if a buyer will be found before your hair falls out. There are ways of making the process easier.

Pricing

There's an old real estate saying – 'every property is saleable at a price'. So, even if the house 'would suit a handyman', the property is still saleable as long as it's priced appropriately.

Most sellers think their home is worth more than anyone else does. This is because it's special to them – often their blood, sweat and tears have gone into it. Try not to fall into the trap of allowing your sentiments to inflate your property's price. Most buyers will value a property on their perception of its intrinsic merits and shortcomings and not on the fact that you have spent weekends sanding back and varnishing the beautiful bathroom door. They probably won't even notice it!

What they will notice is the price, and arriving at a realistic one that reflects current market values takes some time and effort on your part.

- Start by obtaining a number of market appraisals from local real estate agents who are actually making sales. 'Sold' signs will indicate their strike rate. Appraisals are free and take around half an hour, and agents are more than willing to provide them.
- Average out the suggested values to give yourself a guide. Don't automatically accept the highest appraisal. Some agents provide deliberately inflated appraisals to win listings – it's a fairly

common and particularly irritating practice which invariably leads to vendor disappointment.

■ Go and look at comparable local houses or units being offered for sale and most importantly, those that have recently sold.

Should you use an agent?

The next thing to do is decide whether you put the property in the hands of an agent (normally one of those who has already appraised it) or whether you sell it yourself. If you have priced your property realistically, and you have time during the week to show prospective buyers through it, and you are prepared to advertise it adequately, there's no reason why you shouldn't try to sell it yourself and save what can be a significant agent's fee. (These vary from state to state and are increasingly open to negotiation – but work on an approximate range of 1% to 3% of the property's value.)

The reality is most vendors don't price their properties realistically – they are usually too expensive – and they don't have the time to show prospective buyers through because many of the genuine buyers are not weekend window shoppers. Also they're often reluctant to spend much on advertising. The result is a slow sale or no sale. An even more distressing scenario for a private seller is discovering too late that the house was underpriced. Employing the services of a real estate professional is therefore the right move in most cases.

Choosing an agent

Choosing the right real estate agent is like choosing any professional in whose hands you rest your fate. The key things you are looking for are integrity and ability. Unfortunately, real estate is one of those industries with more than its fair share of dubious practices and the last thing you need as you go through the rigours of selling is to be in the clutches of a dud.

So how do you find a good agent? The best way is the same way you find most good professionals – through personal recommendation. It simply involves you asking around. If this method fails, have three or four local agents appraise your property. Choose one who has been making sales, who has drive, who seems genuine and who you think you can get on with.

Don't bother with agents outside your area. Local ones have the best idea of local values and they are best placed physically to show potential buyers through the property. This might seem like stating the obvious but it's remarkable how many people engage agents outside the area simply because they have a high profile or are 'fashionable'. You don't need this. What you do need is someone who is close at hand and on the ball to efficiently service the job.

Selling by auction

After you've chosen an agent, the next question to address is – should you sell your property by auction or by private treaty? Most agents associated with the large, franchise real estate groups push auction pretty vigorously – generally more so than independent agents. This is partly explained by the franchise networks having well-established auction procedures and regular auction dates in place, and a culture which they describe as 'auction oriented'.

The advantages of selling by auction:

- If there is more than one buyer at the auction, competitive bidding can lead to a higher price being paid than under the lower pressure of the private treaty method.
- Sale by auction requires a 10% non-refundable deposit being submitted by the buyer on the day meaning that there is less likelihood of the buyer dropping out of the sale than under private treaty where there may be a cooling-off period.
- Auction is the best way of establishing the market value of, and hopefully selling, genuinely unique or special properties where, under conditions of competitive bidding, the property's 'difference' can achieve a premium price.

The disadvantages of selling at auction:

- Some agencies levy non-refundable auction marketing charges of up to around $1,000 – and sometimes more – whether or not the sale is successful on the day or afterwards. This money goes towards costs like auction room rental, the auctioneer's fees, signboard and pamphlets. Also, by strange convention, the vendor pays for advertising which can run into thousands of dollars depending on the property's estimated worth. Advertising costs under private treaty, while normally not as high, are usually free to the vendor. Many have suggested that this is the main reason why agents love auctions.

■ The intensive advertising/marketing period under auction is relatively short – an average of three to four weeks of inspections prior to the auction day. This may be too short a time to find the buyer who will really fall for your home and pay top dollar for it.

■ Under normal market conditions, average auction clearance rates – those that actually sell on the day – only hovers around 50%. During recessionary times, average clearance rates are lower. If you fail to sell at auction on the day it can have a very demoralising effect on you which may be capitalised upon by the agent where he heavily pressures you to drop the price. A consequence of this is that you could end up receiving less than the property is really worth.

I need to point out here that the auction method involves more than just trying to sell a property under the hammer. It can be sold beforehand, during and after the auction but trying to sell the property on the day is still very much the focus of the whole marketing exercise. This is because it's believed that the auction is where the highest price is likely to be obtained.

Private treaty

Selling by private treaty can take longer than auction as it's not such a hot-house, concentrated, time-specific technique, however, private treaty is generally cheaper as there are minimal or no advertising charges levied on the vendor by the agent. Because private treaty tends to be a slower process than auction, it can provide more time to find that special 'top paying' buyer. It also tends to be a less traumatic experience than auction.

Private treaty penalises the buyer far less than under auction if she wants to back out of the sale, which vendors and agents rightly see as a major relative flaw. Under auction the buyer loses

10% of the value of the property if she does not proceed with the sale after successfully bidding, whereas she can walk away from a private treaty sale after placing a deposit and lose as little as 0.25% of the agreed purchase price. Clearly, the amount of buyers who renege on a sale under private treaty is much higher than under auction.

Under private treaty, whatever you do, don't give your house to a number of agents to sell. An 'open listing' almost guarantees the property won't be properly advertised. The reason is that one agent who advertises the property is loath to see another agent (who hasn't advertised it but with whom the property is also listed) selling it to some buyers excited by *his* ad. The upshot is that no one advertises it properly for fear of giving the opposition a free kick – which does the vendor no good at all.

Whatever you do, don't give your house to a whole lot of agents to sell. An 'open listing' almost guarantees the property won't be properly advertised. You see, an agent doesn't want to see the property being sold by a second agent off their ad.

An 'exclusive listing' – where there's only one agent authorised to sell the property, normally for a specified period of, say, a month or two – gives the agent real incentive and a fair go at selling the property. If it isn't advertised well, the agent loses the listing.

To sell by private treaty, I recommend an exclusive listing. But beware – once you grant an exclusive listing, only the agent to whom you have granted it is entitled to sell the property. This not only excludes all other agents – it also excludes you. So if *you* find a buyer, you must still pay the full commission to the agent whether he has anything to do with the sale or not.

This, however, is an extremely rare occurrence, and I stick to my recommendation to sell via an exclusive listing if you choose to sell by private treaty. And, in most cases, unless you have a genuinely unique property with a value that's hard to gauge, private treaty is probably the way to go. It's less expensive, less traumatic and works just as well as auction – which, I sometimes suspect, is pushed hard by real estate agents too often for their own interests rather than for those of their clients.

For further information

If you need information or help on any real estate matter a call
to the Real Estate Institute is a good starting point:
NSW   (02) 264 2343
VIC   (03) 9882 9188
QLD   (07) 3891 5711
WA   (09) 380 8222
SA   (08) 366 4300
TAS   (002) 234 769
National Office/ACT (06) 282 4277

CHAPTER SEVEN

Mortgages

There is little doubt that having a mortgage or, more to the point, paying one off, shapes our adult lives enormously. While it's the ticket that enables us to enjoy all the benefits of home ownership, it's also the millstone that can bind us to a dreary job and an irritating boss that we otherwise wouldn't put up with. Like a marriage, a mortgage is a major commitment, and possibly an even more scary one. If you don't play your cards right, it can last for all of 25 awful years.

Actually, mortgages need not be too painful. What you have to do is make sure you find the right one to start with, and then pay it off as quickly as possible, thereby saving yourself many thousands of dollars and much heartache in the process.

Finding the right mortgage

For starters, be aware that as a potential home-buyer you will find yourself popular – there is strong competition out there in the mortgage marketplace which means you can shop around for the best deal.

Despite the large number of home loan providers and variability in home loan rates, mortgages are quite basic products with a fairly limited number of variations. These are the options you can choose from:

- interest-only loans
- principal and interest loans
- variable rate loans
- fixed rate loans
- combination of fixed and variable rate loans (including capped rate loans)
- equity credit loans.

All of these loans can range in duration from 15 to 30 years.

Making Money

Interest-only vs principal and interest

With an interest-only loan, your regular repayments are comprised of nothing other than interest charges. You do not repay any of the principal (or 'capital') at all. I can't recommend interest-only loans to the average home-buyer because at the end of the loan period, you still have all of the principal to repay!

Interest-only loans – which have smaller repayments than principal and interest loans – are really designed for investment purposes. They enable you to hang on to a property which, during the term of the loan, hopefully generates some rental income and undergoes capital gain.

Interest-only loans often involve selling the property to repay the principal – which is not what the average home-owner has in mind.

If you are buying a property with the intention of turning it into your home and living in it for some years, take out a principle and interest mortgage. This way you are repaying the debt and, at the same time, increasing your equity in the property. At the end of the loan period you will own the property outright.

Variable rate vs fixed rate

A variable rate loan is one where the rate of interest you pay on your mortgage can be raised or lowered by the lender at its discretion. The changes to the interest rate you are being charged, in turn reflect changes to the official level of interest rates set by the Reserve Bank of Australia.

When the official interest rate changes it does so in response to pressures applied by a wide range of local and international economic and political factors – which could range from a boom in Australia to a crash on Wall Street to a war in the Middle East. Many of these influences are beyond the Government's control and cannot be predicted. Consequently, not even the experts can be quite sure just how interest rates will move in the coming years.

Do you remember, for instance, how high home loan interest rates climbed during the late 1980s? In June 1989 the major banks were charging 17% on home loans. On a $100,000 mortgage over 25 years this meant a monthly repayment of $1,438. Compare this with a repayment of $909 on the same loan with interest rates at only 10%. If you have a variable rate loan you must be prepared for the possibility that interest rates could rise during the long course of your mortgage.

The alternative is a fixed rate mortgage which you enter for a specific period, commonly three to five years. This means that whether market rates go up or down, your rate remains the same and you know exactly what your monthly (or preferably fort-nightly) repayments will be.

You can agonise forever about which is the best option and you'll find that interest rate predictions are notoriously inaccurate. Even the best-informed people get it wrong. A friend of mine, a financial director in a major Australian company, took out a fixed-rate mortgage in 1990, locked in at 15% for three years. He then sat by, scratching his head, while standard variable (bank) home loan rates dropped 15 times to a low of 8.75% in September 1993. His decision to take a fixed rate loan could not have been more ill-timed – and he is a financial professional!

I do realise this isn't very comforting for the average home-buyer. What should you do? Well, pretty obviously if you think interest rates will fall you'd go for variable; if they are likely to rise you'd fix your loan. Unfortunately no one really knows this with any certainty, so my advice is that if you can afford the mortgage repayments at the current rate, but would be in great difficulty if rates increased by more than say, 2%, I advise you take a fixed loan for three or four years. At least this way you know you will be able to afford your mortgage for that time. On the other hand, if your finances aren't so tight, in the present economic climate, I'd go for the variable rate.

Another thing you will want to consider with variable and fixed rate loans is the facility to make extra repayments. With variable rate loans you are entitled to make additional payments in order to pay your mortgage off faster but this isn't the case with standard fixed rate loans, where payments over and above the regular minimum repayment are not normally accepted (except under rare promotional circumstances). You need to think carefully about this before you sign anything, as the ability to make extra repayments is very beneficial.

Making Money

Split and capped

For those of you who want to take an each-way bet on interest rates you have the option of a 'split loan'. These are loans which are part fixed and part variable, in almost any ratio you wish. With split loans it doesn't matter so much which way the rates go – you'll win a bit, lose a bit either way.

Then, there are capped rate loans. These usually feature a very low introductory rate lasting for the first 6 to 12 months, then reverting to the standard variable rate. With these loans the interest rate you are charged during the introductory period cannot exceed, but can be less than, the capped rate (though it rarely is).

Capped rate loans might appear attractive at first glance but really they are little more than marketing gimmicks. Generally, the capped rate period is too short to be of any value. Sure, the honeymoon period is better than nothing, but it should not be the sole determinant for giving your mortgage business to the lender offering it.

You may be borrowing money for 25 years, so look at the cost over the full 25 years, not just the 6 months or 1 year 'special offer'.

Longer vs shorter term loans

Whether you choose a 15- or 30-year loan depends simply on what you can afford. The longer the term, the less your monthly or fortnightly repayments will be, however, the longer the term the more you end up paying and the longer you will have the weight of a mortgage around your neck.

If you take out a $100,000 mortgage at 10% over 15 years your fortnightly repayments are $494. During the term you will pay back a total of $192,660. Now, if you take this mortgage out over 25 years, your fortnightly repayments drop to $418, 15% less than for the 15-year loan – but the total amount you end up paying over the 25 years will be $271,700, 41% more than for the 15-year loan. (*Source*: National Australia Bank.)

Clearly, the less time you take to pay your mortgage off the better, so my advice is to take out as short a term loan as you can realistically afford.

Equity credit loans

Equity credit loans are mortgage-based loans. They are a form of financing secured against your home which should be considered carefully because of the impact they can have on the time you take to pay off your mortgage.

There are two versions of equity credit loans. One is a 'draw back' or 'redraw' loan, where you can withdraw any excess money from your mortgage account. That is, what you have paid into it over and above the minimum amount required. An example of this is the Westpac 'Options' loan. You are required to make a minimum repayment that will pay your loan off over 25 years but if you get in front you can take that amount out again. This is rather clever because it forces you to pay off your loan, but you can put extra money in, and effectively earn around 10%, risk free and tax free, yet still have access to the money.

The other type of equity loan is one where you are effectively granted a line of credit against the equity you have in your home, which is the difference between how much the property is worth and how much you still owe on it. These types of loan are often called 'equity overdraft loans', because you are really being granted an overdraft secured by your home, at lower than standard overdraft rates. Most banks offer these loans.

Citibank's home equity loan, for example, allows you to have a chequebook with which you can draw up to a predetermined limit. This limit, which takes into account your income and other debts, has a theoretical maximum of 90% of the value of the property at the time the loan is struck. The money can be used for all sorts of purposes including investments in property or shares, working capital for a business, your childrens' education, or a holiday. With most home equity loans the amount you borrow against your home is repayable at an interest rate normally around 1% above the lenders' standard variable rate.

This is a very convenient and easy form of finance. Too easy, some might say. If you are not disciplined enough there is a real danger of dipping too deeply into your home equity and 25 years on, still having a substantial debt outstanding against your home. At least with a redraw loan, after 25 years your mortgage is fully paid out.

Both types of equity loans have offset benefits. This means that any additional payments you make towards the mortgage over and above the minimum repayment give you a tax-free return on those additional payments – at a rate of interest equivalent to the mortgage interest rate.

What to look for in a mortgage

These are the things you should look for when shopping for a mortgage, regardless of the type you prefer.

Consistently competitive interest rates

Some lenders are more able or willing to consistently offer keener rates than the competition. This may be because they are a low-cost operation, or simply a more aggressive organisation.

The mortgage market *has* become far more competitive in the 1990s. This is mainly due to the entry of major insurance companies including MLC, FAI and GIO and of an army of smaller lenders specialising in mortgages, known as mortgage originators or mortgage managers. These include Aussie Home Loans and Austral Mortgage Corporation.

Generally, the mortgage managers are low-cost operations which, unlike the banks, don't have extensive and expensive branch networks to support. This enables them to sometimes significantly undercut the banks.

Low fees and flexibility

When you apply for a mortgage you will probably be up for an administrative charge known as an *establishment fee*. This covers the cost of:
- preparing the loan application and any supporting documents
- obtaining details of the Certificate of Title
- attending the settlement of the property
- lodging documents at the Land Titles Office.

The establishment fee may or may not include the lender's solicitor's fees and valuation fees. However, it *does not* include government charges such as stamp duty on the mortgage or charges by the Titles Office.

Establishment fees are a growing area of negotiation between lender and borrower. They can range from $0 to $1,000 on a $100,000 loan, and average around $600. When you are applying for a loan ask for a discount in this area – you might be pleasantly surprised.

You might also be up for a *valuation fee* – the cost of having your property professionally valued. Like establishment fees these fees can vary tremendously, for example, on a $180,000 property the valuation fee would range from $0 to $300, averaging around $150.

There may be times when you are late with your regular mortgage repayment. Most lenders have a *late payment penalty* which is where you are charged a higher rate of interest on the overdue amount. The penalty rate is usually around 1% above your normal rate, though it can be several percentage points higher.

Like all loans there will be *ongoing bank fees* and these can vary from as little as $3 per month to $120 per year.

Refinancing and switching fees

Two other fees you need to investigate are the early pay-out penalty fee when you refinance with another lender and the switching fee when you change from a variable to a fixed rate loan, or vice versa, with the same lender. Refinancing from one mortgage to another can be an expensive business, depending on the policies of the lenders involved and the current level of interest rates.

Let's say you're thinking about refinancing your mortgage with a mortgage manager because it offers a better rate. Lenders don't like losing customers, so to discourage you from taking your business elsewhere they normally charge a significant exit penalty fee which can range from one to six months interest payments. On the other hand it may be just a flat fee.

You may have a fixed rate loan and want to switch to a variable rate loan – but with the same lender. Some lenders are very flexible and allow you to do this at no cost. However, others will charge a fee for what is really a form of refinancing. The fee can be very high, particularly if there is a significant gap between the fixed and the variable rate.

0━ Key thought

Remember, it's not the end of the world if you take the wrong mortgage. You can always bail out of the loan you are in and refinance elsewhere.

A good mortgage

Look for the following features in your mortgage:
- consistently competitive rates
- flexibility – about exiting, early pay-out, or switching to a different mortgage
- low or no establishment fees (including low or no valuation and mortgage documentation fees)
- low exit/early pay-out penalty fees
- low or no switching fees (from variable rate to fixed rate, or vice versa)
- ability to make additional repayments
- offset savings facility
- written in plain English and easy to understand.

Mortgage checklist

Have this checklist handy when you are shopping for a mortgage. Photocopy it and take it with you to different lending institutions.
- What is your variable rate now?
- What was the rate six months ago?
- How is your variable rate set?
- What are the terms (duration) of your mortgages?
- What are your fixed rates over one to five years?
- What happens to the loan at the end of the fixed term?
- Can the rate be refixed then?
- What is the capped rate?
- For how long is it capped?
- What happens at the end of the capped period?
- Do you have split loans?
- What are the maximum and minimum ratios between the fixed

and variable components on your split loans?
- What are the terms of the split loans?
- What are your establishment fees?
- What is your valuation fee?
- What is your mortgage documentation fee?
- Are there any other up-front fees?
- What is the exit fee?
- What is the early pay-out fee?
- Can you switch between fixed and variable loans or vice versa?
- What is the switching fee?
- Can I make additional repayments on all your mortgage products?
- What is the late payment penalty?
- Can I see a copy of your mortgage document?
- How long will it take to arrange finance?
- Is there anything else I should know about your home loans?
- What do you recommend?

When looking for a mortgage, take your time, shop around and ask plenty of questions. Don't sign any mortgage contract without fully understanding what it all means and what it legally binds you to. If you're not satisfied with what's offering (or with the mortgage you already have), go elsewhere. There are plenty of home lenders out there bending over backwards to do business with you, so, go and take advantage of it.

The benefits of extra payments

Let's assume you borrow $100,000 to buy your home and it's to be repaid over 25 years, with an annual interest rate of 10% that remains constant for the life of the loan. (This is a totally unrealistic assumption, but it does serve to make an important point.)

Look at the table below and see how much you save and how much time is shaved off the term of the mortgage by paying an additional $25 and $100 per month over and above the standard repayment set by the bank. As you can see, the amount of time cut off the loan and the size of the savings these additional repayments make are quite extraordinary. And when you remember that all these savings are totally tax-free, it's pretty clear just how smart an investment making extra repayments really is.

$100,000 loan over 25 years at an interest rate of 10%:

Paying the minimum repayment	$909 per month
Term length	25 years
Total interest paid	$172,748
Paying an additional $25 per month	($934 per month)
Term reduced to	22 years and 6 months
Total interest paid	$151,033
Saving	**$21,715**
Paying an additional $100 per month	($1,009 per month)
Term reduced to	17 years and 8 months
Total interest paid	$112,700
Saving	**$60,048**

(*Source*: National Australia Bank)

Adding a bit extra to your regular repayments is one way of paying your mortgage off earlier but there are some other ways:

- Making your mortgage repayments fortnightly instead of monthly. This simple change in repayment frequency can save you a small fortune and cut years off the loan. Using the same scenario as above, that is, a $100,000 loan over 25 years at 10% per annum, paying your mortgage fortnightly would save you $53,629 and reduce the life of the loan by six years and six months.

    How does it work? Well, when you pay fortnightly, you end up repaying the equivalent of 13 monthly instalments per year, not 12. It's this extra month's worth of instalments that makes all the difference. The key is that paying fortnightly really does not seem any more painful than paying twice as much monthly, particularly if you time your repayments to the day you are paid.
- Running an offset account means you have the interest earned on a separate savings or cheque account paid into your

mortgage account. Now, when you earn interest on your savings or cheque account, ordinarily up to almost half can be lost through tax, taking a lot of the shine off the investment. But when the interest earned on your savings or cheque account is offset against your mortgage account, you get the full benefit of the interest because there is no tax involved. As well as this, these relatively small extra contributions will make a big reduction in your mortgage over time.

■ Lump sum repayments on your mortgage can also dramatically accelerate its reduction. Let's say you put $5,000 towards your $100,000, 25-year, 10% p.a. mortgage at the end of the mortgage's first year.

The $5,000 lump sum payment would reduce your mortgage by a mighty 3 years and 11 months and knock $39,200 off it. However, if you were able to put $10,000 into your mortgage you would wipe 6 years and 10 months off the term and save $65,700! (*Source*: National Australia Bank)

Consider putting your tax refund, share dividend cheque or similar large payment straight into your mortgage account if possible. No other investment will provide the fabulous result of strong tax-free returns without any risk attached (because you are effectively investing in your own home).

How extra repayments work

All the methods of paying off your mortgage faster and saving thousands of dollars in the process are facets of the one basic strategy, namely, putting more money into your mortgage account than the minimum monthly repayment required by the lender.

But why do these extra payments, even when they are quite small, have such a major impact? The answer is really quite simple.

In the early years of your mortgage most of your repayments are comprised of interest only, not the principal. That's why on a 25-year, $100,000 loan, after one year you still owe $99,943, after two years $97,446 and three years $94,732.

Now, if all you do is pop just an extra $20 into a $100,000 loan this $20 is immediately deducted straight off the *principal*, so the amount you owe now is $99,980.

Making Money

However, your regular repayments are calculated on a debt of $100,000, so not only does your extra $20 help, but importantly, *it does not reduce your regular repayment*. This double effect – the extra money and the normal repayment, really get stuck into reducing the amount you owe.

CHAPTER EIGHT

Insurance

Insurance is all about protecting what you have now and what you would like to have in the future. But, as you go through life, the protection you need for the present and your future changes. The key to insurance, therefore, is being attuned to these changes, to make sure you always have the right sort and in just the right amounts. It's a waste of money having too much, but you can't afford to have too little.

What I'll look at in this chapter are the types of insurance relevant to your journey through life, showing when you need what protection, and how much.

Insuring your possessions and you

First up, there are two fundamental areas of insurance – your possessions and yourself. Most people don't question the need for insuring their assets – whether it's their home and its contents, their car, boat or jewellery – and to varying degrees most people do insure these things.

Considered less important by many people (and incorrectly so) is insurance directly concerned with you – this includes your life, income and health. The reality is that, at certain times in your life, these insurances are at least as important as the insurance on your possessions, arguably even more so. Yet it is an area where many are under-insured, based on the assumption that 'it won't happen to me' – but unfortunately it can, and sometimes it does. So you need to be prepared.

Shop around, read the fine print

Now, when you decide to buy insurance, regardless of what sort it is, there are two important steps to take. The first is to make sure you shop around energetically. This is because there are significant differences in the prices and conditions of the policies offered by the various insurance companies. The second, which follows from this, is to make sure you know exactly what each policy covers, or, more to the point, what it doesn't. If this involves quizzing the insurance salesman or broker closely and reading through the policy (as boring as that may be), do it. It's your life or your possessions being insured so it's up to you to make sure the cover is right.

Insurance checklist

Apart from the obvious questions about the premium and, depending on what type of insurance it is, the questions you need to ask before you buy include:

- Is there an excess? (an initial amount you pay in the event of a claim)
- Are there no-claim bonuses? (where the premium reduces over time if you make no claims, particularly common with car insurance)
- Is there a waiting time for benefits?
- Are there any discounts? (for example, for a fitted car alarm with car insurance, for non-smokers with life insurance, for people aged over 50 with household insurance)
- What are the exclusions of this policy and under what conditions will the insurer not pay a claim?
- What proportion of claims does the insurer pay?
- How long does it take to process a claim?
- Can I have a copy of the policy to read?

You also need to pay close attention to the way insurance companies *define* things. With income/disability insurance, for instance, the definition of what a 'disability' is varies.

Choose a reputable insurer

The company behind the policy is also important. Some insurance companies have a reputation for paying more readily than others.

When you see a hitherto unknown insurance company burst onto the scene with a glitzy advertising campaign saying they have the lowest premiums and the best service in town, beware. It may also be that they'll be the hardest people in town to get any money from.

In the event that you do have to claim you don't want the added stress of having to battle for the cover you thought you had been paying for. Give your business to a company that's well established, that enjoys a good general reputation, that people you know have had trouble-free claims against, or which has been recommended to you – and if that means paying a bit more, let me tell you, it's worth it!

Be accurate and honest

Another thing you must be careful about with insurance is to ensure you are accurate and honest when filling out the proposal or application form. If, when you make a claim, the insurer discovers a pertinent fact was incorrectly entered or not entered at all they can legally refuse the claim.

Under the Insurance Contracts Act you have a 'duty of disclosure' to tell the insurance company 'every matter which you know or could be reasonably expected to know is relevant to (the insurance company's) decision to accept the insurance risk'.

Please don't try to fudge on this and when you make a claim don't fudge on that either! If the insurance company suspects a phoney or exaggerated claim you can be prepared for a long delay until settlement, and possibly even legal action.

Now, let's look at the insurances you'll need as you travel through life, beginning with the ones that protect your material assets.

Household insurance

Home building insurance covers your home against an array of calamities including damage or destruction from fire, wind, hail, earthquakes, vandalism (other than by tenants or people you've invited), water, riots and so on, *but normally excludes damage by flood*. (Do check exactly what is and what isn't covered before you buy.) Contents insurance simply covers what's inside your house against the same calamities, as well as covering them against theft.

Household insurance policies come in different forms. Firstly, you can insure your home and/or its contents on separate policies, or you can have a combined house and contents policy. Buying a combined policy is generally cheaper than buying two separate ones.

Secondly, you can chose between an indemnity policy and a replacement/reinstatement policy. Indemnity policies allow you to insure your home and/or contents for their value, minus an amount for depreciation based on the home or item's age and condition.

The increasingly common replacement/reinstatement policies, on the other hand, allow you to insure your home and/or contents for the full cost of totally rebuilding your home and/or replacing your damaged or stolen contents with – in most cases – new items of an equivalent standard. (This can be a problematic area and it's one where you really need to check the fine print. Some replacement policies may not, in fact, fund the replacement of all old items with new items. For instance, some insurers will not replace damaged carpets older than five years with new carpets.)

Replacement policies have higher premiums than indemnity policies because they cost the insurance companies more, but I recommend them nonetheless. The depreciation factor with indemnity policies means that money will have to come out of your own pocket to restore your property to its former state, and that can be a killer in the event of a major claim.

Most contents policies only pay a maximum amount for each item in your home, normally between $1,000 and $2,000. So if you have a piece of jewellery worth, say, $5,000 or a painting worth $10,000 you would need to list each item separately and probably pay an additional premium.

In the event of a loss, the claim should proceed more smoothly if you can easily prove the existence of the destroyed or stolen items. This proof ideally takes the form of receipts or valuations but photos are also helpful, particularly in the case of stolen jewellery. They also give the police a much better chance of recovery as does engraving items such as stereos with a means of identification.

Insurers will generally not require you to prove the prior existence of stolen items, but they can if they wish, and without proof the claim can get messy. Of course, any proof you had may have disappeared as well – that's why it's a good idea to keep photocopies of documentation in a safe place other than your home. Around Australia you will find services that will do this documentation and take photos for you. The cost is typically $150 to $250.

Under-insurance

Under-insurance is one of the great financial hazards. Let's say you have a replacement policy on your home, and your home is destroyed by fire. The policy will cover the costs of replacing the house, *but only up to the value for which the original one was insured*. If the destroyed home was under-insured you will have to dip into your own pocket to rebuild another as valuable.

Most people under-insure out of ignorance of their property's current replacement value; others, foolishly, do so to save a few dollars on insurance premiums. And while the consequences can be clearly catastrophic, under-insurance is surprisingly widespread. When the Ash Wednesday fires raged through Victoria in 1983 around 40% of damaged or destroyed homes were found to be under-insured. When Newcastle was struck by earthquake in December 1989 30% of homes were found to be under-insured, and these by an average of around 30% each (where the maximum insurance payout only met around 70% of the total damages bill).

According to the Insurance Council of Australia, the average national level of under-insurance on Australian houses is 30% of their real and total replacement value. In older established suburbs with many elderly residents and in new suburbs with many younger homebuyers on tight budgets the average level of under-insurance is closer to 50%.

On household contents the average national level of under-insurance is about 40%, rising to 60% for the elderly and low income young home-buyers. Items that householders perennially under-value and hence under-insure are record, CD and book collections, clothing, tools and goods in storage.

Most people do not realise they are under-insured until they claim, and under-valuation is generally the cause of the problem. The way around this is to have a professional value your house (and contents) for insurance purposes. The valuation normally costs around $300, and it remains valid up until the time you make any capital changes to your property (the valuation is indexed for inflation on your policy).

If you choose to value your home yourself, make sure you allow for expenses such as the removal of debris from the site, architect's fees and other contingencies. Normally you would add somewhere between 10% to 20% to the replacement building cost to cover these. Also, take into account the potential costs of relocation and temporary accommodation that can arise from a claim, or consider the loss of rent that may arise from damage to an investment property. Most house policies can provide adequate cover for all these eventualities, so make sure the one you choose does.

What does it cost to insure your house?

In early 1995 the average cost of replacement house insurance, based on the following, three-bedroom, full brick houses was:

Location	Sum insured	Average annual premium*
Sydney (Baulkham Hills)	$172,000	$324
Melbourne (Glen Waverley)	$174,000	$297
Perth (Kingsley)	$157,000	$325
Brisbane (Kedron)	$157,000	$288
Adelaide (Modbury)	$152,000	$289
Hobart (Kingston)	$159,000	$213

* the average premium was drawn from a survey of 22 insurers including AMP, Colonial, Mercantile Mutual, GIO and MLC.

(*Source*: *Property Investor*, BRW Publications, January 1995.)

Public liability

Household insurance frequently includes a public or legal liability component, generally up to a limit of $10 million. This covers you for the accidental death or personal injury or damage to property suffered by another party for which you may be held legally liable due to your negligence. This, of course, excludes damage caused deliberately or injuries that occur as a result of motor vehicle accidents which are covered by Compulsory Third Party Insurance.

Car insurance

There are three types of car insurance:

Compulsory third party

Compulsory third party is the insurance you have to pay when you register your car. It insures you (the driver) or anyone else driving your car against any claim for personal injury brought by another person or their family, for any injury or death caused to them by your car, assuming your car was at fault.

This insurance, which costs around $250 per year, does not cover you against any damage your car may cause to property – so if you ran into someone's Rolls Royce and you were at fault, your compulsory third party insurance would not cover the bill.

Third party property

Third party property insurance costs around $150 p.a. and protects you against claims from a third party for damage to their property caused by your car (assuming it was at fault) whether or not you were driving. Some third party property policies also offer limited cover for damage to your car if you can prove someone else was at fault. The NRMA, for instance, will pay you up to $3,000 for damage done to your car assuming it was not at fault. Anyone who drives is crazy not to have at least this level of car insurance.

Comprehensive

Comprehensive car insurance covers damage not only to anyone else's property but also to your car, up to an 'agreed value', which is theoretically your car's current market value including all added options and registration costs.

Most comprehensive car insurance carries an excess – where you pay an initial proportion of the claim out of your own pocket regardless of who is at fault – as well as an additional excess if the car is driven by a high-risk category driver, such as an under 25-year-old male.

Your car insurance also generally accumulates no-claim bonuses, rising over some years to a maximum of 60% – which represents a major discount. (An example of how this works is: with one major car insurer it takes five years to build your no-claim bonus (NCB) up to 60%. If you make a claim and you can prove the accident wasn't your fault you'll retain your NCB. If it was your fault or you can't prove it wasn't, your NCB will be reduced by 20%.)

The idea of the excess and the no-claim bonus is to discourage you from making small claims. The cost to you of paying the excess and increased premiums over the coming years needs to be calculated before you claim for any minor damage. (Your insurer will do this calculation for you.)

Car insurance premiums are calculated taking into account many variables such as the car's market value, its make, its type, the age and gender of the driver/s, whether the car is for private or business use, where you live, if the car is garaged or parked on the street, whether it has a car alarm and so on. Exotic and powerful sports cars, particularly turbos, are especially expensive to insure.

It's very important to shop around for car insurance. There can be an enormous difference in premiums between insurers due to the different ways they measure risk. But remember there is more to insurance than just the premium. Make sure you compare conditions and exclusions, and pay particular attention to the treatment of no-claim bonuses. Most importantly don't get involved with an insurer with a reputation for being a difficult payer.

Insurance for other material items such as boats, motorbikes, aircraft etc work along similar lines. An insurer assesses the risk based on a number of variables and offers you a premium.

Life insurance

'Life insurance' is actually a misnomer – it should really be called 'death insurance' because death is what you are insuring against. More to the point, you are insuring against an untimely death. There are two types of life insurance – term and whole-of-life (or 'endowment') insurance – which I compare later.

Who is life insurance for? Well, it's a product designed for anyone with a family, dependent relatives or debt. If you die and your life is insured your beneficiaries receive a lump sum pay-out.

In the case of families it makes sense that both parents are insured even if they don't both work. Too often the economic worth of the child-rearer's work is overlooked. Both professional childminding and housekeeping are expensive services and it makes sense to insure the housewife's (or househusband's) life at a similar level to the breadwinner's.

So, how much should you insure your life for? Well, many insurance agents suggest a reasonable figure is 10 to 15 times the annual expenditure needs of your dependants. Others say anywhere between 3 to 10 times your annual salary in addition to an amount necessary to cover your debts is appropriate.

Let's look at my situation. A mortgage, three young children, school fees, and it's my income that makes it all tick over. If I get run over by a bus and die it could cause my family real problems. So I have term insurance that will provide an amount of money that will take care of them all until the kids have finished their education.

How did we work out how much we needed? Well, it's quite simple really. Our budget identifies our yearly spending and our 'balance sheet' (our list of assets and liabilities) shows us what we have and what we owe. I carry enough insurance to pay out our debts and provide sufficient capital to provide for my family and the kids' education, with a balance to help my wife rebuild her future.

As a rule of thumb, the following guide will help. For each $5,000 of income your family would need each year, you should have the following amount of capital.

How much capital do you need?

The amount of capital required to generate $5,000 of income per year is:

$22,000 if the income is to last for 5 years
$41,000 if the income is to last for 10 years
$56,000 if the income is to last for 15 years
$68,000 if the income is to last for 20 years.

Note that these figures assume you use up all your capital. In other words, if you wanted an income of $30,000 per year to last for five years you would need $132,000 to generate it and, at the end of the five years there would be nothing left. You would have spent the lot!

   Also note that these figures assume your investment portfolio is diversified across a mix of cash, fixed interest, shares and property securities. Average annual portfolio returns are assumed to be 8%, and inflation to be 4%. Be aware that different returns and a different inflation rate would produce different final figures, therefore, *this table is to be treated as a guide only and cannot be guaranteed.*

Whole-of-life insurance

Whole-of-life insurance (WOL) is structured on the understanding that you contribute towards it for virtually the whole of your life. The premium doesn't change as you get older (apart from indexation), and is determined by the age at which you sign up. The idea is you stop contributing towards the policy either when you die or when the policy matures, normally at age 60 or 65.

WOL has an agreed pay-out to your beneficiaries in the event of your death and also has an investment or savings component which part of your premium goes towards. If you are still alive at policy maturity it is wound up and you receive a lump sum pay-out which is the return on the investment portion of your premium.

WOL policies can be cashed-in prior to maturity, however you will only recoup the full amount of annual premiums paid in after around 5 to 10 years of contributions. If you cash-in (or 'surrender') the policy before this you will get back less than you have put into it. While things are improving, commissions and insurance company costs can see many WOL policies having no cash value for their first three years.

Term life insurance

Since WOL policies have been falling out of public favour, insurance companies have promoted term life policies which insure against death only and have no investment component. This has substantially reduced the cost of obtaining death cover and presently term cover is very keenly priced. (Indeed, term insurance is one of the few products to have come down in price during the last decade.)

The cost of term life insurance, for someone with a good health record, depends on your age, sex and whether you are a smoker. Through one major insurer, for example, a 30-year-old non-smoking male will pay only 88 cents per $1,000 of cover per year. A 30-year-old male smoker, on the other hand, will pay $1.54 per $1,000 of cover per year. (If smoking doesn't kill you the costs will!)

A 30-year-old female non-smoker will pay 66 cents per $1,000 of cover per year and a smoker will pay $1.10 for the same cover. Commonplace to all insurers is an added standard annual policy fee (in this case $34.10) which does not vary, regardless of the amount insured, your age, sex or whether you smoke.

While other insurers' premiums are comparable to these it is worth shopping around as you will see from the table below. You also need to look for certain features in your policy, such as the option of renewing the policy regardless of changes to your health. Some companies, for example, guarantee that a policy, once accepted, will be renewable to age 70 at the appropriate premium level. Another feature to look for is the ability to link the amount insured to the Consumer Price Index. This ensures that the level of cover is maintained in real terms.

Term insurance annual premiums for $200,000 sum insured as at April 1995

	GIO $	AMP $	MLC $	Mercantile Mutual $	Legal & General $
Male non smoker					
30	200	194	202	200	220
35	200	194	206	200	220
40	244	238	254	241	270
45	352	340	358	341	392
50	540	572	584	553	640
55	906	1114	1070	1001	1066
60	1646	2032	1952	1779	1908
65	3054	3636	3554		3460
Male smoker					
30	304	336	332	285	306
35	324	380	384	331	350
40	422	484	506	449	476
45	628	704	728	705	728
50	970	1174	1214	1159	1238
55	1622	2086	2062	1887	2068
60	2924	3444	3846	3247	3648
65	5366	5596	6330		6506
Female non smoker					
30	200	176	200	200	220
35	200	176	200	200	220
40	200	194	212	200	222
45	244	254	266	259	294
50	300	416	434	403	456
55	630	716	696	657	762
60	986	1088	1156	1071	1228
65	1662	1882	2246		2058
Female smoker					
30	200	302	266	227	276
35	204	336	302	255	296
40	280	412	386	323	392
45	408	608	546	467	538

50	682	916	854	699	886
55	1064	1474	1322	1123	1490
60	1642	2434	2320	1651	2274
65	2712	3956	4280		3854

Notes: All premiums are quoted for age next birthday and include any annual policy fees. Conditions may vary from insurer to insurer.

Term vs whole-of-life

Some people will still tell you that whole-of-life insurance is better than term insurance because it provides a fixed price for your insurance (that is, the annual premium does not increase as you get older), and it has an investment component. In my opinion these arguments don't stack up.

Consider this. A healthy, 32-year-old, non-smoking male taking out life insurance with a death cover of $200,000 through one of the major Australian life offices would pay an annual WOL premium of around $4,200 based on policy maturity at age 65.

The cumulative amount of premiums paid by this policy holder between ages 32 and 65 would be around $140,000. If the policy was surrendered at age 65 it would be worth around $290,000. But I don't believe roughly doubling one's money over 33 years is such an impressive investment result.

The same individual taking out $200,000 death cover through term insurance at age 32 would pay very much less per year as the table above indicates.

Okay, the annual WOL premium remains constant meaning WOL is relatively cheap in our later life but most of us need high levels of insurance in our thirties and forties (when term cover is cheap) and none in our sixties (when term cover is expensive).

As far as the savings/investment component of WOL goes, you would be far better off investing the savings differential between it and term premiums in other investments such as shares, property, super or accelerated mortgage repayments which show much better long-term returns.

You may find those who argue for WOL have a personal financial interest in the matter, namely that salesmen's commissions on WOL are much more lucrative than the amount earnt on term insurance.

> ⊙━ **Key thought**
>
> When young, put your money into savings. When married and with a family, take plenty of term death cover. With the kids at work, retain your death cover and establish an investment portfolio. When older, build up your contributions to your investment fund and reduce or eliminate your term insurance.

Income (disability) insurance

Income insurance, also known as disability insurance, protects what is probably your most valuable asset – and if you think that's your car or your house, think again. Unless you've retired, chances are your most valuable asset is your ability to earn an income.

Let me illustrate this. If you are 30 years old on $30,000 p.a. and you expect your earnings to increase by 7% per year, you will earn $4.1 million in total income by 65 years of age. If you are 40 years old on $40,000 p.a., given the same growth, you will earn $2.5 million by retirement.

But, while no one would buy a new car or house without immediately insuring it, surprisingly few people take action to insure their income against an inability to work due to illness or injury. This is despite income/disability insurance being widely available at reasonable cost, and also being fully tax deductible.

The reason the vast majority of people don't take out disability insurance probably reflects the fact that not many people believe that they are likely to be disabled. But the chances are probably much higher than you think.

A 25-year-old male, for instance, has a 24% chance of becoming disabled for some period in his life by age 65. If he is disabled for more than three months then the average claim duration is 2.2 years.

Many of us take out life insurance policies to financially protect our dependants against our untimely death and yet during our working life, we have an eight to nine times greater likelihood of being seriously injured than being killed.

The idea of disability insurance is pretty straightforward. You can insure yourself for up to 75% (sometimes 80%) of your income in the event of sickness or an accident rendering you incapable of carrying out your normal work duties. So if, for example, your annual income was $35,000 you could insure yourself for a yearly amount of $26,250 (75%). This benefit would be paid to you until the expiry of the agreed term, or until your recovery allowed you to return to work.

Like life insurance, you should have income/disability insurance if you have a job, unless someone else will take care of you if you get sick or injured – with the possibility of it being until you die!

Premiums vary depending on your age, sex, occupation and whether or not you are a smoker. Another determinant of the premium is how long you wait for the insurance payments to kick in after you fall ill or the accident occurs. The usual range of waiting periods is 14, 30 and 90 days. The longer the waiting period you opt for, the lower the premium. You can also vary the length of time the benefit is paid to you, from two years through to a maximum term of up until age 65. Clearly, the longer the term the higher the premium.

Income insurance costs

The annual premiums below are for income insurance where the benefit is 75% of gross income, payable to age 65 and indexed for inflation.

The premiums include stamp duty and policy fee, and are for the standard income insurance policies offered by the three companies. All policies are guaranteed renewable.

1 Male doctor aged 45; non smoker; $6,250 gross income per month; 30 day waiting period.
2 Female real estate agent aged 35; smoker; $3,750 gross income per month; 14 day waiting period.
3 Male plumber aged 50; smoker; $3,437 gross income per month; 30 day waiting period.
4 Female nurse aged 30; non smoker; $2,500 gross income per month; 30 day waiting period.
5 Female hairdresser aged 50; non smoker; $2,500 gross income per month; 14 day waiting period.

	Prudential	Mercantile Mutual	MLC
	$	$	$
1	813	1139	749
2	1114	1554	951.
3	2094	3283	2481
4	868	771	654
5	2844	3188	2586

Quotes accurate at May 1995.

A vital thing to check before you go out and sign up is how each insurance company defines 'disability'. This can be critical in the event of a claim. You will come across three broad definitions:

- an inability to perform your normal occupation (due to illness or injury)
- an inability to perform each and every duty of your normal occupation
- an inability to perform each and every duty of *any* occupation for which you are reasonably qualified by your training, education and experience. Be wary of this one. The insurer would not consider you could work as a lawyer, for instance, if you were an office clerk (pre-claim), but they may think you could work as a office clerk if you were a lawyer (pre-claim), and terminate payments as a result.

The common and reasonable definition is one that will compensate you if an illness or accident renders you unable to perform your normal duties, where you are not working and where you are under the ongoing care of a medical practitioner.

In some cases the definition of disability is modified after you have claimed for a minimum period (usually two years) so that the payment stops if you are able to undertake a job which you are qualified to do, but which might not necessarily be your usual occupation.

What to look for

The sort of income protection policy I recommend you take is one:

- with an unambiguous definition of 'disability' – being, an inability to perform normally your usual occupation
- where the benefits are indexed in the event you are disabled for a long time
- where the policy cannot be cancelled by the insurer, no matter how often you fall ill or for how long.

Whatever you do, make sure you shop around. Premiums vary significantly as do policy conditions – which you must make sure you fully understand.

Total and permanent disability cover

Some people confuse income/disability insurance with total and permanent disability cover (TPD) – which is often an add-on to life insurance. As its name implies, TPD covers you only in the event of *total* disability caused by accident or injury, rendering you incapable of work (and probably much more) for the rest of your life.

A six months waiting period normally applies to TPD. Not only that, up to age 50 you are 30 times more likely to be disabled for three months than to suffer a TPD qualifying disablement.

Another area of confusion that arises in connection with this area of insurance is how it fits into the protection offered to you by worker's compensation insurance.

Worker's compensation

Everyone in paid employment must be covered by employer paid worker's compensation but this insurance only covers you for accidents that happen while you're at work or travelling to and from work. It does not cover you for accidents that occur at home nor does it cover you for non-accident related illnesses.

Worker's compensation will provide you with your salary or a proportion of your salary for up to six months and will pay any medical expenses up to a point. There are set guidelines for benefits such as to what type of treatment is acceptable; how many hours of physiotherapy you get; what sort of rehabilitation and so on.

Worker's compensation certainly has its place but income/disability insurance extends your protection.

Crisis insurance

Also known as trauma insurance or 'vital cover' insurance, crisis insurance pays you either a lump sum or a monthly benefit in the event you experience a major physical trauma. The conditions that qualify you for a pay-out generally include heart attack, heart disease involving bypass surgery, stroke, malignant cancer (excluding skin cancers other than melanoma), chronic kidney failure and any disease requiring an organ transplant.

Crisis insurance generally doesn't cover you for a medical condition resulting from an accident – you need disability insurance for that. Some life insurance policies have a crisis insurance component, or you can buy it as a stand-alone product.

Private health and hospital insurance

The big health question most people have been asking since Medicare was introduced in 1984 is 'should I take out private health insurance or not?' It's a question a growing number of people have been saying 'no' to.

When Medicare was introduced, 63% of Australians had private health insurance. By June 1988, the figure was down to 47% and by December 1994, it was around 36% and still trending downwards.

So, why the flight from private health insurance? There is no definitive answer but a few observations should provide some clues.

- Private health insurance isn't cheap. According to the Canberra-based Consumers' Health Forum, for someone in the bottom 20% of incomes, private health insurance premiums can represent up to 6% of total income.
- At the family rate – which may account for only two people – the highest level cover, including ancillary benefits (such as routine dental and optical cover), can cost near to $200 per month. When you consider that our 1.5% Medicare levy will

generally give us free medical and hospital care in the public ward of a public hospital, this sort of hefty monthly slug is too much for many people, particularly for a young, fit, childless couple.

■ To compound the problem of high premiums, the highest supplementary level of health insurance can still leave you with some significant hospital (and doctor's) bills to pay out of your own pocket.

Despite the popular belief that private health insurance will take care of all your medical bills, it doesn't. Private health insurance is actually designed to cover part or all of a hospital's or approved medical day centre's accommodation and theatre costs. It should also cover the 'gap' between the Medicare schedule doctor's fee and the Medicare rebate. However, it does not cover any portion of a doctor's fee which is over and above the scheduled fee for a given service – which doctors are entitled to charge, and which can be very substantial. You pay this additional amount yourself no matter what level of private health insurance you have.

With some, but not all health funds, even when you have the highest level of hospital insurance, described as '100% cover', you may still find yourself out of pocket with hospital bills. According to the statutory Private Health Insurance Administration Council, 100% in this context can mean your fund will meet *100% of its remunerative agreement with any particular hospital*. However, the full remunerative agreement between your fund and your hospital may not be enough to fully cover the hospital's bills, in which case you pay the difference. If you have health insurance you must look into this before you admit yourself to any hospital.

What are you covered for?

Consider this case taken from a 1994 episode of 'Money'. We profiled a young woman who had top level health insurance who gave birth in a private hospital. After her health fund and Medicare had paid their portion of the bills, the couple paid, out of their own pockets:

Specialists*	$ 797
Hospital charges	$ 594
Pathology	$ 20
Sub-total	$1,411

Add to this the annual health insurance premium of $1,352

Total	$2,763

If this woman had gone to a public hospital for the birth it would have cost absolutely nothing, because she would have been completely covered by Medicare.

Of course, there is far more to health insurance than just the money. There's also peace of mind. With private insurance you have your own choice of doctor in hospital. You also have immediate access to private hospital treatment meaning you can avoid the queues clogging some areas of the public hospital system, particularly in elective surgery.

As an insured patient you will have free or close-to-free access to a private room in a public or private hospital and will be able to enjoy a more comfortable environment than many patients in the public system, particularly those in public wards.

An insured patient will be able to go to the best and most expensive private hospitals without breaking the bank. However, it does not follow, *at all*, that the standards of care in private hospitals should be any better than in public hospitals – for many it's just good to have the choice.

For first-time insurers, do plenty of homework before choosing a fund, paying particular attention to the limits of its cover. And be aware that you are most likely to get the maximum value from health insurance if you are old, sick or have a big family. This is because the premiums for the same level of benefits don't vary according to your age – strapping 20-year-olds pay the same as

* The Medical Benefit Schedule Fee for obstetric care, including delivery and pre- and post-natal care was $629.45 in early 1995. The Australian Medical Association's recommended fee (which many doctors follow) was $1,605.

frail 90-year-olds, and those paying a family rate will pay the same if the family is comprised of two people or 10.

Mortgage insurance

Mortgage insurance can be worthwhile but there are two types and you have to be sure you have the right one. One type is designed to protect the *lender*, not you, in the event you can't meet the repayments and the property is repossessed. This is the type of insurance most banks insist you take out if you are borrowing more than about 80% of the property's value, or, in the case of some building societies, more than 65% of the property's value.

Under this insurance, if, when the lender sells your property it doesn't recoup the full amount of borrowings still outstanding against it, the insurer will make up the difference to the lender. When you are obliged to take out this insurance as a condition of receiving a home loan you are effectively buying insurance for the lender. I stress, you receive no protection whatsoever from this type of mortgage insurance.

The other type of mortgage insurance, which is voluntary, is designed to protect *you*. It is sometimes distinguished from (lender protecting) mortgage insurance by being called, confusingly, *mortgage protection* insurance.

This insurance is designed to keep up your mortgage repayments in the event an accident or illness prevents you from being able to work and earn an income. Of course, if you had disability/income protection insurance – which I recommend to most people – you probably would not need mortgage protection insurance.

0—🔑 Key thought

With your mortgage insurance pay particular attention to the definitions and the conditions under which you will and won't be entitled to a benefit.

Travel insurance

Travel insurance is a product that I recommend to all travellers, particularly if you are going overseas. What happens, for instance, if you end up in a American hospital and are presented with a pile of notoriously expensive US medical bills? What happens if your $1,000 camera gets ripped off in Bangkok or you cancel your trip due to illness and face a loss of deposits and cancellation fees? Travel insurance is designed to recompense you for these and many other similar dilemmas that commonly befall travellers.

There can be tremendous variation in the specific cover offered by the various travel insurers, therefore I suggest you compare at least three or four different policies before you put your money down. Read the fine print closely, note what is and what isn't covered, and make enquiries about how and when you can make a claim and how and when you will receive payment. And remember, there is much more to selecting an insurance policy than going for the one with the lowest premium. It's the nature of the protection the policy provides that matters.

Travel Insurance

Underwriter	Top cover	Med cover	Budget cover
	$	$	$
Thomas Cook (HIH Casualty)	378	340	245 (for 22 days)
NRMA	260	200	
AFTA Travel (CU Insurance)	364	318	233
Cover More (CIC Insurance)	367	308	231
HCF Travel	378/316	271	205

Notes:
1. Premiums are based on family cover for 31 days (or 32 for Thomas Cook)
2. The benefits are not the same for each insurance package
3. Top cover is generally advised for North America, Japan, Europe and the Middle East; Medium cover for Asia and Budget cover for Australasia and the Pacific region.
Quotes accurate at April 1995

Disputes

Insurance is an area with a virtually unlimited scope for disputation between the insured and the insurer. However, disputes can be minimised if you:
- select a reputable insurer
- keep proof of your belongings' existence and condition
- don't fudge on the proposal or the claim
- ensure you buy the right insurance policy to start with.

Where to find help

Despite your best intentions and planning you may feel you are being hard done by, in which case I recommend you contact the General Insurance Claims Review Panel, on 008 034 496 or the Life Insurance Complaints Board on 008 335 404.

⚿ Key thoughts
- Insurance is a fundamental component of wealth creation. It protects the assets you have now and therefore helps secure the future. It is not a luxury, it's a necessity.
- Being over-insured or having the wrong insurance is a waste of money, and being under-insured is false economy and downright dangerous.
- To make sure the insurance you do have is sufficient and appropriate to your present stage in life, I recommend you contact an independent insurance broker or financial planner for an assessment of your insurance position.
- Remember, there is no point working hard over the years to accumulate wealth if, through inadequate insurance, you expose yourself to losing it in a flash!

CHAPTER NINE

Superannuation

Raise the topic of superannuation next time you have a few friends around for a barbecue and you'll get a range of reactions. Some people will look at their watches and ask 'is that the time?', some will pour themselves extremely large drinks, some will slip into a type of coma, others will become completely absorbed by a spoon or salt shaker, and a few will say 'I think super is okay because people keep telling me it is, but I'm not really sure why'. The majority will tell you that it is confusing, keeps changing and is all too hard.

Well, I'm one of those people who keeps saying super is okay, and what I am going to try to do here is explain why. And I hope as you read this your mind won't drift off to a palm-fringed beach on a tropical island. Bring it back here if it does, because, confusing as super may be, it's worth knowing about. Indeed, if you play your superannuation cards properly, you'll actually be able to accompany your mind to that tropical paradise when you retire as well as doing many other things you've only dreamt about during your working life.

What is superannuation?

Basically, superannuation is designed to provide for us financially in retirement. It's built up over our working lives from contributions made by our employers and, hopefully, topped up out of our own pockets. It's also taxed lightly – both to encourage our active contribution towards it and to increase the size of its pay-out at the end.

That's the good news. The bad news is that it's confusing, your money is locked away for a very long time, and the Federal Government continually fiddles with the rules. While this may bring us no joy, the fact is, we need super.

Consider this. In 1994 we had around six people in the

workforce for every person in retirement. That was a large pool of taxpayers from which to fund the aged pension. But because we are living longer and having fewer children, by 2030 there will be only three people working for every retired person.

Let's look at it another way. Today we have around 1.8 million Australians aged 65 or more. In 25 years time, when I reach 65, there will be around 5 million of us! Already pensions are a major funding burden, accounting for more than 30% of the Federal Budget, so can you imagine what it's going to be like then? Either taxpayers in the future will have to be taxed to within an inch of their lives if the aged pension is to remain at its present (modest) real level, or (far more likely) the pension will fall.

But 'what about the value of the family home?', I hear you say. Who cares about a pension if you're sitting on good real estate? Okay, but do you really want to find yourself at retirement where you have no option but to sell the home you're perfectly happy living in and don't wish to leave? And after you've sold and put aside sufficient proceeds to live off comfortably for the rest of your life you will be faced with taking a very substantial down-grading in the type of housing or the location you can afford. No, relying on the value of your home is not the way to plan for your retirement.

A comfortable retirement can only be funded by a separate nest egg of investments, which has been built up for that purpose during your working life. And your success in building up a suitably sized nest egg will depend on your success as a saver. The reason is very clear. If you don't save you don't invest, and if you don't invest you will have nothing (apart from your home) to retire on.

The problem is, however, that we are not good savers. Certainly earlier generations who lived through tougher times were much better at it than we are. Indeed, Australians now are amongst the worst savers in the world – currently we only save around 4% of what we earn. That's why, I am sure, the government, has decided to force us to save, and the way they have chosen to implement this is through compulsory superannuation.

The key word here is *compulsory*. If there was only voluntary superannuation there's little chance we'd contribute enough for it to do what it is supposed to do – provide for a comfortable retire-ment and head off a society increasingly burdened by taxation to pay for the aged.

What is a super fund?

Super funds come in two basic forms.

Defined benefit funds

With defined benefit funds your final pay-out is 'defined' by a set formula. For example, you may get four times your salary if you retire at 55, five times at age 60 and so on. You know in advance what you will get.

These are quite common in public sector super funds and with some private companies. The advantage of defined benefit super-annuation is certainty about the size of your payment upon retire-ment or leaving the company. The bad news is that it may be less attractive if you don't stay with the one company until retirement. I know many people who feel trapped by this type of super. The end benefit is so attractive, they just can't afford to leave. Low motivation is bad for the employee and employer and what a sad situation it is, because no one wins. These people wait for 5 o'clock so they can go home, and long to retire.

With defined benefit funds, how the investments in the fund perform is of no interest to you. Your end benefit is paid anyway (unless your company goes broke and defrauds the super fund). Your employer will be very interested in investment performance though because the better the fund does, the less he has to put in! You may have seen very public arguments about 'surpluses' of defined benefit funds. A surplus means simply that your super fund has more money in it than it needs to pay out to its members in entitlements. Often employers will try to reclaim this surplus, and employees fight to hang onto it.

Providing the surplus is accurately measured, I have no doubt who it should belong to – the employer. He guarantees the member will receive a set benefit and dips into the company coffers if the money is not there. So, given he must meet any shortfall, I have no doubt any surplus, if it occurs, also belongs to him.

Accumulation funds

Accumulation funds are increasingly common and are also very simple. Whatever you or your employer puts in, plus investment earnings, less expenses, is yours.

While with defined benefit funds you concentrate your attention on the documentation describing your end benefit and don't worry about investment, with accumulation funds you do worry about investment and you need to ask lots of questions. With accumulation funds what you get is determined by what goes in, but the expenses of the fund and, in particular, the performance of the investments it holds, is critical to what you end up getting.

Things you should know about your accumulation fund

- How much is your employer putting in?
- How much do you have today?
- Where is the money invested?
- What are the fees and charges?
- Do you get any insurance cover, if so how much?
- Can you add your own money to your employer's super fund?
- Do you have any choice about how the money is invested?

If you don't know the answer to these issues – ask! No reputable employer would not want to answer these questions.

Just for the record, the Superannuation Guarantee legislation sets out the compulsory employer contributions to your super fund to the year 2003 expressed as a percentage of your gross income. They are:

1994/95	4%
1995/96	5%
1996/97	6%
1997/98	6%
1998/99	7%
1999/00	7%
2000/01	8%

2001/02	8%
2002/03	9%
(and beyond)	

The employer's contribution of 9% of your salary going to super in 2002 (and beyond) might appear pretty good but unless you are 18 in that year, it won't be enough! (More on this later.)

Choice of investment options

An issue that causes much debate is what choice you should have in terms of investment options. Some argue that we aren't smart enough to be given a choice. This is nonsense and we should treat it as such.

Think about it. How can a super fund with members aged between 18 and 65 have an investment strategy that suits everyone in it? It can't!

We need choice to maximise our final pay-out and this could be as simple as making a choice between three options – 'cash' funds; 'balanced' funds and 'growth' funds which have the following characteristics:

1. **Cash funds**
- Investing in cash and short-term fixed interest investments.
- Suitable for low-risk investors, such as those near or in retirement.
- Your capital will not go backwards in any 12-month period.
- Projected long-term returns above inflation of 0% to 2%.

2. **Balanced funds**
- Investing in cash, short-, medium- and long-term fixed interest, shares and property.
- Suitable for medium-risk investors with a minimum time frame of 3 to 5 years.
- In any one year your capital can fall in value. For example, in 1994 – the worst year for 20 years – the average balanced fund fell in value by some 6% to 8%.
- Projected long-term returns above inflation of 3% to 5%.

3. Growth funds

- Investing in all the main asset classes but with a strong bias to long-term fixed interest, shares and property.
- Suitable for higher risk investors with a time frame of more than five years.
- In any one year your capital can fall in value. In 1994 the average growth fund fell in value by more than 10%.
- Projected long-term returns above inflation of 5% to 8%.

I don't think that this choice is too hard and really don't believe that you should be denied the opportunity to make a decision. It's a choice that could *double* your superannuation pay-out! Here is one place where you need to stand up for your rights – the right to choose how your money is invested.

The basic issues

When it comes down to it you only need to understand the *basics* of super (and, unless you are going to make super your hobby, I'd stick with the basics). Your car runs perfectly well without you understanding the operations of its electronic ignition or what its catalytic converter actually does, and my advice is to take the same approach to super. The rapidly changing minute detail of superannuation you should leave to your super fund administrator, company or personnel adviser. However, you *do need* to know about the investment performance of your fund and you *should* know about the following:

- How do you contribute?
- How much money can you put in?
- What happens to your contributions?
- How much should you put in?
- How do you get your money out?
- Rolling over your benefits.

How do you contribute?

There are two ways of putting money in to super. Firstly, your employer will put an amount in for you, unless you fall into the following categories (in which case your employer can ask for an exemption):

- if you are aged over 65
- if you are aged under 18 and working less than 30 hours a week
- if you are earning less than $450 per month
- if you already have more than you are entitled to in super under the pension Reasonable Benefit Limit (don't worry I'll explain this shortly).

The second way you can put money in is to add your own money to your employer's contribution. This can sometimes be done with what is called 'salary sacrifice'. A 'salary sacrifice' is typical industry jargon meaning that you choose to take less salary and have the amount you don't take added to your super. On the face of it this may sound silly but it is actually a very smart move. Why? Well, like your employer's contributions which go into your super with only 15% tax taken out, your 'salary sacrifice' contributions are also taxed at only 15%.

To illustrate – if your personal tax rate was 40%, $1 of salary less income tax would leave you with only 60 cents in your pocket for investment in some other (non-super) area. However, $1 going into your super, less the 15% contributions tax would give you 85 cents invested in your name. In this case you'd be 25 cents or about 42% better off for every dollar that was invested in super rather than in some other asset. It's a very good deal.

Now, if your employer's fund won't let you make a salary sacrifice, you can put in after-tax money (that is, money after your normal income tax has been taken out). For those of you covered by the Superannuation Guarantee, you won't generally be able to claim a tax deduction on your own contributions made out of your normal after-tax income. These contributions for which no tax deduction is allowable are called '*undeducted contributions*'.

Having said this, there are circumstances under which you may be entitled to a few small tax concessions if you 'top up' your employer's contributions made under the Superannuation Guarantee. Firstly, if your assessable income is less than $27,000 you can get a tax rebate of up to a maximum of $100 on your contributions. Secondly, if your assessable income is between $27,000 and $31,000 a maximum rebate of up to $1,000 is available, reducing by 25 cents for every dollar of assessable income over $27,000. Lastly, if your assessable income is more than $31,000 you are not entitled to any tax rebates on your super contributions.

The good news is that the 15% contributions tax does not apply to the contributions that you pay into your employer's fund out of your own after-tax income. In addition, you can take these undeducted contributions out of your employer's fund if you change jobs or leave the employer. They are returned to you tax-free (meaning there is no lump sum exit tax) under the current legislation. And while your contributions are in the super system, a maximum rate of tax of 15% is charged on their investment earnings – which is a real advantage for the majority of working Australians.

Okay, but what if you are self-employed or an employee *not* covered by the Super Guarantee? In this case you get a tax deduction for either the lesser of your 'maximum deductible contribution' (which is explained below); or the first $3,000 you contribute, plus 75% of everything over $3,000.

Be aware that you don't have to put your extra contributions into your *employer's* fund. You can use what is known as *personal super*, offered by banks, building societies, fund managers and insurance companies. The personal super fund is 'yours', meaning it goes from job to job with you and you can choose your own investment options, but a note of caution – some personal super funds have very high fees and life insurance companies are the worst offenders here. Plans offered by banks tend to have lower fees – so shop around carefully!

How much can you put in?

You, or your employer can put quite a lot of tax-advantaged money into super. Money on which you or your employer can claim a tax deduction is limited by your *'maximum deductible contribution'* (MDC) which is age determined. The MDC limits for the financial year ending in June 1996 are:

Age	Maximum (tax) deductible contribution
Under 35	$ 9,405
35 to 49	$26,125
50 and over	$64,790

For the purpose of most readers of this book, you can put as much of your own money that you *do not* claim a deduction on (undeducted contributions) as you like. However, if you are thinking of doing this please get expert advice as every case requires an individual approach depending on your personal circumstances.

How much can you have in your super?

The limiting factor to how much you can have in super is related to a dreadful piece of jargon called Reasonable Benefit Limits (RBL). Since 1 July 1994, this has been based on a flat dollar limit which is increased each year in line with wages.

For the financial year ending in June 1996 the RBL for a lump sum is $418,000, and the RBL for a pension is $836,000 (where you can take $418,000 as a lump sum and $418,000 as a pension).

If, prior to 1 July 1994, your RBL was *above* these amounts, fear not – there are some special rules to protect you. If you were aged 50 or over on 1 July 1994, you get your RBL on that date. Those aged less than 50 are protected by a complex formula best explained to you by your adviser. (Remember, you're here to get the 'big picture' not the minute details, which can be very confusing).

Any amount you have above the new RBL levels plus adjustments for wage increases, are called an *'excess benefit'*. Excess benefits when taken as a lump sum are taxed at the highest marginal rate plus the Medicare levy. Sadly, I doubt many of us will have such a 'wonderful' problem. Remember, an excess benefit means you have more than $418,000 (plus inflation) in super if you want it all as a lump sum, or more than $836,000 (plus inflation) if you want 50% as a lump sum and 50% as a pension.

What happens to your contributions?

In a *defined benefit fund*, as we discussed earlier, it does not really matter to you how the underlying investments perform – so long as your employer has the money to pay you when you leave or retire.

If you are employed by a shonky outfit whose boss has gone bankrupt two or three times and you are in a defined benefit fund then I'd be very nervous. In reality, though, defined benefit funds are usually offered to employees by government bodies and large companies and are therefore normally safe.

For those of you in an *accumulation fund* what happens to your money is of vital importance – investment earnings minus fees equals what you get!

Let's follow your money through the superannuation system and look at *deductible contributions* first. Remember a deductible contribution is usually put in by your employer under the Super-annuation Guarantee and some employers will put in more than they have to. You may be putting extra in by salary sacrifice or, if self-employed, you may be making deductible contributions to a personal superannuation fund.

This is what happens to your money.

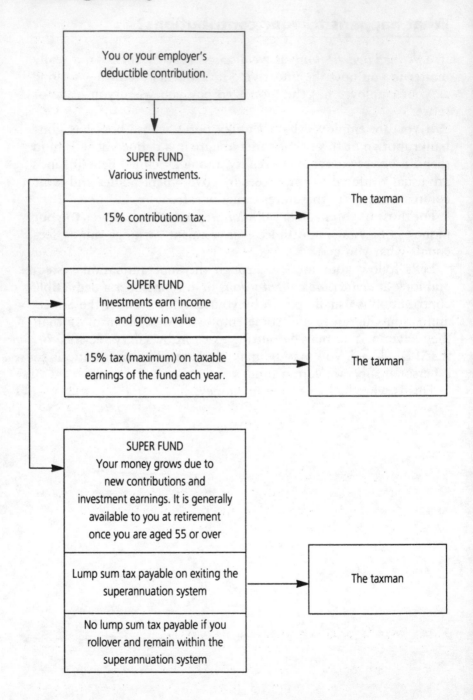

The process for *'undeducted contributions'*, which is money you put in and get no tax deduction on, is the same as above except there is no 15% contributions tax.

Your own contributions will pay a maximum 15% annual tax on the taxable earnings of your super, but remember this is a very attractive rate. If, for instance, you were earning over $5,400 p.a., you would be paying a higher rate of tax than 15% on any other (non-superannuation) investment income you received. Indeed, if you were earning over $20,700 p.a. you could be paying up to 47% tax on any (non-superannuation based) investment income you received.

The chapters on investment will give you the information you need to know about making the right investment decisions for your super money, but I really want you to consider the following issues:

- Money in super is your money. Understand what is happening to it.
- Ask your employer about your ability to choose investment options.
- For those of you more than five years from retirement, super is a long-term investment. I recommend you consider choosing an investment option that holds long-term growth assets like shares. (Yes, they are more risky in the short-term but in the long run will show better returns.)

☞ Key thought

I cannot stress how important it is that you understand how your super fund is investing the money, what the fees are, how it is taxed and how much you have in super.

How much should you contribute?

This is where theory and reality collide. The theoretical, ideal life-time financial plan is to buy a home; contribute enough towards super to give you 75% of your final salary each year in retirement, and acquire a significant level of other investments such as property, cash or shares.

This is all very well of course, but the reality is that very few people manage to do all three. With this in mind, my general advice about contributing to super is:

Young people (under 25)	Concentrate on building a deposit for a home. Do not add to employer super.
Middle ages (26 to 45)	Accelerate your mortgage repayments. Make additional super contributions if possible.
Planning for retirement (46 to 65)	Concentrate on building super up as kids leave home and you pay out your mortgage.

Technically, I can argue that super is your best asset – better than your home – due to its tax advantages. Unfortunately, this all falls down when our regulators keep stuffing around with the rules. By maximising your super contributions later in life, you reduce the risk of being disadvantaged by rule changes. It would be a brave 18-year-old who decided that super was going to be their main asset in 47 years time at age 65.

Equally, in your early years you may be on a lower tax rate on your personal earnings making super less tax effective. In your later years, you are likely to be earning your maximum salary, and thus paying a higher level of income tax. This makes deductible super contributions and the 15% tax rate on super investment earnings very attractive.

This is not to say, though, that starting super early is not a good idea. If you start contributing at age 18, you would need to put in around 12% of your salary to have 75% of your final salary in retirement. You might think 12% sounds like a lot but, if you start contributing to super later in life it will cost you much more than 12% for the same end benefit as the table below shows.

Percentage of salary you would need to put into super to give you 75% of your final salary each year in retirement commencing at age 65

Males aged	% of gross salary into super	Females aged	% of gross salary into super
25	16.3	25	19.9
35	24.2	35	29.5
45	40.3	45	49
55	89.0	55	108.3

I suspect you're wondering why females need to put in more. It's simple. Women live around four to five years longer on average than males and, therefore, need their money to last longer.

⊖━ Key thought

Even if you think that it's too hard to put such a high percentage of your salary aside and feel like giving up – don't. These numbers reflect the 'perfect' world. Remember, even $1 a day saved every day is worth real money over 10, 20 or 40 years.

How do you get your money out?

How you get your money out of super depends on whether your benefits are '*preserved*' – another piece of jargon. Contributions are generally preserved if:

■ They are made under the Superannuation Guarantee (employer's contribution).

- They are company contributions made after 1 July 1996.
- They were a contribution made to a personal super fund before 1 July 1994.
- They are a deductible contribution made to a personal super fund after 1 July 1994.

You generally can't touch a preserved contribution until you have retired and are aged 55 or over. About the only way you can get your hands on this money before 55, is to obtain approval from the Insurance and Superannuation Commission based on permanent incapacity to work, severe financial hardship or permanent departure from Australia. If you change jobs, you can rollover your preserved benefit – but it remains preserved in the rollover fund until you hit at least 55.

In your super fund you may have a mixture of benefits – preserved and not preserved. (Your benefits that are not preserved are likely to be employer contributions where super funds were set up before 22 December 1986.) You can get your hands on benefits that are *not preserved* if you change jobs or retire (even under age 55). Then, basically you have two options. You can either cash them in or roll them over, which means transferring your money from one concessionally taxed super fund to another concessionally taxed super fund.

Cashing in your benefits

When you cash in your benefits, your payment, called an '*eligible termination payment*' (ETP), is broken up into various categories. The main ones are:

- your pre-1 July 1983 component
- your post-30 June 1983 component
- your undeducted contributions
- your excess component (excess benefits).

Luckily, your super fund administrator will do this for you but it is worth knowing that with your 'pre-' and 'post-' component, the administrator will look at your total days of work while in the super fund. Let's say you have worked 7,000 days: 3,500 were pre-1 July 1983 and 3,500 were post-30 June 1983. Your split between 'pre-' and 'post-' is the same, so 50% will be called pre- and 50% post.

Now, let's look at how lump sum tax is applied if you take your money out of the super system.

ETP Categories	Lump sum tax rates on withdrawal
Undeducted contributions	This is the bit you put in after 30 June 1983 and received no tax deduction for. The lump sum tax rate is zero.
Excess benefits	Bad news here. On withdrawal from super you pay the highest personal rate of tax, plus the Medicare levy.
Pre-1 July 1983 Component	95% is tax-free and 5% is added to your income for the year and taxed at your marginal tax rate, plus Medicare levy.
Post-30 June 1983 Component	This bit is broken into two bits – money on which 15% contributions tax has been paid and money on which contributions tax has not been paid.

Age	Lump sum tax payable on post-June 1983 *taxed* component	Lump sum tax payable on post-June 1983 *untaxed* component
Under 55	20%	30%
Over 55, $0 to $81,168*	0%	15%
Over 55, $81,168 plus	15%	30%

* The $81,168 is the 1995/96 rate and it is indexed to weekly earnings each 1 July.

Rolling over your benefits

While 'rolling over' (where you transfer your money from one concessionally taxed super fund to another) sounds like something your pet dog may do, it does have a number of advantages including:

- Lump sum tax is not paid. Therefore, you have more money working for you.
- You continue to pay a maximum rate of tax of 15% on investment earnings in 'lump sum' rollovers such as approved deposit funds or deferred annuities, and zero tax if you rollover into an annuity or pension.
- If you at least rollover until age 55, your lump sum tax on taking the money drops quite significantly as you can see in the table above.

So far so good, but just what are your rollover options? You actually have quite a few. You can rollover into:

- another super fund
- an approved deposit fund (ADF)
- a deferred annuity (DA)
- an immediate annuity
- an allocated pension.

A brief description of these will help here.

Approved deposit funds and deferred annuities

Approved deposit funds and deferred annuities are managed investment funds within the superannuation environment into which you can transfer (rollover) any eligible termination payments you receive when you change jobs or retire. You can remain invested in a ADF or DA until age 65.

There's no real difference between approved deposit funds and deferred annuities except most banks, fund managers and credit unions offer ADFs while life insurance companies and friendly societies offer DAs.

Inside an ADF or DA you can choose your investment options and alter these as you see fit. You can also rollover from one organisation's ADF or DA to another – but watch the fees! Your investment income will be taxed at the maximum 15% concessional rate while inside an ADF or DA.

Immediate annuities

Typically you would buy one of these from a life insurance company. In exchange for your lump sum investment you get a regular income stream. The amount of income you get depends upon your age, sex and interest rate at the time you buy.

You can nominate a *'lifetime annuity'* but I'd suggest you'd want to be in good health to do this. With a traditional lifetime annuity, if you buy it one day and die the next, you lose all your money.

A *'term-certain annuity'* is just the same as a lifetime annuity except payments are guaranteed for a fixed time. If you bought a 10-year term-certain annuity on Tuesday and died on Wednesday, your estate would receive the annuity payments for 10 years – a much safer bet for your beneficiaries.

Part of your income may be considered tax-free and you may also be able to get a tax rebate.

Allocated pensions and allocated annuities

You can choose to rollover into an allocated pension or allocated annuity with your ETP benefits. These can be benefits that are not preserved if you are under 55, are 55 or over and retired, or over 65 and not retired.

The big pluses for an allocated pension annuity are, that you do not pay any tax on your investment earnings, and you are likely to qualify for a 15% tax rebate on part of your income. You determine what level of income you want, and you can access lump sums at the normal lump sum tax rate.

Do be careful though. Unlike a normal lifetime annuity which pays you for your lifetime, with an allocated pension or annuity you can spend all of your money by taking a higher income stream (or cash withdrawals) than your money earns in income and capital growth.

This should be carefully planned for in your retirement strategy. I don't mind you spending capital, in fact I encourage it, but not so that you run out of money too soon!

⚷━ Key thought

How you get your money out of superannuation depends on your age and your personal plan. But always ensure you look at all the options and weigh them up before you do anything. A mistake here can be very expensive.

What about insurance?

If you need life insurance, your super fund is likely to be a good place to buy it. Many funds offer automatic cover, other funds allow you to choose what you want. Make sure you know where you stand with your fund.

Do remember that any death benefit you get will count against your RBL. Your fund administrator can help here.

The reason I like to buy my death cover inside my company super fund is that it is done on a group, wholesale basis. In 1995 my premium as a 40-year-old non-smoker was $95 per $100,000 of death cover. Now that's cheap, and rather than buying it with an after-tax dollar that I get in my pocket, it's paid for with a dollar which has only had the 15% contributions tax taken out.

⊙━ **Key thoughts**

- Super should be a part of your financial strategy.
- The ideal plan is to build three pools of wealth – home, super and other investments.
- Concentrate on your mortgage first, then build up your personal contributions to super.
- At present super is complex, confusing and the rules change. But if super is made unattractive or the Government 'steals' it with increased taxes, future governments will just have to pay us a pension.
- Super must remain an attractive option, and most new rule changes are making things simpler – not harder.
- Super *is* terrific. It is tax advantaged, it compounds in value over the years, and more importantly, you can't touch most of it until you retire!

CHAPTER TEN

Tax

Death and taxes – life's only certainties, so the old saying goes. It's certainly true that you can't escape from one, but what about the other? Well, to varying degrees you can.

For instance, you don't have any reason to worry about tax if you don't have any income. I am always amused when people complain to me about how much tax they're paying. No one *enjoys* paying tax but, it seems to me, that if someone is paying a small fortune in tax then they're also making at least twice as much.

Having said this, there's no sense in paying more tax than you need to. And there are a number of perfectly sound and legal ways of reducing your tax bill which you should take advantage of if you can. In other words, you should try to *avoid* tax where possible as distinct from *evading* tax which is illegal as well as quite unproductive.

So this means that you shouldn't participate in an investment simply because it will reduce your tax bill. You should only ever invest in something if you are well satisfied it will increase your wealth, treating any tax reductions that an investment receives or generates along the way as a bonus. Think about it – no one has ever become rich by building up tax deductions.

> ### 0━┳ Key thought
> Try to reduce your tax, certainly, but aim to increase your wealth.

Steps to tax minimisation

Regardless of any tax benefits that may flow to you from participating in certain investments, from the method in which you invest, or from how you structure the way you receive your income, on a day-to-day basis there are a few fundamental and simple tax reducing steps you need to follow.

Step 1. Check permissible tax deductions

The most fundamental step is to make yourself aware of all the permissible tax deductions that relate to your job. I can give a few examples here – though I wouldn't attempt to nominate and detail all the possible tax deductions that relate to all jobs because they are so varied. Some deductions are cost of toys for nannies, black suits (but not shirts) for funeral directors, calculator batteries for draftsmen, safety boots for doctors, the depreciation of television sets and anti-VDU-glare tinted glasses for advertising executives, and self-education expenses for students studying in the same field they are working in.

The way to find out what work-related expenses you can claim is to speak to an accountant, to a representative of your union or industry association, or to someone in your company's accounting or personnel department. The other place to make inquires of course, is at the Australian Taxation Office (ATO).

Step 2. Keep good records

Making sure you record all your expenses properly and having adequate proof of incurring them is fundamental to good tax management. In the likelihood of undergoing a desk audit – where you get to meet very inquisitive representatives from the Tax Office face to face – make sure you can verify whatever work-related expenses you have claimed as deductions in your tax returns. If your records are inadequate and you cannot substantiate your claims, you may have to pay additional tax and a penalty. In more serious cases, you can be prosecuted.

If the total of your claims is $300 or less, you must keep a record of how you worked out each of your claims. If the total of your claims is more than $300, the records you will need are receipts, invoices or similar documentary evidence. Cheque butts are not acceptable.

Whatever you do, make sure you keep your records for five years from the date you lodged your tax return. This is the period stipulated by the Tax Office.

Step 3. Strategies and investments

There are a number of worthwhile tax minimisation strategies and preferentially taxed investments available to everyone, no matter what your occupation is. These include:
- income splitting
- income timing
- negative gearing
- franked dividends
- superannuation and managed investments in retirement
- offset accounts.

Now, let's look at these tax minimisation ideas in some detail.

Income splitting
Income splitting is a highly effective way in which couples can minimise the total amount of tax they pay. The principle is very simple – income is held in the name of the partner on the lower marginal tax rate so that the actual amount of tax paid is minimised.

Let's say we have a couple, Kevin and Fay. Kevin earns $38,000 p.a. and Fay, who does some part-time work when not looking after the children, earns $3,000 p.a. Fay's income is below the (current) tax-free threshold of $5,400 so she pays no tax. Kevin, a PAYE (Pay As You Earn) employee, has $8,942 in tax deducted from his annual pay.

Now, let's assume the couple have $15,000 cash which they wish to put into a term deposit paying interest of 10% p.a. ($1,500). If the term deposit is put in Kevin's name, his annual income will rise to $39,500 ($38,000 + $1,500). At this income level his marginal tax rate will be 43%. Therefore he would pay $645 in tax on the $1,500 income, retaining only $855. ($1,500 x 43% = $645.)

It would make much more sense from a tax point of view to put the term deposit in Fay's name. The $1,500 income flowing from it would raise her overall income level to $4,500 – which is still below the $5,400 threshold at which tax kicks in. Therefore Fay would pay no tax on the $1,500 interest income.

Timing income

Income is generally taxable only in the year in which it is *received*, not the year in which it is *earned*. So if you did some extra paid work towards the end of one financial year knowing that you were going to do less paid work in the following financial year, it would be a good idea to defer payment for the work until July. This payment would be counted as income for the new year where your lower overall level of income could attract a lower marginal tax rate.

This is especially relevant if you are just about to retire, because you can save yourself thousands of dollars in tax liabilities by retiring in July rather than June. It's also relevant as far as capital gains tax is concerned. If you choose to sell assets which are subject to capital gains tax you should always try to do so at times when you are receiving the least amount of income.

To illustrate, let's say you decided to have six months off work to take an extended overseas holiday, and decided to sell some shares (purchased after 19 September 1985 when capital gains tax was introduced) to help pay for the trip. The best time to sell the shares would be in the tax year where you weren't earning a full year's income. So, for example, if you intended to leave in June you'd end up paying a full year's tax on that financial year's income plus the capital gains tax on the sale of the shares – all of which could raise your marginal tax rate for the year. But, if you delayed your trip by one month to July, the capital gains from the shares would be your only income for the next six months – meaning your total income for that tax year (and thus your marginal tax rate) could be much lower.

You can also maximise your deductions in years of high income by early payment of deductable expenses. For example, you could pay your income protection insurance – which is fully tax deductable – for 12 months in advance. If you're self-employed you could also put extra money into superannuation in the high-income years.

Making Money

Negative gearing

An investment is said to be negatively geared when the costs of holding it – including interest charges on the loan used to finance it – exceed the income the investment produces. In other words, the investment is negatively geared if it produces a running loss when all income and costs, including interest, are taken into account. In most cases negative gearing occurs in connection with property investment, though it can arise when borrowing to invest in any income-producing asset, such as shares.

The significance of the running loss is that it is tax deductible against the investor's other assessable income including their salary or wages. This has the effect of reducing the real size of the loss, especially so for those on higher marginal tax rates.

Let's say, for example, you borrowed to buy an investment property that after 12 months generated a loss of $2,000, including interest repayments on the loan. This $2,000 would be a tax deduction against your other income.

If your marginal tax rate was 47%, this tax deduction would reduce the *real* cost of holding the property to $1,060 ($2,000 x 47% = $940, $2,000 – $940 = $1,060). If your marginal tax rate was 20%, the *real* cost of holding the property would be reduced to $1,600 ($2,000 x 20% = $400, $2,000 – $400 = $1,600).

Now, borrowing is a perfectly legitimate way to fund select investments. But be very aware that when you borrow to invest you are using money you don't own. If the investment fails you still owe this money – and you can imagine how happy that would make you feel.

The key thing about borrowing to invest is to make as sure as possible that the underlying investment is sound, meaning that when you realise the asset you stand a good chance of making a positive return – after all costs of buying, holding and selling are accounted for. While negative gearing generates tax deductions which minimise the real cost of borrowing to invest, it should never of itself be the reason for investing. For more detail on negative gearing see Chapter Twelve, 'Investing in Property'.

⊙━┳ Key thought

⊙━┳ Key thought
Don't ever participate in an investment simply because it promises good tax deductions. You should only ever invest if you believe the asset will ultimately realise a profit and, if you enjoy tax deductions along the way, treat that as a bonus.

Franked share dividends

Share dividend income is taxable but if it is 'franked' it can be very tax-effective compared to income from other investments. 'Franked' dividends are those distributed from *after-tax* company profits. Because tax is paid by the company before you receive these dividends, they are deemed by the Tax Office to be after-tax income in your hands, effectively meaning income on which *you have already paid tax*. The amount of tax that has already been paid on the franked dividends you receive is tax deductable against any other assessable income you may have.

Dividends can be 'fully franked', which is where they have been distributed from profits taxed at the full company tax rate of 36%. They can also be 'partly franked' – where tax has been paid against them at anything up to 36% – and 'unfranked', which is where no tax has been paid against them, making them fully taxable as income in your hands.

If you receive fully franked dividends (pre-taxed at 36%), and your marginal tax rate is (theoretically) also 36%, you will owe no further tax on this dividend income. If your marginal tax rate is higher than the fully franked dividend tax rate, say 47%, you will still owe the Tax Office some tax on these dividends, being the difference between the fully franked rate of 36% and your marginal rate of 47%. In this example you will need to pay tax equivalent to 11% of the dividends' value (47% – 36% = 11%).

Conversely, if your marginal tax rate is below the rate at which the dividends have been taxed, you will receive a tax credit equivalent to the value of that difference to reduce your tax liability.

Again, just as you shouldn't borrow to invest in property just to take advantage of the tax benefits of negative gearing, nor should you buy shares in companies simply because their dividends are fully franked and will give you tax benefits. Only buy shares in a company if you believe that they will show decent and steady growth over time. If their dividends are franked, that's great, but it's not the main game. As ever it's the quality of the underlying asset that really counts. (See Chapter Thirteen, 'Investing in Shares' for more information about franked dividends.)

Superannuation and related managed investments

Superannuation is taxed very preferentially in order to encourage good long-term growth and a high level of public support. In the simplest terms, your contributions to super are generally taxed lightly, your earnings whilst in the fund are also taxed lightly, and the tax on your eventual pay-out is favourable too.

Once in retirement, your superannuation pay-out can be put towards a range of other preferentially taxed managed investments including rollovers, annuities and allocated pensions. The tax provisions applying to these investments are substantial and can be very complicated, particularly in the case of exiting super, so I have chosen to detail them in Chapter Nine, 'Superannuation'.

So should you just invest in these retirement-related investments simply because they receive good tax treatment? Well, super does generate respectable returns which alone would make it worthy of an investor's attention. At IPAC our research shows that you can expect real, long-term returns from balanced super funds in the range of 3% to 5%, and for growth super funds in the range of 5% to 8%, all after fees and tax, and there is nothing wrong with these numbers.

The fundamental answer to the question is that, once again, you should not participate in these investments simply because of their tax treatment. The sometimes stringent conditions that apply to them may not suit your circumstances or wishes and, as ever, the quality of the investment's asset base, earning potential and financial structure should remain the most important considerations. However, that said, the tax treatment of these investments (super especially) is so attractive that you would need some pretty serious doubts about the products' underlying worth or appropriateness not to make them a part of your retirement plans.

Offset accounts

If you have a savings account earning interest and the interest is added to the balance of the account, you'll obviously pay tax on it. But, if instead of having the interest added to your savings account, you can 'offset' it against a loan account such as your mortgage where it will reduce the size of the debt – *and attract no tax*. Interest earned on one account and offset against debt in another account is tax-free – because you haven't really earned any income.

If you do offset interest against a mortgage account you can benefit from the double-whammy effect of putting a real hole in your long-term interest costs without any dilution through tax.

To give an example, an additional $25 per month (in this case, offset interest) coming off a 25-year, $100,000 mortgage at an interest rate of 10% would reduce the interest costs by $21,715 and cut two and a half years off the loan. One of the best things about this sort of debt reduction is that you are getting a full 'return' ($21,715) on your investment (offset interest of $25 per month) which is itself not subject to tax.

Personally, I use an 'equity credit' mortgage where I can pay money into my mortgage, effectively earn my current rate of interest on my mortgage tax-free, yet access the money when I need it.

End-of-year tax schemes

End-of-year tax schemes sit at the other end of the tax minimisation spectrum – the bad end. With depressing regularity, my in-tray overflows with prospectuses for tax-driven investment schemes at the end of each financial year.

My general advice on tax schemes is like the old saying about trading the futures market, that is, 'if you feel like becoming involved, lie down until the feeling goes away'. Sadly, many tax-driven investment schemes offer little more than a tremendous opportunity for shysters to separate you from your money.

Often the investments promise outstanding longer term returns, coupled with short-term, indeed immediate tax write-offs while the venture is in the establishment phase. These immediate tax write-offs can be used to reduce your tax liability in the current financial year – and this is their significant selling point.

Now, there is normally nothing intrinsically wrong with the products at the heart of these investment schemes. They may be wildflowers, farmed prawns, yabbies, pine plantations, or feature films, which, in the right hands and circumstances, can generate good returns. What is wrong is that many of the schemes are put together by, to put it politely, 'city financiers', whose main interest is in raising money for a fee.

How do the schemes work?

Normally, the investor purchases a share in a venture in the form of one or more monetary units. Each unit may be worth $1,000, $5,000, whatever. There are a finite number of units for sale. The venture is often a start-up operation and the proceeds from the sale of the units are designed to fund its establishment.

Let's take the theoretical example of a cut flower venture, a plantation comprised of proteas. Financial projections for the first two or three years will show a loss while the plants are still too young to bear commercial quantities of flowers. During this stage the investor generates ongoing tax losses to be offset against other income. So far so good, if you don't mind making losses, that is.

Projections show that the protea plantation will generate positive cash flows from Year 4 when the plants have reached maturity. From Years 5 through to 15 the money will roll in and the investor will supposedly laugh all the way to the bank.

Odds are, though, this won't happen. What is more likely to happen is that the scheme will fail. Any amount of things can go wrong. The market may be weaker than predicted or harder to crack, the plants may be struck by one or more fatal diseases, a killer frost may strike, some plants may have a commercial life of only five years instead of 15, the operators may be incompetent or even downright crooked. (Most of these problems actually did befall a major wildflower investment scheme featuring proteas. There have also been a string of badly performing investment schemes based on blueberries, macadamias, avocados, yabbies, pine trees and movies.)

Generally, the highly optimistic projections of tax-driven investment schemes are rarely achieved, and investors invariably end up taking a bath, getting far greater tax losses than they had hoped for. And no matter how you dress them up, tax deductable losses are still just that, losses.

The trick is not to get into an end of financial year panic about paying too much tax and then jumping into a tax minimising investment scheme. If you really have a swag of tax to pay (meaning you have earned an even bigger swag of income) try a short-term tax minimising strategy instead, like borrowing to invest in shares or property (as a long-term investment) and, pre-paying the interest on your borrowings, thereby getting a tax deduction this financial year.

O—ᵣ Key thought

The correct approach to tax planning is to start on 1 July. Making tax decisions in consultation with a tax accountant, and making sensible investment decisions throughout the year will see you much richer in the long-term, and much less stressed in the lead up to 30 June.

Should you do your own tax?

In the 1993 financial year one third of Australian taxpayers, or some 3 million individuals, completed their own tax returns. Remarkably, some 10% failed to sign their forms. Another very large proportion of tax payers forgot to attach their group certificates to the returns. (This type of oversight is par for the course.)

Now, given the relative difficulty and potential pitfalls of completing your own tax returns, 3 million do-it-yourselfers may seem to be a surprisingly large number. But if you take care, doing your own tax is a sensible and inexpensive choice – so long as your financial affairs are uncomplicated.

If you are a salaried PAYE employee with simple work deductions and no involvement in, say, a family trust or company, there really should be no need to seek the assistance of an accountant or tax agent to handle your return. But just remember you can seriously short-change yourself by not knowing what work-related expenses you are legitimately entitled to claim as tax deductions, and by keeping inadequate records.

Also remember that acceptable work-related expenses vary tremendously from occupation to occupation and advice from friends and colleagues should not be acted upon until its accuracy can be checked. The Tax Office is the right place to get this basic advice.

Do-it-yourself tax returns are the wrong choice, however, if you have complex financial affairs. By 'complex', I mean, for example, being involved in a family trust, partnership or company; receiving income from property which involves depreciation adjustments; receiving franked dividends from shares; and almost any matter involving capital gains. (In other words, the present or future financial affairs of many of the readers of this book!)

It's been my overwhelming experience with clients in these circumstances that employing a competent accountant to do your tax returns (and provide you with tax advice throughout the year) is a move which more than pays for itself. It saves you time and headaches, you'll probably pay less tax or get bigger rebates, you'll be better prepared in the event of an audit, and, your accountant's fees are fully tax deductible!

Tax and investment

The taxes that will be most relevant to anyone involved in investment are (personal) income tax, provisional tax and capital gains tax.

Personal income tax

Income is clearly more than just your salary or wages. It also includes returns from investments such as interest on term deposits or from bonds, rental income or dividend income from shares. This investment income, over and above the income you generate from your paid employment, is fully taxable at your highest rate of tax (your marginal rate) as per the current personal income tax rates.

The income tax rates are subject to change at any time but in 1995 were:

Taxable Income $	Tax$	% on excess
5,400	Nil	20.0
20,700	3,060	34.0
38,000	8,942	43.0
50,000	14,102	47.0

To this tax a Medicare levy of 1.5% of your total gross income should be added. It applies to most residents whose income exceeds a certain level, which in 1995 was $12,688.

Let's say your annual salary is $40,000. Based on the scale above, up to $38,000 will be taxed $8,942, and on the $2,000 between $38,000 and $40,000 you will be taxed at 43% (the marginal tax rate). The total tax on your salary will therefore be $9,802, which represents 24.5% of your salary. ($8,942 + $2,000 x 43% = $8,942 + $860 = $9,802.) To this tax on salary of $9,802 must be added the Medicare levy of $600 ($40,000 x 1.5% = $600) making the total tax payable $10,402.

If on top of your salary you received $900 in interest income from a term deposit, the $900 would be added to your salary to produce a total income of $40,900. The $900 would, therefore, be taxed at the relevant marginal rate which in this case is 43% (plus the 1.5% Medicare levy).

Provisional tax

Now, where you earn more than $1,000 per year from sources other than your wages/salary, such as investment income from shares, fixed interest or managed funds, you will have to pay provisional tax. (Self-employed people also face provisional tax, as do those who earn extra income from a second job.)

When you are charged provisional tax by the Tax Office you are being charged tax on anticipated income for the full current financial year, based on your actual income for the past financial year.

The dodge about provisional tax is that you have to pay it at the same time as you pay your personal income tax for last year, so, the first year you pay provisional tax you can have a very hefty tax bill. This can be particularly unpleasant if you have spent all of your investment income and saved none for the tax man!

⊙━ Key thought

I recommend anyone incurring provisional tax or anyone thinking they might incur it to speak to an accountant. Provisional tax can come as a rude shock so it's best to try to anticipate it and be prepared for it. It's really important that you don't spend money that belongs to the Tax Office!

Capital gains tax

Capital gains tax (CGT) is the other tax of great relevance to investors. It's enormously complicated and, personally, I leave the calculations to my accountant. Having said that, it's useful to know how CGT is calculated and to understand the principles behind it.

Now, the Tax Office can provide you with quite detailed booklets on the subject explaining (after a fashion) how capital gains tax is calculated for shares and other investments; for assets acquired after divorce; for assets acquired from a deceased estate, and when capital gains tax needs to be paid on your home.

If you think you may be liable for capital gains you should read this material – and then ask an accountant to explain it to you! Also, make sure you keep good records for any investment prone to capital gains, such as shares or property investment, otherwise you'll end up paying too much.

- Capital gains tax is payable on any capital gain made after the disposal of non-exempt assets (the family home is exempt from CGT, for example) acquired after 19 September 1985.
- A 'capital gain' is the difference between the cost of the asset and the amount you receive when you sell it (so long as you get more than you paid for it).
- The 'cost' includes the original purchase price, the incidental

expenses of acquisition and disposal, and any capital improvements in between.

- If you own an asset for 12 months or more you can convert the investment's costs into today's dollars by using a calculation based on an inflation index. This has the effect of reducing the amount of tax you have to pay.
- Capital gains tax can apply whether you acquired the asset by purchase, inheritance, construction or received it as a gift.
- Similarly it will be considered 'sold' (that is, it will have a 'disposal cost') even if you give it away, if it is lost, or if it is destroyed.

The following illustration of how CGT is calculated is based on an example in the Australian Taxation Office's booklet, *Capital Gains Tax – What you need to know*, published by AGPS, Canberra, 1995, (Commonwealth of Australia copyright reproduced by permission).

Let's say Jim bought an investment property for $150,000. He paid a deposit of $15,000 on 24 June 1988, and the balance at settlement on 5 August 1988. However, because he became liable for the full amount on the exchange of contracts on 24 June 1988, he is deemed (as far as CGT is concerned) to have incurred the full cost of $150,000 on 24 June. As you will see, timing is significant with CGT.

Jim paid stamp duty of $5,000 on 20 July 1988, and paid his solicitor's fees of $2,000 on 5 August 1988. On 28 April 1989 he spent $3,000 on a pergola, which is a 'capital improvement'.

Jim subsequently sold the property on 17 July 1990 for $195,000. He then incurred costs of $1,500 in solicitor's fees and $1,000 in real estate agent's fees on 19 August 1990.

To calculate Jim's capital gain you need to arrive at a total base cost which has been indexed for inflation. To do that, each cost in each time period is multiplied by a special 'indexation factor', and then these costs are added together to give a total indexed base cost (a 'real' total cost adjusted for inflation at the time the capital gain is realised).

$$\text{The indexation factor} = \frac{\text{sale date CPI figure}}{\text{expenditure date CPI figure}}$$

Making Money

CPI indexation figures used for calculating CGT can be obtained from the Tax Office but here are the relevant CPI figures for these transactions:

24 June 1988	88.5
20 July 1988	90.2
5 August 1988	90.2
28 April 1989	95.2
17 July 1990	103.3
19 August 1990	103.3

Each cost is multiplied by the indexation factor to give you the indexed cost base in real dollars at the time the capital gain is made. So, in Jim's case . . .

Purchase price: $150,000 x $\dfrac{103.3}{88.5}$ $\qquad$ = $175,050

Stamp duty: $5,000 x $\dfrac{103.3}{90.2}$ $\qquad$ = $ 5,725

Solicitor's fees (on purchase): $2000 x $\dfrac{103.3}{90.2}$ = $ 2,290

Pergola: $3,000 x $\dfrac{103.3}{95.2}$ $\qquad$ = $ 3,255

Solicitor's fees (on sale): $1,500 x $\dfrac{103.3}{103.3}$ $\qquad$ = $ 1,500

Agent's fee (on sale): $1,000 x $\dfrac{103.3}{103.3}$ $\qquad$ = $ 1,000

Total indexed cost base $\qquad\qquad$ $188,820

Therefore the real capital gain is $6,180*
($195,000 (sale price) – $188,820 (indexed cost) = $6,180).

* To calculate how much tax is payable on a (real) capital gain, the real capital gain is:
1. firstly, divided by 5
2. this amount is then added to your assessable income
3. tax payable at your relevant marginal personal tax rate is then calculated on the added amount
4. this additional tax liability is then multiplied by 5 – and that becomes the total capital gains tax payable on the real capital gain.

So, out of the $45,000 *nominal* capital gain Jim made on the sale, ($195,000 − $150,000) he only has to pay capital gains tax on $6,180 (the *real* capital gain for taxation purposes − which, incidentally, in this example, ignores real holding costs such as interest).

While I repeat my recommendation that anyone facing CGT should leave it all to an accountant, what is instructive about these calculations is that they throw a revealing light on the capital gain one *appears* to make from an investment and the capital gain one *actually* makes, not only once certain costs but also once inflation are taken into account.

Working out the CGT payable on shares is calculated using the same principles as above (that is, you have to work out the indexed costs of shareholding to calculate the real capital gain) but in practice it is even more complicated.

Tax Office scrutiny

Australian taxation is based on self-assessment − the Tax Office trusts you to work out your own tax liability (perhaps with an accountant) and then to submit a tax return which reveals what you owe them or what they owe you.

However, the Tax Office does random checks just to keep everyone honest. And, if the tax man finds there is a mistake your way in your tax return it may cost you a lot of money. You can be fined on any amount found owing − as well as still having to pay the outstanding tax itself.

The Tax Office also has a thorough and comprehensive program of audits. Every so often it picks an industry and starts hunting so you may be unlucky enough to be called on. This could be a simple check of just one deduction claim, or it could involve someone from the Tax Office wanting to inspect every document or every tax return you've submitted for up to the last five years. It's critical therefore to keep your tax records (receipts etc) for that long.

You may be asked to send information into the Tax Office or to show up in person. You are not required to give the tax man original copies of your receipts etc − good photocopies will suffice.

If you have an accountant who has been doing your tax returns you should contact him or her immediately after you are contacted by the Tax Office and discuss the situation. If the Tax Office is doing an-indepth audit it would be a good idea to have your accountant present at all meetings with tax officers.

If a tax officer calls on you you don't have to let him or her in the door the moment they appear. They are required to arrange a mutually suitable time with you to examine your records.

Look, audits might be a cause of much anxiety but, if you keep all your receipts, maintain good records and don't fudge on your tax returns you won't have anything to worry about!

CHAPTER ELEVEN

Ten Keys to Successful Investing

How often have you had one of those great moments where, when you least expect it, you notice a detail that puts everything into perspective? I once had such a moment at Warwick Farm racecourse once. And no, unfortunately, I didn't suddenly realise a 100 to 1 outsider was going to win and put all my money on it.

The revealing detail was the nature of the car parks that you walk past on the way into the course. There is a large one for the public – the punters – and another, smaller one for the book-makers, and what really struck me was the stark difference in the types of cars in the two parking areas.

One was full of old, clapped-out Valiants, Datsuns and Kingswoods, the other full of gleaming new BMWs, Jaguars, Mercedes Benz and the odd Rolls Royce. There are no prizes for guessing which cars belonged to the bookies, and the extreme contrast between theirs and the punters spoke volumes about who was (and is) making all the money at the track.

Why is it that over time the bookies always seem to win? What do they do right that the punters do wrong?

Well, apart from having a better idea than the punters about which horses are good and which are not, what they do is spread their risks, while the punters concentrate theirs. And, over time, it's clear which is the better strategy.

A bookie spreads his risks by continually changing the odds in such a way as to encourage punters to back as many different horses as possible in each race – ideally, every horse in the race. And, if despite this technique of encouraging a wide spread of bets, one particular horse is very heavily backed, the bookie then minimises his exposure to it by backing it with other bookmakers. This way, no matter which horse wins, the bookie will have a mix of wins and losses. If he has spread his risks well, his wins should outweigh his losses.

Making Money

The punter takes the opposite tack. He doesn't spread his risks at all. He concentrates it all on one or two horses in each race without knowing too much about them and, if he is anything like me, they usually run backwards. At the end of the day, pockets empty, all he has to show for his efforts is his 20-year-old Datsun to limp home in.

What punters do at the track is lay bets against horses which generally have a low chance of winning. They punt, bet or speculate. Call it what you will, they 'gamble' – looking for a spectacular, instant gain. They take a chance on something performing well. If it does, they're rewarded handsomely, if it doesn't, they lose the lot. Not only that, the more they do it the more they increase their chances of losing.

This is not what I call 'investing'. In my book investing means putting your money on something that has a good chance of winning in the short to medium term, and an even better, if not dead certain chance of winning *in the long-term*. The wonderful thing is, there are money making vehicles which fit this description, and they are the classic asset classes of shares, property, fixed interest securities and cash deposits.

To strengthen your returns from these, you should, ideally, invest a little in all of them, not a lot in one. Investors call this diversification, bookies call it hedging their bets. They both mean the same thing, which is, not putting all your eggs in the one basket.

Let's take a look at my 10 keys to successful investing. Ignore them at your peril because they represent a combination of everything I have learnt from all the books on investment, from the professional investors that I have spoken with over the years, from the real-life experience obtained from my own clients and from the many people who write to me about their investment experiences.

You'll find a number of these keys very simple. Commonsense always works best, but you'd be amazed at how often people forget the basics.

1. Understand that risk equals return

Carve the words 'risk equals return' into your bathroom mirror so you can see them every morning. Taking excessive risk in looking for a big return is the number one reason why investors lose their money. They get too greedy – and investment sales-people know this.

The only way you can breach risk and return is to obtain information that is not widely known. With shares it is called insider trading and the penalties are high if you get caught. With property, inside knowledge about things like rezoning can be very valuable but unfortunately, over the years, a number of people have abused their position of trust on such matters. For most of us, inside knowledge isn't available and we must invest on the premise that the return we get will be related to the risk we take.

If you see an investment offering a high return, don't say 'oh good' ask 'why?' Examples such as Estate Mortgage and Pyramid Building Society spring to mind. To attract money they offered higher rates of interest than their competitors. To pay this higher rate they lent the money on more risky projects. The result? Investors lost most of their money when it all collapsed.

Now, I'm not saying risk is to be avoided. If you take no risk you get no return. Everything has some risk, but you must be aware of risk. The real trick is to consider how much risk you can sleep with, and to invest accordingly.

To illustrate this, let me describe my family's investment strategy.

For my young kids, I put around $500 a year into a managed share fund purchasing South-East Asian shares. Now this is very risky, but over 20 years I think it's where my kids will get the highest return. If the kids make 60% one year and lose 60% the next, it doesn't matter – they don't even know about it! At their age, investment risk is irrelevant to them.

At my age (40), I would not invest all my money in South-East Asian shares because of the high risk. However, I have been more than willing to invest some of my super money in this area – because I won't be touching it for many years.

My main plan at this stage is to pay off my mortgage, build up my super and build up a portfolio of other investments, such as Australian shares and perhaps even an investment property.

Making Money

As I age, my attitude to risk will change. I'll be more concerned with protecting my wealth, not growing it, so I will gradually switch to lower risk investments such as cash, fixed interest and blue chip shares.

My Dad, who is semi-retired, invests mainly in blue chip shares and property. Once he retires, he will hold increasing amounts of fixed interest investments to generate the income he will need.

> ### ⚷━☞ Key thought
> Be aware of risk. Ask questions and understand the true nature of risk in any investment before you do anything.

At IPAC Securities we put investors into five categories which we describe (in increasing order of risk) as:
- income defensive
- low growth
- balanced
- growth
- high growth.

The table below shows the actual portfolio returns for these five groups over the years 1982-94. As you will note, the higher the risk taken, the higher the return over the 12 years; however, the higher the risk the greater the likelihood of a negative return in any given year.

Type of investor	Value of $10,000 after 12 years	Numbers of years in which money was lost
Income defensive	$59,000	1 (1994)
Low growth	$63,000	1 (1994)
Balanced	$68,000	1 (1994)
Growth	$72,000	2 (1990, 1994)
High growth	$74,000	2 (1990, 1994)

The following table gives the type of return you can expect above inflation over the very long-term, by which I mean 10 years

146

plus. This is a 'real' return, meaning that it is the projected return in excess of inflation. It's important to look at long-term returns because short-term returns (under three years) are very unpredictable.

As you can see again, the higher the risk you take, the higher the expected return. Conversely, if you take very low risk and pop all your money into the bank, your long-term returns will be very low.

The real return (this is the return in excess of inflation) that I would expect from the main asset classes over 10-year periods is as follows:

Investment	Risk	Projected real annual return
Cash in bank	Very low	0% to 1%
Term deposits (1 to 3 years)	Low	0% to 2%
Long-term fixed interest and bonds (3 to 10 years)	Medium	0% to 3%
Residential property	Medium	1% to 3%
Commercial property	Medium – High	3% to 5%
Australian shares	High	5% to 8%
International shares	High	6% to 9%
Emerging markets (e.g. South-East Asia, Latin America)	Extremely high	10% to 25%

The trick to managing risk is to consider how much risk you can tolerate given your personal situation, and to then build a portfolio of assets that suits you.

Put simply, a youngster with $500 may be happy to take very

high risk. This would see a 100% exposure to shares. A middle-aged person may want to be moderately aggressive and invest in a mix of medium- and high-risk investments. A retiree is likely to take a low-risk approach and invest mainly in low-risk assets like cash and fixed interest with a smaller exposure to high-risk investments such as shares.

2. Don't try to time the market

Now, it's pretty obvious that you should buy when things are cheap and sell when they are expensive. It's so delightfully simple, but guess what most investors tend to do?

When the news is good and investments are expensive they buy and when the news is bad and investments have fallen in value, they sell. It's a recipe for financial ruin.

Good market timing is buying at the bottom and selling at the top. Being a market timer means trying to do just this. Unfortunately, except by sheer good luck, no one I know can do it year after year. IPAC Securities has put together the following table which illustrates the point very well.

The best performing investment classes 1982 – 94

		Annual return
1982	International fixed interest	38.31%
1983	Australian shares	66.80%
1984	International shares	15.26%
1985	International shares	72.36%
1986	Australian shares	52.22%
1987	Australian fixed interest	18.60%
1988	Australian shares	17.88%
1989	International shares	26.48%
1990	Australian fixed interest	18.24%
1991	Australian shares	34.24%
1992	International fixed interest	18.24%
1993	Australian shares	45.36%
1994	Cash	5.36%

Let's say you were genius enough to invest solely in these top performing assets every year – your average annual return would have been a very healthy 33.0%. Not bad!

But do you really think you could have picked the best investments every year? I'll bet you couldn't!

The worst performing asset classes 1982 – 94

		Annual return
1982	Australian shares	-13.87%
1983	Cash	11.93%
1984	Australian shares	-2.26%
1985	Listed property trusts	5.25%
1986	Cash	12.38%
1987	Australian shares	-7.86%
1988	International fixed interest	-10.58%
1989	Listed property trusts	2.35%
1990	Australian shares	-17.52%
1991	Cash	11.20%
1992	Australian shares	-2.31%
1993	Cash	5.39%
1994	Australian shares	-8.67%

If you had managed to invest solely in the worst performing assets every year during this period – your average annual return would have been -1.54%.

Fortunately, your chances of picking them all wrong are the same as getting them all right – about zero. So, most investors over the period would have earned somewhere between our best average annual return of 33.0% and our worst annual return of -1.54%.

Punting (and it is punting) on the 'best' investment for the next year really is a mug's game. Even the maths is against punters.

A gambler's lament

- Invest $1 and lose 50%. You now have 50 cents.
- Invest 50 cents and earn 50%. You now have 75 cents.

Try it the other way around

- Invest $1 and earn 50%. You now have $1.50.
- Invest $1.50 and lose 50%. You still have 75 cents!

Two equal returns sees you losing money. And in the context of investment dealing, this is before you pay any commission, stamp duty or brokerage. Pretty obviously, you need to be right with your investment timing decisions two-thirds of the time to break even and it's just too difficult to get it right that often.

I'm not saying don't use research to guide you to better investment areas. But when it comes down to it, determining how much risk you can live with and then buying investments that suit your risk profile and monitoring these is a better strategy than switching from one investment area to another on a regular basis. The only winner in this is the broker or salesperson who is doing the buying and selling – or the Stamp Duties Office!

3. Diversify

In broad terms, I recommend that you have a plan to create three pools of wealth – your home, your superannuation and other investments. This is based on a simple view about diversification. This strategy gives you exposure to property (your home), shares and fixed interest (through your super) and other investments you buy yourself. These might be shares, money in the bank or an investment property.

It also gives you diversification from a tax and legislative perspective. Super is a highly regulated area, and the main reason I would not rely solely on super is another type of risk – the risk of changing legislation.

How you diversify depends upon your age, income, family and so on. The younger you are the less diversification you are likely to have, but as you get older you will diversify more as your wealth grows and you want to reduce the amount of risk you are taking.

Remember my kids? They are concentrating into one high-risk area – South-East Asian shares. My retired clients on the other hand have a very diversified portfolio because they are trying to minimise risks.

You can also take diversification into a more narrow context. For example, with a share portfolio you should diversify by choosing different sectors within the market. You might invest in the following areas:

- banking and finance
- building and construction
- media
- health
- resources.

Inside, say, the banking and finance sector you might further diversify by choosing several shares such as Westpac, National Australia Bank and a smaller bank such as St George.

With international shares, your level of diversification can become very extensive as the following graph shows.

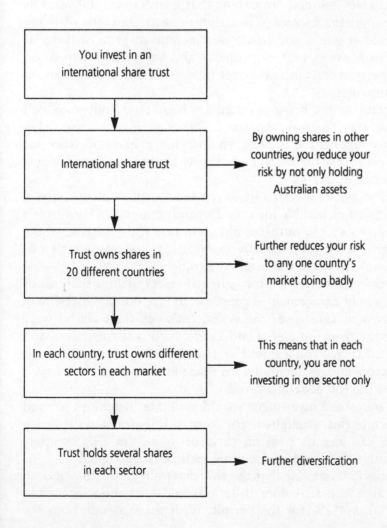

4. Invest in growth assets for the long term

A growth asset is simply something that grows in capital value as well as producing income. To maintain your standard of living once you stop work, you need your income to grow with inflation. Growth assets such as property and shares will help to do this. Property rentals increase over time as do share dividends on good companies.

Be careful about being seduced by high (and fully taxable!) income returns on bank deposits or other such investments. Let me try to highlight this with an imaginary investor who has $10,000 to invest for her future. She is 40 years old and wants to stop work at age 55.

If the $10,000 is invested in, say, a term deposit at 9%, it will generate $900 of taxable income. Depending upon our investor's income, up to 48.5% of this could go in tax. If the balance of the income gets spent (as it usually does) in 15 years at age 55 our investor will still have the original $10,000.

By investing the $10,000 into growth assets such as shares, our investor would earn much less income today, but the investment would grow in value over the years. Let's say three shares were purchased with the money: Lend Lease, National Australia Bank and Coles Myer. (You'll note I've chosen a share from three different sectors and, incidentally, investing in a managed share trust would do the job equally as well.)

Now, our share investment would generate income of around 5%. Much of this would be in the form of fully franked dividends and have tax already paid on them at 36%, but let's compare apples with apples and assume this income is also spent.

It's realistic to assume that the shares would grow (in price) on average at 6% p.a. (before inflation) and that inflation would average around 4% for the period. With these assumptions the shares would be worth around $24,000 in 15 years. So at retirement at 55, our investor would have $24,000 worth of shares earning 5% income ($1,200) and this $1,200 would have tax paid on it at 36% (being, for the sake of this example, fully franked dividends).

Compare this income to that provided by the $10,000 still sitting there in the term deposit (and getting eaten by inflation). It's still only earning 9% ($900) – and this $900 is fully taxable.

If the investor's effective tax rate was 36%, the shares would provide an after-tax income of $1,200, and the term deposit an after-tax income of $576.

In 15 years time, would you rather have $900 of taxable income or $1,200 of income with tax advantages?

Sure, growth assets are far more risky in the short-term, but over 10 or 15 years, quality growth assets will tend to grow in value, and so will the income they generate for you.

0—⚷ Key thought

Growth assets increase in value, have tax advantages and, therefore, generate more income as time goes by.

5. Rebalance your investments regularly

I can't tell you how often I have seen investors get bitten by a failure to rebalance their investments. So, what's 'rebalancing'?

If you have constructed a diversified portfolio of investments, I would hope that you have made a deliberate decision about how your investments are spread – the technical jargon for this is 'asset allocation'.

This means that on Day 1, your investment portfolio may look like this:

Australian shares	30% (in value)
International shares	22%
Australian fixed interest	25%
International fixed interest	15%
Property	8%
	100%

If, as was the case from 1985-7, the sharemarket roared ahead and, if you did nothing, your portfolio could look like this sometime later:

Australian shares	36%
International shares	26%
Australian fixed interest	18%
International fixed interest	11%
Property	9%
	100%

Your share weighting (the value that shares proportionally comprise of your portfolio) has increased dramatically without you having done anything to it. The higher share weighting now means your overall portfolio risk is higher than on Day 1, because shares are the riskiest of the main investment classes.

Unless your attitude to risk has changed, you should rebalance back to your correct portfolio mix at least twice a year. Yes, you may incur switching fees in some cases and pay capital gains tax on profits, but if you don't rebalance, don't be surprised at how much you might lose when markets fall!

Rebalancing also has the added attraction of enforced discipline. It forces you to sell when assets are expensive and buy when they are cheap. How? Well, if you always keep the original 30% value of your portfolio in Australian shares and rebalance if this falls or rises by 2% (at 32% you sell some shares, at 28% you buy some shares) by definition you *must sell when expensive* and *buy when cheap*. It's a simple discipline, but believe me, it works.

6. Watch your gearing

Gearing, meaning borrowing to invest, can multiply your profits – and your losses. Many investors in the late 1980s unwittingly borrowed money to buy unlisted property trusts, some of whom had also borrowed money to buy property. This was gearing on gearing and led to some terrible losses.

I give a lot more detail on this subject in Chapter Twelve but as one of your central investment rules, please watch carefully any gearing that you use – and any gearing inside investments that you make.

In brief, this is how gearing works:

- Invest $100,000 of your money into a $100,000 property. If the property rises by 10% you make $10,000.
- Invest $50,000 of your money into a $100,000 property. If the property rises by 10% you make $10,000 on your $50,000 investment, or 20%.
- Invest $10,000 of your money into a $100,000 property. If the property rises by 10% you make $10,000 on your $10,000 investment, or 100%.

In the last example, you double your money if the $100,000 property only increases in value by 10%. This sounds terrific and many investment salespeople use this to great advantage. What they don't mention is the fact that gearing can multiply your returns – *in both directions*.

In our example, if the property falls by 10%, you lose $10,000 – or all of the money that you put in. If the investment falls, by say $20,000, you lose not only your original $10,000, but another $10,000 which you still have to repay.

θ━ Key thought

Only gear your investments if you fully understand the risk you are taking.

Borrowing against your home – don't!

A number of so-called 'advisers' strongly promote borrowing against your own home to buy shares. They may give you a very attractive presentation about how you will get tax deductions and pay off your mortgage more quickly.

This is a great deal for them as they typically make a commission on arranging the finance and on the investments they buy for you. On a $100,000 investment their take could be as high as $6,000.

Now, if the shares go up in value, (and in the <u>long term</u> they will), their presentation shows that you are well in front. What they seem to forget to tell you (except in the fine print), is that if shares fall in value you will lose borrowed money if you have to sell and this will jeopardise your home.

Sure, you should buy some shares, but not with borrowings against your home. It's one asset you should not risk.

7. Invest internationally

One of the truly historic changes during my time in the money industry has been the fact that when it comes to investment, the world really is a global village. By this, I mean that money flows instantly from country to country via the banks' computer systems. You can buy assets such as shares, fixed interest or even property in practically any country you like.

Okay, you may be thinking that it has nothing to do with you but, for better or worse, it does. Our long-term standard of living depends on how competitive we are as a nation. If we are under-productive and we continue to allow our economy to build foreign debt, a fall in our dollar is inevitable. If our dollar falls, imports cost more and, no matter how hard you try, you cannot buy only Australian.

Arun Abey, one of my partners at IPAC, is fond of making this point by asking people, 'How much more Australian can you get than a steak sandwich?' I must admit, at first, I couldn't quite understand what he was getting at. 'Of course, it's Australian,' we all say, 'Australian meat served with Australian salad on Australian bread.'

Then he points out that the cattle the meat comes from are looked after with foreign pharmaceuticals; eat pasture grown with foreign fertiliser; transported to the abattoirs in an American, Japanese or German truck; cut up by German equipment; transported again in a foreign truck; wrapped in Taiwanese plastic; and then served to you on a plate, knife and fork also made in Taiwan. Even your cash will be put into a cash register that may not be made here! All in all, our $3 steak sandwich could have 40% of its cost determined by 'foreign' value-added items.

What am I getting at? Well, many of you may have had an overseas holiday 10 or 15 years ago. Do you remember that at one stage your Aussie dollar bought you nearly $US1.50, £1 stg, 3 Swiss francs and so on?

What does it buy today? Around 75 cents American, 50 English pence and 1 Swiss franc. Our dollar has fallen in value significantly over the last 20 years. If you had held American, English, Swiss or, even better, Japanese investments you would have been protected from this fall in the value of our currency.

Look, I'm very positive about our country. In fact, I can't think of a better place to live, work and bring up a family but I do want to protect my standard of living and I can't do that by investing all of my assets in Australia. Sure, the Aussie dollar may hold its value or even rise against other currencies in the next 20 years – but I doubt it. We still have a number of problems such as too much debt, some poor workplace practices, and too high a dependence on welfare for me to be absolutely confident that we will be competitive and productive in comparison to our trading partners. So, for me, having some of my money invested offshore is a matter of commonsense.

While protection against our currency is a negative reason for investing offshore, there is another, very positive one. It allows you to participate in a range of exciting investments. You can buy shares in companies in the huge economies of the world such as the USA and Japan. You can participate in the rebuilding of Eastern Europe, or the new fast growth markets in South-East Asia or Latin America. You could even have a stake in the biggest potential market of all – China.

Not only are these exciting thoughts, but they are also sensible. The graph on the next page looks at the performance of various investments over the last 12 years. As you can see, international shares have performed best. And, interestingly, investment in the major international sharemarkets is actually less risky than investment in the Australian sharemarket. You need to remember that our market accounts for less than 2% of the world's stockmarkets, and we have a market with a high percentage of resource stocks (companies mining coal, aluminium, gold, copper and so on). Resource prices move rapidly on world markets – and so do resource stocks' values!

I've mentioned before that I invest around $500 ($10 a week)

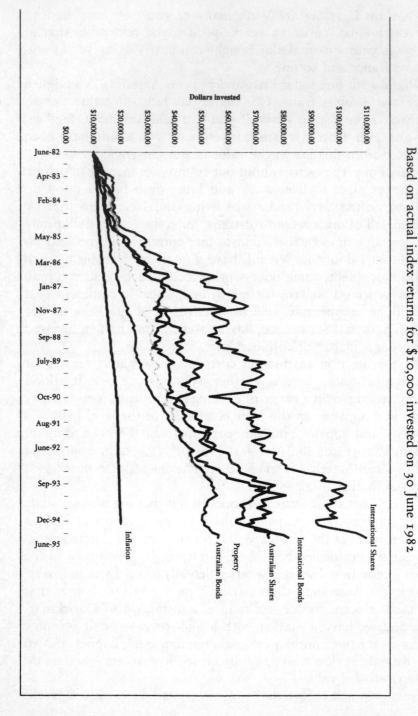

Investment markets to 30 June 1995

Based on actual index returns for $10,000 invested on 30 June 1982

Dollars invested

$0.00
$10,000.00
$20,000.00
$30,000.00
$40,000.00
$50,000.00
$60,000.00
$70,000.00
$80,000.00
$90,000.00
$100,000.00
$110,000.00

June-82
Apr-83
Feb-84
May-85
Mar-86
Jan-87
Nov-87
Sep-88
July-89
Oct-90
Aug-91
June-92
Sep-93
Dec-94
June-95

Inflation
Australian Bonds
Property
Australian Shares
International Bonds
International Shares

for each of my three children into 'emerging markets' – mainly in South-East Asia. This is where I see the fastest economic growth and my children can benefit from this by owning shares in companies in these economies.

I do this by using a managed 'emerging markets' share fund. These typically invest in a dozen economies and hold hundreds of different shares in Thailand, Korea, Malaysia and so on. There is no way I'd try to pick international shares myself – it's all too hard. For an initial investment in one of these funds of between $1,000 and $2,000 you do get an amazing spread of economies and individual shares.

However, don't let the spread trick you into thinking that the risk is therefore low. It's not. The actual economies and companies are risky. A standard salesperson's line might be that the average annual return from emerging markets over the eight years (1987 to 1994) was 32%. Now, while this is true, what they don't tell you is that the actual returns year by year were:

1987	22%
1988	40%
1989	90%
1990	-9%
1991	60%
1992	12%
1993	63%
1994	-22%

See? The average is terrific but year-by-year things are very risky.

Why invest overseas?

- to spread risk
- to protect yourself against a falling Australian dollar
- to invest in the world's major economies
- to participate in exciting opportunities in Asia, Europe and Latin America
- to protect your long-term standard of living.

> ## ⚿ Key thought
> While I want to live in Australia, I want to protect my
> standard of living in a global context. I invest offshore because
> it makes sense to me not to have everything in one small
> economy such as ours. It allows me to participate in the major
> world economies and dynamic smaller economies.

8. Avoid tax schemes

When it comes to tax and investment, please do be cautious about tax schemes. Prawns, salmon, flowers, horses, helicopters and port. You name it, I've seen it! Tax schemes in every colour, shape and size that are typically bought in a desperate panic in June by people with a tax problem.

The typical scheme will arrange finance so that you can borrow the money to get the tax deduction. If, say, you borrowed $10,000 for one of these schemes, a maximum taxpayer would get a reduction in tax of $4,850 (including Medicare levy). Now that's not to be sneezed at. But if, as inevitably happens, the scheme fails you might have a $4,850 tax deduction but you have lost another $5,150. This doesn't sound very appealing to me.

My advice is quite simple. Unless you *really* understand the nature of the investment, don't do it. Looking at my own clients, I find that those who have simply concentrated on minimising their tax in the usual ways, paid what they owed, and concentrated on a sensible investment strategy, end up miles in front. You can read more about it in Chapter Ten, 'Tax'.

9. Try dollar cost averaging

This is a great tip, simply because it works so well. In 'Don't try to time the market' (page 148), I pointed out how hard it is to pick the right investment except with hindsight. Well, dollar cost averaging makes things very easy. All you have to do is to simply decide how much and how often you are going to invest. You may decide to invest on a monthly, six monthly or yearly basis – it really doesn't matter.

Let's imagine you decide to invest $1000 twice a year into a particular share. Its price, like all shares, rises and falls over time. This is what could happen:

	Share price	Number of shares you get
1 January 1996	$1.00	1000
1 July 1996	$1.20	833
1 January 1997	$0.80	1250
1 July 1997	$1.00	1000
1 January 1998	$1.40	714
1 July 1998	$1.30	769

Look at when you bought the most shares – in January 1997, when our imaginary share's price was 80 cents. When did you buy the least? In January 1998, when the share price was $1.40.

Human nature tends to lead us to sell when things are cheap (times are bad) and buy when they are expensive (things are good). Dollar cost averaging forces you to buy most shares when they are cheapest, and buy the least when they are the most expensive. This must be a discipline worth using.

10. Take advice if necessary

I'm the first to argue that the more you know about your money the better off you are. But there are some things you don't need to know nor, unless you have a huge amount of spare time, will you be able to know. It's like your health – you don't have the time or training to be able to self-diagnose and treat your own health problems. When necessary you go to see a doctor. With money matters you go to a financial adviser. But if you thought finding a good doctor was hard, finding a good financial adviser is even more difficult.

The reason is that the whole field of professional financial advice is reasonably new. Commissioned salespeople have been around for years, but it has only been in the last decade that qualified, professional advisers have started to appear in reasonable numbers. You'll find more about this in Chapter Nineteen, 'Choosing an Adviser'.

Take action!

Anyone can be a successful investor rather than a losing punter by following a pretty simple prescription – spreading risk over a diversified range of assets, and hanging on to these assets for the long-term, through the good and the bad times.

And yes, there is something else – taking action. No one ever gets rich by doing nothing (unless you're lucky enough to inherit a fortune). You generate wealth by *doing something*. This might seem obvious, but it needs saying.

Look, all of the main investment classes produce reasonable returns over time. And even if you only invest in one or two of the poorer performing ones, this is still far, far better than having invested in none at all. Yes, I know I say that diversifying across all the main asset classes is the *best* investment strategy, but let's say you have only invested in residential property, well, good, at least you have invested in at least *one* viable asset class. In fact, in the end it doesn't really make an enormous amount of difference which quality assets you invest in, be they shares, property, cash or fixed interest, just so long as you *do invest!*

Keys to successful investing

1. Understand that risk equals return.
2. Don't try to time the market.
3. Diversify.
4. Invest in growth assets for the long term.
5. Rebalance your investments regularly.
6. Watch your gearing.
7. Invest internationally.
8. Avoid tax schemes.
9. Try dollar cost averaging.
10. Take advice if necessary.

CHAPTER TWELVE

Investing in Property

When Australians think investment, many think property, particularly residential property. Indeed, figures from the 1991 Census indicate that 20.9% of Australian dwellings are rented to private sector tenants which is a massive show of support for residential property as an investment.

Like buying a home to live in, buying a property to rent out and, hopefully sell at a profit one day, is an easy concept to grasp. It's not as abstract as investment in shares or bonds and I am sure this goes a long way towards explaining its enormous popularity.

Don't let me give you the impression that residential property investment is straightforward, though. It may appear to be, but getting it right can take a lot more than meets the eye. Anyone with the money can go out and buy a property but, if you don't choose carefully, you may find your returns are low or even negative. What you need to ensure is that you do your homework properly and make sure you buy the right property at the right price.

It's fair to say in fact that direct investment in property normally requires greater care, is more complex and has more pitfalls than investment in any of the other main asset classes.

Returns from property

Like all investments, returns from residential property investment depend on which period you look at because all investments have their good and bad years. To get an accurate picture of an investment's performance you have to look at returns that have been calculated over as long a term as possible.

Consider the following table, compiled by Associate Professor Graeme Newell of the University of Western Sydney, comparing the medium-term returns of Australian residential, commercial and retail property to Australian shares, 10-year bonds and 90-day bank bills in the period 1985 to 1993.

163

Making Money

Performance of investments 1985-1993

	Average annual return
Residential property	
Sydney	15.3%
Melbourne	14.2%
Brisbane	14.8%
Adelaide	11.1%
Perth	17.6%
Canberra	13.8%
Australian shares (based on the All Ordinaries Index)	17.9%
10-year bonds	18.5%
90-day bills	12.4%
Office property	
Sydney	8.0%
Melbourne	5.4%
Brisbane	9.7%
Retail property	
NSW	17.1%
Victoria	15.8%
Queensland	16.4%

(*Source: Real Estate Journal of NSW*, October 1994.)

Professor Newell's residential property performance figures are pre-income and/or capital gains tax and are based on the performance of three-bedroom houses only. His results are derived by adding together *capital growth* (the increase in the average three-bedroom house price over the period) and *net income growth* (the increase in the average rental income of three-bedroom houses, less all outgoings, over the period). All the calculations are based on raw data supplied by the Real Estate Institute of Australia (REIA).

Note how good the residential returns generally are. Though please remember that they are over a nine-year period and include the boom of 1985–87. The lowest average annual residential return of 11.1% from Adelaide was still 5.5% above the average rate of inflation over the nine years, and the performance of Perth property exceeded the inflation rate by a very healthy 12%. It's these sort of figures that help explain why residential property is such a popular area of investment.

Through its 'Investment Monitor', ANZ Funds Management also provides residential property returns measured in the same way as Professor Newell's results. But the ANZ survey period covers a slightly different time frame to Prof Newell's, and also provides shorter term results. So it's interesting to compare the two sets of figures.

Investment returns by market sector as at 31 December 1994

	3 Months	12 Months	2 Years	5 Years	10 Years
Australian Shares	−4.48%	−8.67%	15.22%	7.50%	14.91%
Fixed Interest	4.14%	−4.33%	5.61%	12.61%	13.18%
Residential Property					
Sydney	−3.70%	7.63%	10.04%	5.50%	14.19%
Melbourne	−0.32%	6.51%	7.13%	6.22%	12.77%
Brisbane	2.73%	10.02%	9.44%	10.91%	14.59%
Adelaide	3.10%	7.21%	5.25%	8.72%	11.22%
Perth	1.89%	15.70%	16.27%	10.27%	16.00%
Total Australian					
Property	−0.43%	8.76%	9.56%	7.74%	14.65%
Cash	1.99%	6.27%	5.67%	8.28%	11.80%
CPI	1.00%	2.73%	2.37%	2.66%	5.33%

What both surveys indicate is that residential property has been a decent and steady performer over time, but the ANZ figures illustrate how volatile and inconsistent it can be across different markets in the short-term.

Capital improvements

It's worth noting that these REIA based residential property performance figures do not take into account buying and selling costs for residential property, which can be significantly higher than for shares, cash or fixed interest. Property transaction costs include stamp duty, conveyancing fees and agent's fees which are not to be sneezed at and, if factored into these returns, would take some of the sheen off them.

To further cloud the picture presented by these figures, they give no indication of how much of the increase in residential property values is due to *owners injecting their own capital* into their properties through renovations, extensions, landscaping and general upgrading.

Let's say, for example, you bought a house for $200,000 in 1996, then sold it in 1997 for $300,000. These two transactions would go into REIA calculations and could help create the impression that residential property prices were going through the roof. *But, what if you had spent $120,000 renovating the property in the year you owned it?* It might look like you had made a real estate killing but the reality is totally different – you would have been mauled!

Median house price lists which are published from time to time in the press also don't take into account the capital value added to homes by their owners' own money, as distinct from the more mysterious price increasing effect of 'market forces'. Remember this when working out just what sort of returns you would like to achieve from a residential property investment and try to answer this (difficult) question – how much growth in the property's capital value is likely to come from a buoyant market and how much growth is likely to come from your own pocket? If you pick the right property, most of it should come from the market. If you pick the wrong property then you'll generate most of the growth yourself.

Micro markets within larger markets

Remember, that the REIA-derived returns are based on the average price and rental values of three-bedroom houses across entire Australian cities. But be very aware that particular areas within a city or township and other types of dwellings produce both higher and lower returns than these.

To illustrate how variable the property market can be within just one city let's take the Sydney housing market in the year between the September 1993 and September 1994 quarters. In the council area of Woollahra, largely comprised of affluent eastern suburbs close to the city, average prices for three-bedroom homes rose by 45.6% over the 12 months but during the same period in the mid-western council area of Strathfield, average three-bedroom housing prices fell by 2.8%. (These were the extreme results from Sydney's 43 local government areas and the average increase in three-bedroom housing prices across the city was 10.3% for the year. *Source*: NSW REI.)

The best performing micro markets

It has been a trend for some years that areas close to the centre of a city tend to show stronger price growth than areas further out, not only in Sydney but also in other state capitals, particularly Melbourne and Brisbane.

What's happening is that the oldest and closest suburbs to the city are being done up and gentrified, and then attention is turning to nearby, similar suburbs a bit further out. Urban renewal of this type thus tends to spread out in concentric circles from the centre of the city. To illustrate:

- The value of a typical Sydney inner-city house (0 to 6 kilometres from the city centre) was $52,000 in 1977. By the end of 1994 it had risen to $388,000, a 746% appreciation and the strongest growth shown in the metropolitan area over the period.
- The average Sydney house price in the middle distance suburbs (6 to 25 kilometres from the centre) was $46,000 in 1977 which grew to $285,000 by the end of 1994, an appreciation of 620% over the period.
- Outer suburbs (more than 25 kilometres) showed the slowest growth, with an average house price of $37,000 in 1977 growing to $185,000 by 1994, a 500% appreciation over the period.

The highest specific growth came from Paddington terrace houses. (If you are unfamiliar with Sydney, Paddington is an old and picturesque suburb on the eastern boundary of the city. It consists largely of 19th century terraces built as inexpensive workers' housing which since the 1970s have undergone major renovation, changing the demographic nature of the suburb dramatically.) In 1977, the average value of a Paddington terrace was $45,000; by the end of 1994 this had grown to $550,000, an appreciation of 1,222% over the 17 years. (*Source*: *Sydney*

Making Money

Morning Herald, 4 February 1995 based on Valuer-General's data).

Of course a much higher than usual proportion of Paddington's appreciation would have been attributable to the residents' own capital injections into their properties – many Paddington renovations have been virtual rebuilds – but there are some lessons here for residential property investors.

In general (and I stress *in general* – there are *always* exceptions) try to buy a property that:
- is close to the city centre
- is in an area where gentrification is underway or is likely to be soon
- is aesthetically pleasing or at least has potential to be
- has a unique or rare positive characteristic. Remember that scarcity adds value to any asset. (This is one of the reasons why Paddington's Victorian terraces have performed so well – there is a limited number of them.)

Now, if your foresight is good and you buy into an area just before gentrification takes off, your property will show very good capital returns – but be aware of the risks. Some areas take ages before they become popular and in some areas it may not happen at all. These include places where there has been haphazard industrial development, often accompanied by high levels of air and noise pollution. You find such areas in all Australian cities, and I advise you to ignore them for investment.

Obviously, everyone wants to live in a place that is as pleasant and as attractive as possible. And being an investor you can't afford to hang on to a property in an unattractive locality for too long waiting for the renovating and cappuccino set to move in and smarten the area up. The longer a property sits around effectively doing nothing, the less money you are making. And, if you have borrowed to buy you will actually be losing money while the property stagnates.

⚿ Key thought

One of the basic truths in buying real estate is position is paramount. Beauty, scarcity and convenience are some of the qualities to look for.

Satisfy the baby boomers

What sort of individual property is likely to produce the best investment returns, both in terms of capital (price) and income (rental) growth? You can see how hard it is to answer this question just by looking at short-term property results for specific areas, the sort of information regularly presented to us in the newspapers.

An answer however, begins to emerge if you look at Australia's changing demographic patterns and use this as the basis for your real estate decisions. There are two key points to consider. Firstly, Australia's largest demographic grouping, the post-war baby boomers (born between 1945 and the late 60s) are now moving into middle and older age. Secondly, due to lower immigration and a reduced birthrate the aging baby boomers will remain the largest demographic grouping for many years. This means the overall Australian population is aging – *and older people have different housing requirements than younger people.*

When the older baby boomers were young parents they mostly wanted as big a house as possible with a backyard for the kids – like parents of any era. This invariably meant living in the suburbs but now, as they slowly age and the kids move out, they don't need the big family home and garden any more. Increasingly, baby boomers will sell their large suburban houses and move to smaller dwellings such as townhouses closer to the city or to coastal retirement enclaves. Without a family to feed, few or no debts and possibly a superannuation pay-out, many will be able to afford to move more or less where they please.

The dwellings they move to will be low-maintenance (little or no gardens), made of good quality materials, and will be well appointed and well positioned. They will want as few stairs as possible, good security, ample parking and storage, proximity to all amenities, and preferably a level stroll to shops and transport. They will prefer localities that are attractive, as well as clean, quiet and safe.

If you want to buy an investment residential property I recommend you buy something that fits these parameters. The type of housing that will appeal to many of the aging baby boomers will remain in greater demand than the type of housing appealing to other, less robust demographic groups – and hence show greater growth. It should also mean that the general localities best suited to baby boomers' needs should show relatively stronger price and rental growth than other localities.

> ### 8━━ Key thought
> Pick a property and a location that will appeal to aging baby boomers. They've got the numbers, they've got the money. There will be more than 5 million Australians aged 65 or older in the year 2031.

Residential property – problems ahead?

A lot of concern has been expressed by investment commentators about Australia's slowing rate of population growth which the following figures illustrate. In 1921 the number of Australian-born residents was increasing at 2.2% per year; by 1991 the rate had fallen to 1.2%. The average number of births per Australian woman peaked in the 1960s at 3.55; by 1991 the figure was down to 1.85. In 1970 there were 20.6 births per 1,000 of population; in 1991 the rate had dropped to 14.9 births per 1,000, a fall of 27.7%.

Our declining birth rate has been accompanied by an immigration intake that has remained more or less steady at around 70,000 per year in the 10 years to 1995, excluding the large one-off intake of Chinese students in 1991-2 following the Tian'anmen Square massacre. (*Source: ABS.*)

Now, the relevance of all this to residential property is that population growth is the key driver of real property price growth. So, if there is a decline in population growth there should also be a decline in property returns.

It's important to recognise that a house is not like a business. Other than renovating it, extending it or getting it rezoned you don't have much influence over it's financial performance. To what extent it appreciates is largely beyond your control. You're in the hands of the market – and where population growth is slow market growth is likely to be slow too.

Now, I don't believe the rate of our population growth will ever be allowed to get so low as to bring on a major collapse in property values but it is quite likely that residential property returns in general will not be as good in the future as they have been. Australia's slowing rate of population growth is partly to blame for this, and so is our changing demographic structure.

Let me explain. The older 45 to 65 year age group is the fastest growing segment of the working population, and it will continue to grow until about the year 2020, when every other age segment will be in decline. Significantly, the younger 25 to 45 year age group will fall sharply as a proportion of the total working population over the same period. And because the 25 to 45 year age group is the one most involved in the formation of new households, its relative decline over the next 20 years is likely to lead to a corresponding relative decline in the demand for new housing. Therefore, I would advise you to look to other areas of the residential market to invest in rather than investing in property primarily designed for new, young families.

The practicalities

You will recall the REIA-derived residential property returns reflect the total investment performance of three-bedroom houses, arrived at by adding both the average price growth and the average net rental growth of this type of dwelling, *minus all outgoings*. So, what do we mean by 'outgoings? Well, they include:
- council and water rates
- insurances
- body corporate fees

Making Money

- property management fees to real estate agents
- maintenance
- bookkeeping fees
- accountancy fees
- legal fees (for drawing up leases)
- advertising costs to find tenants
- costs involved in employing people, for example, worker's compensation
- bank charges
- petrol, phone, postage and stationery.

While ongoing costs vary from property to property, a reasonable rule of thumb is that residential outgoings average 25% of gross rentals. (This is the percentage used by the REIA, based on three-bedroom houses. Net rent is, therefore, around 75% of gross rent.)

Some property costs are unavoidable, like insurance and rates, but it may be possible to save some money by managing your own property, doing your own maintenance or finding your own tenants. These chores might give you a headache but they will help you achieve a better than average net return (yield) from your investment property. Take note, however, that increases in your rental income will also increase your tax liability, while management fees and maintenance costs are tax-deductible.

Buying costs

When you buy a property there is no agent's commission to pay but you will be up for stamp duty and legal fees and probably some other costs. Stamp duties and legal fees in particular vary across the states, and are calculated on a (normally sliding) scale dependent on the value of the property.

The following is an approximate breakdown of what buying a house for $200,000 (with a mortgage of $150,000) can cost. I stress that all these costs, apart from stamp duties, are open to market forces and negotiation and there may be no need to pay for pest and/or building reports if they have already been done.

Property price – $200,000
Location – Sydney
Mortgage – $150,000

Stamp duty on property	$5,490
Stamp duty on mortgage	$ 541
Buyer's legal fees	$2,000
Bank's legal fees	$ 500
Bank's loan application fee	$ 600
Survey	$ 325
Pest and building reports	$ 350
TOTAL	$9,806

In this example buying costs represent 4.9% of the $200,000
purchase price.

Selling costs

When you sell your investment property you will be up for some
or all of the following costs: agent's commission, advertising, solicitor's fees (to prepare the mortgage and exchange documents),
early mortgage pay-out fee, building and pest reports, surveys and
possibly cosmetic renovations.

Agent's fees vary from state to state and, in some instances, are
simply arrived at through negotiation between the vendor and the
agent. As a guide, work on the agent's selling fee being 2% to
2.5% of the value of the property.

Here is approximately what it would cost to sell the same property for $200,000 in Sydney. (Bear in mind that lenders may not
charge an early repayment fee or may charge more than is quoted
here. Also, some vendors make no financial contribution towards
a property's advertising campaign while others contribute significantly more than quoted here):

Solicitor's fees (including contract preparation)	$1,800
Early mortgage pay-out bank fee	$ 500

Making Money

Agent's fees 2.5% (negotiable)	$5,000
Vendor's contribution costs for advertising	$ 500
TOTAL	$7,800

In this example selling costs are 3.9% of the $200,000 selling price.

Recouping costs

You can see how buying and selling costs add up to a very significant proportion of a property's value. In this case – based on real quotes taken in Sydney in early 1995 – transaction costs total $17,606 or 8.8% of the property's total value (assuming that the purchase price and selling price are the same).

A property has to appreciate by this much before you recoup these transaction costs. Remember, too, that these are not the only costs of investing in property. If, like most property investors, you have borrowed to buy you will have interest payments to make, possibly tax to pay on the rent you receive, and capital gains tax to contend with on selling the property (if you bought it after 19 September, 1985). Of course interest repayments, income tax and capital gains tax can be a feature of any other investment you make, and though not unique to property, you still have to account for them in working out your overall returns.

While all this might sound as though I'm a little down on residential property as an investment, that's not really so. Over time it has proved to be a reasonable investment, and so long you *pick the right property in the right location at the right price*, it should continue to be so.

Take a long-term position

As is the case with other mainstream investments taking a long-term position in residential real estate is generally the best policy. The reason is simple. Property prices can go through major swings which can occur with little warning. Consequently, if you buy and sell over a short time frame, you are just as likely to catch a bust as you are a boom and while you can make a lot of money in real estate in two or three years, you can lose your shirt just as quickly.

The thing to be aware of is that growth in property prices does not occur smoothly over time. A relatively common pattern includes a price surge of one to two years' duration followed by a price fall, in turn followed by a period of stagnation and/or modest price growth lasting around four to five years. And while there are examples to the contrary, the accepted view in real estate circles is that Australian residential property works in seven-year cycles roughly following this scheme.

Now, not only is residential property prone to irregular price movements but the rate at which it appreciates (or depreciates) and by how much it moves also varies from market to market.

In 1988 for example, the median price of Sydney houses increased by 43.6%, (from $122,400 in January to $175,800 in November). In the same year, median Melbourne house prices increased by 23.5% ($91,500 to $113,00) and in Brisbane prices increased by 17.9% ($62,700 to $73,900).

Two years later, in 1990, the median Sydney house price dropped by 11.7% from $198,100 in January to $175,000 in November (prices had peaked at $208,500 in July/August 1989). But during 1990 in Melbourne the median house price *rose* by 3% ($135,700 to $139,800), and in Brisbane the median house price also rose, by 11.4% ($96,300 to $107,300). (*Source:* REIA.)

Results like these (and they are not isolated) may confuse potential property investors, but that's not my intention. My aim is to show you that trying to pick where and when the next big price surge is going to happen is for the birds.

If you invest in residential property for the short-term with the hope of buying in at the start of one of its periodic upward surges you are adopting a punter's strategy. There's more luck than science in picking the right times. The solution is to buy and hold property for the long-term (meaning at least for seven years). This way you increase the likelihood of catching a price surge and consequently generating good *average* annual returns. You can also stop worrying about *when* to buy because, over time, this question becomes irrelevant. So, when is the right time to buy? When you're able to!

Making Money

As we have noted above, too, you need to hold on to property for as least as long as it takes to appreciate to the point of covering the buying and selling costs. Under flat market conditions just meeting this requirement alone could literally take years.

Cash flow

Investing in property is a bit different from other asset classes. With shares and bonds you hand over your money and then sit back and wait for the investment to start producing (all being equal). With property it's a different story. You hand over the money ... and then you hand over some more ... and then you hand over some more ... Just like your home, a property investment is a constant source of expense.

Your rental income should more than cover the ongoing costs of holding a property (approximately 25% of gross rentals). But for most property investors the biggest cost is interest on the loan and, in most cases, in the early years of a property investment net rentals do not cover interest costs. (Of course this is dependent on what proportion of the property's value is borrowed, what the interest rate on the loan is, what the rental income is and what the ongoing costs actually are.)

Because most property investors will be out of pocket for the first years of the investment, a very important question to consider before you start looking for funds is what other sources of income do you have to make up any shortfalls, and how secure is this other source of income? And, when thinking about this, bear in mind that there are bound to be times when your property is vacant – indeed, it's common practice to allow for at least two weeks of vacancy per year.

Lenders will clearly want to know how you intend to repay the loan. What you should do for their sake (as well as for your own) is to prepare a cash flow analysis on the property you are interested in, projected out for as many years as it takes income to at least equal outgoings. The point of this exercise is to find out how long (if at all) the investment will leave you out of pocket.

This projection should list all anticipated rental income and all anticipated expenses against the property, including interest.

Starting at the beginning of Year 1 with a $0 balance, by the end of the first year it will indicate a cash surplus or shortfall for the year. This amount is then carried forward as the starting balance for Year 2, and so on, for every following year. Just make sure that from Year 2 onwards all income and expenses are adjusted for anticipated inflation. A rate I am comfortable with at present is 5% p.a.

At some stage the cash flow analysis will indicate you have moved into a cash surplus, as rentals, boosted by inflation, finally outstrip expenses (though at this point you will have another expense to contend with – income tax). That's when you decide if you have sufficient other income to afford the holding costs of the investment.

If you decide you can fund the initial losses that your property investment is likely to make (and be aware that these losses are a tax deduction against your other income – see 'Borrowing to invest' page 181), show the projections to your lending institution and demonstrate how you intend to make up the cash shortfall in the first few years. If you do all this credibly there is little reason why you shouldn't get the loan.

Preparing cash flow projections involves a fair amount of homework, effort and time – and a personal computer spreadsheet is perfectly suited to the task if you know how to use one. If you don't feel confident about doing this yourself, don't worry, an accountant will gladly do it for you for a reasonable fee – and I suggest it's money well spent given the stakes involved.

Below is an example of a property investment cash flow analysis, prepared by Peter Wills, Lecturer in Property at the University of Western Sydney. It is based on the following assumptions:

Property purchase price	$150,000
Purchase costs	$6,000 (stamp duty, legals etc)
Real capital cost	$156,000
Size of loan	$100,000
Type of loan	Interest-only fixed rate
Interest rate	12% p.a. (calculated annually)
Starting rent	$190 per week

Making Money

Cash flows under three different annual growth rates are calculated below. These are at a 'most likely' case scenario growth rate of 5%, a 'least likely' case scenario growth rate of 2%, and a 'best' case scenario growth rate of 10%.

In each scenario the property's value, the rent and the outgoings are increased annually in line with these growth rates. Do note though, that:

- annual changes to gross rent and outgoings are derived from changes to the weekly rent which, as in real life, is rounded off to the nearest $5
- annual changes to property values are non-compounding. They are derived from the change in the price from Year 1 to Year 2
- all amounts are rounded off.

Cash Flow Tables

'Most likely' case scenario with all growth calculated @ 5% p.a.

Purchase price $150,000	Year 1	Year 2	Year 3	Year 4	Year 5
	$	$	$	$	$
Weekly rent	190	200	210	220	230
Gross rent (p.a.)	9880	10400	10920	11440	11960
Vacancy (allow 2 weeks p.a.)	380	400	420	440	460
Outgoings (allow 25%)	2375	2500	2825	2750	2990
Net income p.a.	7125	7500	7875	8250	8510
Interest only @ 12% p.a.	12000	12000	12000	12000	12000
Net return (Loss) p.a.	-4875	-4500	-4125	-3750	-3490
per week	94	86	79	72	67

Property value at end of each period	$157500	$165000	$172500	$180000	$187500

Total capital gain (Over the 5 year period)	$37500
Less: Net return (Loss) (over 5 yrs)	$-20740
Less: Purchase costs	$-6000
Overall capital gain	$10760

'Least likely' case scenario with growth calculated @ 2% p.a.

	Year 1	Year 2	Year 3	Year 4	Year 5
	$	$	$	$	$
Weekly rent	190	195	200	205	210
Gross rent (p.a.)	9880	10140	10400	10660	10920
Vacancy	380	390	400	410	420
Outgoings	2375	2437	2500	2562	2625
Net income	7125	7313	7500	7688	7875
Interest	12000	1200	12000	12000	12000
Net return (Loss) p.a.	-4875	-4687	-4500	-4312	-4125
per week	94	90	86	83	79
Property value at end of each period	$15300	$156000	$159000	$162000	$165000

Total capital gain (over
5 yrs) $15000

Less: Net return (Loss)
(over 5 yrs) $-22500
Less: Purchase costs $-6000

Overall capital gain (Loss) $-13500

'Best case' scenario with growth calculated at 10% p.a.

	Year 1	Year 2	Year 3	Year 4	Year 5
	$	$	$	$	$
Weekly rent	190	210	230	250	270
Gross rent (p.a.)	9880	10920	11960	13000	14040
Vacancy	380	420	460	500	540
Outgoings	2375	2625	2875	3125	3375
Net income	7125	7875	8625	9375	10125
Interest	12000	12000	12000	12000	12000
Net return (Loss) p.a.	-4875	-4125	-3375	-2625	-1875
per week	94	79	65	50	36
Property value at end of each period	$165000	$180000	$195000	$210000	$225000

Total capital gain (over 5 yrs) $75000

Less: Net return (Loss) (over 5 yrs) $-16875
Less: Purchase costs. $-6000

Overall capital gain $52125

Making Money

If you take these projections further (under the 'most likely' scenario of 5% annual growth), you will find the actual weekly cash shortfall would be:

Year 6 $58 pw
Year 7 $50 pw
Year 8 $43 pw
Year 9 $33 pw
Year 10 $22 pw
Year 11 $11 pw
Year 12 $0 pw (at this point the rent would be $320 per week)

The figures simply mean that you will have to be able to dip into your pocket for a total of 11 years to hang on to this particular property investment. The benefit of such a cash flow analysis is that it shows you just how much you will be reaching for on a weekly and annual basis and enables you to rationally answer the question 'Can I afford it?'

Earnings projections

Now, while projecting a long way into the future is a highly conjectural exercise, based on the assumptions given above the overall returns from the three investment scenarios after 10 years would be:

1. 'Most likely' case scenario (5% annual growth)

Total capital gain		$75,000
Less: net cash flow loss	$32,000	
purchase costs	$ 6,000	
		$38,000
Overall capital gain		$37,000

2. 'Least likely' scenario (2% annual growth)

Total capital gain		$30,000
Less: net cash flow loss	$40,500	
purchase costs	$ 6,000	
		$46,500
Overall capital gain (loss)		$-16,500

3. 'Best case' scenario (10% annual growth)

Total capital gain		$150,000
Less: net cash flow loss	$ 15,000	
purchase costs	$ 6,000	
		$ 21,000
Overall capital gain		$129,000

These earnings projections dramatically illustrate how important capital growth is to the viability of a property investment. Note that at only 2% annual growth the investment is still in a net loss position after 10 years and going nowhere.

> **⚷ Key thought**
> Successful property investment is absolutely dependent on good rates of capital growth.

Borrowing to invest

Not many people buy an investment property with their own funds. The beauty about borrowing to invest is that it enables you to participate in investments that would otherwise be closed to you by virtue of their sheer cost, whether it's property, shares, bonds or art works.

There is nothing intrinsically wrong with borrowing to invest, or 'gearing', and as far as property investment is concerned it's the time-honoured method. It's just important that you do it sensibly.

The dynamic of borrowing to invest is that it enables you to increase your stake in an asset (over and above what you could afford out of your own savings) which in turn amplifies the size of its return to you – be this a positive (profit) or negative (loss) return. In other words, the more you borrow the more you stand to gain or to lose. The higher your borrowings, therefore, the higher your risk.

It's for this reason when borrowing that you exercise great caution. You must be as sure as you possibly can that the asset *will show positive returns*, because if it doesn't you will simply magnify your losses.

I receive many letters on this subject and it seems from this correspondence that many people believe the main attraction of borrowing to invest is the tax advantage derived from *negative gearing*. This is worrying so let's look at it.

For a start, an investment property is said to be negatively geared when the costs of holding it (including interest costs) exceed the rent received. Because the property is an investment, this loss is tax deductible and this tax deduction can be put towards reducing the tax payable on the investor's other assessable income.

Let's assume a property investor buys a unit for $120,000. He puts $20,000 of his own money towards it and borrows the remainder ($100,000). Let's also assume that interest on the loan is 10% p.a. ($10,000), and that the weekly rent is $120 or $6,240 p.a.

If the ongoing costs (including rates, water, insurance, maintenance and depreciation allowance) are $1,560 p.a., after-expenses income for the year will be $4,680 ($6,240 – $1,560). However, the annual interest repayments are $10,000 so he has actually lost $5,320 during the year. ($10,000 – $4,680 = $5,320.)

In this example the investor can reduce the tax liability on his other assessable income by the investment property's loss of $5,320.

Now, if the investor was on the highest marginal tax rate of 48.5% (including Medicare levy), this tax deduction would have the ultimate effect of reducing the real loss on the property from $5,320 to $2739.80, a considerable saving. ($5,320 x 48.5% = $2,580.20; $5,320 – $2,580.20 = $2,739.80.)

If the investor was on the lowest marginal tax rate of 21.5% (including Medicare levy), this tax deduction would have the ultimate effect of reducing the *real* loss on the property from $5,320 to $4,176.20, not as great a reduction (but not bad all the same!) ($5,320 x 21.5% = $1,143.80, $5,320 – $1,143.80 = $4,176.20.)

These two calculations clearly demonstrate how negative gearing benefits those on a high marginal tax rate more than those on a low marginal tax rate.

While negative gearing can reduce the real size of your annual loss on an investment – which is certainly welcome – it should not be the main attraction of the investment. A loss, albeit a reduced one, *is still a loss*! And no one has ever grown rich out of tax losses! You should only ever invest if you believe the investment will show genuine positive returns over time. If it provides tax deductions in the process, take that as a bonus but realise that it's not the main game.

Borrowing to invest and negative gearing were particularly popular and successful strategies for accumulating wealth in the 1970s and 1980s. All you had to do was raise a loan, buy a property, sit back and let the high rate of inflation and the relatively high levels of population growth do the work for you. And if you bought the property before 20 September 1985 there was no capital gains tax to pay on it. It was a property investors' dream! Like hundreds of thousands of other Australians I, too, benefited from borrowing to invest in property. In 1983 I went into hock to buy a modest Sydney semi-detached house for what then seemed like an exorbitant price only to find that four years later it had increased in value by 250%! I am the first to admit there was no great skill on my part in generating this fabulous return – it was just the way the market was at the time.

Things are a bit different now. Our current levels of low inflation are expected to remain low for the rest of the 1990s and in a low inflationary environment residential property growth tends to be low too (though not always). This is significant because, when you borrow to invest in property, you are borrowing for capital gains (which are likely to be low for some time).

When inflation is low the inflation-related, tax-free component used in reducing your capital gains liability is also low. In other words, the proportion of your capital gain that's taxable is higher in a low inflationary environment than it is in a high inflationary environment. See more on this in Chapter Ten, 'Tax'.

So, with all these words of warning, is borrowing to invest in residential property still a viable proposition? With qualification, my answer is 'yes'. The qualification is this – do your homework well and select your property with great care, ensuring you pay a fair price for it. Good property will continue to produce good returns over time but whatever you do, when borrowing to invest in property, make sure that your other sources of income are secure enough to cover any running losses. If you do generate some tax deductions from the losses along the way, good, but don't enter into the investment because of them.

⚟━ Key thought

Only borrow to invest in residential property (or any other asset for that matter) if you are as sure as you possibly can be that the investment will ultimately show a decent positive return, which will generally be realised when you sell it.

Selecting a lender

You've done your homework, you've picked the property, you've done your projections, now, who should you go to for finance? Well, assuming the answer is not 'anyone who's game enough', the type of lender to look for is one whose interest rate is competitive and no higher for property investment loans than it is for owner-occupier loans.

Since the recent increase in competition brought to the home lending market by the aggressiveness of regional banks, overseas banks and mortgage managers, getting an investment property loan for the same rate as an owner-occupier loan is possible. Generally though, the majority of lenders still charge property investors a higher rate, usually in the order of an extra 1%.

There is a significant difference between the highest and lowest investment rate so it will pay you to speak to a number of lenders but also bear in mind there is more to a competitive loan than just the interest rate. You should also investigate the lender's establishment fees, ongoing charges, fees for switching from a fixed rate to variable rate loan or vice versa, and policies on additional lump sum repayments and/or total early repayment. (These areas are looked at in some detail in the Chapter Seven 'Mortgages'.

Whichever lenders you speak to, don't be afraid to push for a better deal. There is always room for negotiation. If you're considered a good risk the lender may offer you 'a better than the advertised' rate. In early 1995, for example, the Commonwealth Bank was offering lower interest rates to investors who weren't dependent on the rent from their properties to service their loans.

Another area of difference between lenders is the amount they will lend you against the valuation of the property, known as the 'loan to valuation ratio'. Some lenders are inclined to offer loans to investors on a lower loan to value ratio than they are to owner-occupiers. An example of this is a lender offering a loan of up to 80% or 85% of the valuation on a particular property to an investor, but offering a loan of up to 90% of valuation on the same property to an owner-occupier. The reason is that investment properties tend to change hands more frequently than owner-occupied homes and consequently there's a greater risk of investment loans not being repaid in full, due to an intervening fall in property prices. Having said this however, lenders are negotiable on the maximum amount they will lend you and they consider each loan application on a case-by-case basis.

Your loan

As a potential or existing property investor it's likely you already own the home in which you live, outright or partially. It's also likely when you approach a lender to finance an investment property, the lender will want to take additional security over your home to partly secure the new loan.

If this is the case, try to avoid having the lender bundle up both the mortgage on your home and the loan on the investment property into one big loan covering both properties (unless the new loan is at a lower rate than your home mortgage rate). Generally, it's best to keep the two properties on separate loans, because:

- If the interest rate on the investment loan is at a high investment rate, the bundled loan will also be at this high rate.
- Interest and the costs associated with an investment property are tax deductible whereas the interest and costs associated with your own home are not. If they're covered by separate loans its easier to keep track of both for taxation purposes.
- Separate loans give you flexibility to, say, have your home on a principal and interest, variable rate loan, and the investment

property on a interest-only fixed rate loan (which costs less to service).

- With two loans you can continue to put additional payments towards your home with the aim of making it debt free, both for peace of mind and to allow you to borrow more money against it later for another investment!

Of course, having one loan means you only have one set of fees, however the advantage of having two loans will normally outweigh this.

So, what sort of loan is best for you – variable rate, fixed rate, principal and interest, or interest-only? Well, given that rising interest rates have brought many a property investor undone, a fixed rate loan is generally preferable to a variable rate loan. At least when the interest rate is fixed you know exactly what your interest repayments will be – which is good for controlling your costs, and controlling your costs is essential for successful property investment.

Interest-only loans are useful if your budgeting is tight because repayments are less than on principal and interest loans. However, interest-only loans are rarely available for more than a five-year term, at the end of which you will still owe the lender all of the principal. At that point you will have the option of either refinancing for another term or selling the property to repay the principal, hopefully realising a capital gain in the process.

Be aware that an interest-only loan will not 'buy' you any equity in a property. You will only acquire equity in a property financed this way through capital appreciation, meaning, through an increase in its market value. You can, therefore, look at the loan repayments as simply the price you must pay for the right to hold the property in your name (which also gives you the right to sell it) while the process of capital appreciation occurs.

Take note that if you start with an interest-only loan, you can refinance into a principal and interest loan when the interest-only term expires. Also be aware that if you do refinance rather than sell, your new loan will almost certainly have a different interest rate which will affect your cash flow projections.

If you purchase your investment property with a principal and interest loan, every repayment you make marginally increases your equity in the property but your repayments are higher than with an interest-only loan. For those intending to hold their property investment for the long-term and who are in a position to make additional repayments, a principal and interest loan is probably the best choice.

Investment loan checklist

- Is the income you need to meet interest payments secure?
- Do you clearly understand the risks involved?
- What are the costs involved in holding the investment?
- Can you easily sell the investment if your situation changes, and what is the cost of doing so?
- Are you doing this only for tax reasons or is it a good long-term investment?
- Do you understand the loan documentation?
- Is the rate of interest reasonable, and stable?
- Will you sleep at night if the investment falls in value in the short-term?
- If you do take a principal and interest loan, remember that only the interest component is tax deductible.

Rental income

While long-term capital appreciation is definitely the main attraction of residential property investment, the rental income it can produce may not be insignificant, particularly if you hold a property for some years. Indeed, in time, you may be able to live quite comfortably off the rental income from a portfolio of two, three or four good residential properties.

What sort of rental income does a residential property normally produce? Well, it varies tremendously depending on the type of property and where it is located, however, the gross median weekly rentals for three-bedroom, unfurnished houses for the December 1994 quarter were:

Sydney	Melbourne	Brisbane	Adelaide	Perth	Canberra	Hobart
$245	$150	$160	$140	$130	$173	$145

Median prices for three-bedroom houses during the same period were:

Sydney	Melbourne	Brisbane	Adelaide	Perth	Canberra	Hobart
$193,000	$152,500	$130,000	$110,000	$125,000	$160,300	$113,000

Making Money

Based on these figures, the average gross rental yields (calculated by expressing the gross annual rent as a proportion of the market value of the property) in these markets during the December 1994 quarter were:

Sydney	Melbourne	Brisbane	Adelaide	Perth	Canberra	Hobart
6.6%	5.1%	6.4%	6.6%	5.4%	5.6%	6.7%

Landlords, tenants and property managers

The above yields derived from REIA data are calculated on the assumption your property is let for 52 weeks per year (which is very optimistic – you ought to allow for at least two weeks vacancy per year), and also on the assumption that the relationship between you and your tenants (directly or through a property manager), is a fair and reasonable one. But there are such things as bad landlords and bad tenants and where they are found, below average yields are generated. Conversely, good landlords and good tenants tend to produce better than average yields. It's often said in property circles that landlords get the tenants they deserve, and vice versa.

A good landlord is one who ensures the property is well maintained and who attends to problems promptly and properly when they occur, charges a fair rent and stays out of the tenant's hair.

Good tenants are those who pay the rent on time, take good care of the property, don't generate complaints from the neighbours and don't ask the property manager or landlord to come around and change a light bulb.

Clearly if you want optimum long-term returns from your property be prepared to spend the necessary money on it to make it attractive to good tenants. Not only will you have to spend less on the property after they have moved out (compared to having bad tenants), but they will give you far less headaches while they are there. And if attracting and keeping good tenants means accepting a slightly lower rent, do it. It's much better to have a good tenant at a moderate rent than a problematic one at a high rent.

How do you select a tenant? Whether you place ads in the newspaper and interview candidates yourself or have a real estate agency property manager choose a tenant for you, make sure it's done carefully. It's difficult to shift a bad tenant unless they specifically contravene the lease, and then an eviction can take ages, at least eight weeks, during which time you'll probably receive no rent.

If a property manager finds a tenant for you they will charge a 'leasing fee' which is normally equivalent to one or two week's rent. (You do have the right to veto the choice of tenant until the lease is signed.) If you choose to let the real estate agency manage the property for you on an ongoing basis, the management charge is around 7% to 10% of gross rentals. For this fee the property manager collects the rent (and chases it up if late), organises minor repairs, and represents you in all dealings with the tenant. In other words, you won't have to deal with the tenant at all – which is the way many landlords and tenants prefer it.

Leases – obligations, rights and conditions

A tenancy is not formalised until a lease is signed by both the tenant and the landlord or their agent. The lease is a legally binding document which stipulates the term of the tenancy, the rental and any special conditions which may apply such as the requirement for the tenant to mow the lawn once a month. The lease is designed to protect your interests and the tenant's, and confers rights and obligations on both parties.

Leases come under the jurisdiction of each state's tenancy acts so the rules and regulations that apply to them vary to some degree. Rather than detail all the differences here I have chosen to look at the NSW Tenancy Act because it's probably the most rigorous in Australia, and most other states are moving towards a system like it where tenancy is highly regulated and a tenancy tribunal exists to mediate disputes between tenants and landlords.

Tenancy agreement

A tenancy agreement (or lease) is a standard form which simply needs to be filled in and signed by the parties concerned. There are generally two types of agreement: a fixed term and a continuing tenancy.

Making Money

A fixed term agreement specifies the duration of the tenancy during which time the rent can't be changed (unless otherwise permitted by an added clause). Even though the agreement is for a fixed term, both tenant and landlord must give each other 14 days written notice of an intention or a direction to vacate at the end of the agreed term. And if no further term agreement is signed at the expiry of the original agreement but the tenancy continues, the lease automatically becomes a continuing tenancy with all the requisite rules and regulations.

A continuing tenancy has no time limit on the rental period, however, if the landlord wants the tenant to vacate or wants to increase the rent he or she must give at least 60 days written notice. The tenant, on the other hand, is only required to give the landlord 21 days notice of intention to vacate. The length of notice can, however, be varied where the property has been sold with vacant possession – once contracts have been exchanged the landlord is only obliged to give the tenant 30 days notice to vacate.

Inspections

In NSW it is a legal requirement that either the landlord or the property manager inspect the property before the tenants move in and provide them with two copies of a property report detailing the physical condition of the premises at the time. The tenants are then required to make any changes to the report they think appropriate, sign one copy and give it back to the landlord or agent within seven days.

When the tenants move out another inspection is conducted to check for any damage which could be claimed out of the bond. The original inspection report is designed to establish whether or not any damage to the property is attributable to the tenants or if it was already there before they moved in.

Bond money

You are within your rights (and you are recommended) to ask for bond money as security against any damage tenants may cause or against any rent they may not pay. Generally the bond is equivalent to four to six weeks rent, depending on the nature of the premises and the size of the rent.

In NSW (and other states' procedures, except Tasmania's, are similar), the bond must be lodged with the Rental Bond Board (or equivalent) within seven days of payment to you or the agent by the tenant. The tenant is then sent a receipt from the Board as evidence that the money has been lodged. At the end of the tenancy the tenant fills out a bond refund form which must be countersigned by you or the property manager. Clearly this is only countersigned for a full refund if everything is above board, namely, the property is in as good order as when the tenancy began (taking into account fair wear and tear), the rent is up-to-date, and adequate notice to vacate was provided.

If everything is not above board and you wish to be paid part or all of the bond as compensation for damage, unpaid rent or inadequate notice to vacate, you must apply directly to the Rental Bond Board. If the tenant has agreed to relinquish a part or all of the bond it will be noted on the refund form. The Rental Bond Board will then deduct this amount from the bond and send it directly to you – the remainder, if any, being returned to the tenant. If there is a disagreement between you and the tenant about the return of the bond the dispute is heard before the Rental Bond Board. In other states, bond disputes may be heard before a tenancy tribunal.

Rights of entry

Generally a landlord or agent can only enter rented premises with the consent of the tenant or with an order from your state's residential tenancy authority. However you can go onto the property without the tenant's permission (and without resorting to an order) if your request to enter is 'reasonable' and you give your tenant a 'reasonable' amount of notice. Examples of a reasonable request would be to carry out repairs or maintenance; to show the property to prospective buyers (or to a prospective tenant up to 14 days before the lease expires); or if you have reason to believe that the property has been abandoned.

In NSW you are entitled to inspect the property up to four times per year but you must give your tenant seven days notice before inspection. You are, however, allowed to enter at any time to carry out emergency repairs.

Making Money

Rent

As long as the required notice is given there is no restriction on the number of times you can increase the rent or by how much. However, in NSW, tenants can take the matter to the Residential Tenancies Tribunal if they think the increase is excessive. The Tribunal can rule that a lesser rent be paid but it is only valid for the time specified in the order (generally one year) and for the stated parties. If those tenants leave, you can put the rent up by as much as you like.

Always bear in mind that if you make the rent too steep you may find your property vacant for too many weeks of the year. If holding out for, say, an extra $15 a week rent translates into an extra month's vacancy your cash flow and yield is shot to pieces.

Repairs

As the landlord you are required to undertake urgent and essential repairs, such as a burst water pipe or roof damage due to a storm. If you are unavailable or refuse to go to the property (and this is where having a property manager can be a blessing), the tenant can arrange to have the repairs done and then apply to you for reimbursement of the costs. Under NSW law, the landlord is obliged to repay the tenant within 14 days for reasonable costs up to the value of $500. If the landlord refuses to pay, the tenant can take the matter to the Residential Tenancies Tribunal and the landlord can be ordered to pay.

Landlords are not required to undertake non-urgent repairs but NSW tenants may apply to the Residential Tenancies Tribunal for an order to force the landlord to do the repairs if the tenants think they are essential. If the Tribunal agrees it can order you to:
- carry out the repairs
- authorise the tenant to withhold rent
- authorise the tenant to pay a reduced rent until the repairs are done. The Tribunal can also order you to pay compensation for any damage that may have been done to the tenant's belongings as a result of the delay in repairs.

Evictions

Bad tenants are a nightmare. At best they won't pay the rent and at worst can deliberately damage the property – in which case it's not claimable under insurance.

If you want the tenant to leave your property you must give the required notice, however, unpaid rent is considered a valid reason to reduce the required notice time. If the tenant falls behind in the rent (normally payable in advance) by two weeks you are entitled to issue an eviction notice, which gives the tenant a further two weeks to vacate the premises. And, even if the tenant then brings the rent up to date, the eviction notice still stands and can be enforced if you wish it.

In NSW, if the tenant doesn't vacate the premises by the required date you have 30 days to apply to the Residential Tenancies Tribunal for an 'order of termination and possession'. In NSW the matter will be heard within 14 days. If the Tribunal decides in your favour it will usually give the tenant 7 to 14 days to vacate but if they claim hardship the Tribunal may extend the period. If the tenant doesn't attend the hearing, the Tribunal may give you immediate possession.

All up, the minimum time to evict a tenant will probably take about eight weeks – during which time you won't be getting any rent. And, in case you feel tempted, it's illegal for you to change the locks on your tenant – you could be fined up to $20,000 for this. Finally, under no circumstances try to physically eject a tenant. You may end up with a black eye and being arrested for assault. A sheriff with a valid warrant from a court or a tribunal is the only authority allowed to physically remove a tenant. All this points to the need for good tenants in the first place. If getting one entails compromising on rent or other conditions, so be it. The cost of having bad tenants is just too high. But remember, to attract and retain good tenants you need to be a good landlord!

Residential tenancy tribunals and authorities

Going under different names in different states (other than Tasmania where pressure is being applied to establish one), residential tenancy authorities have been set up to hear disputes between landlords and tenants with the tribunals' judgements being legally binding.

In NSW for example, the Tribunal has the authority to order landlords to carry out work to their property, and can make tenants pay back-rent or direct them to make good damage they have done to the property. The penalties for tenants or landlords who fail to carry out the Tribunal's orders can be fines up to $5000 and/or six months' jail.

Tax on investment property

Land tax

Land tax is an annual tax generally imposed by each state government (including the ACT but excluding the Northern Territory) on land of higher value. Land on which the owner's principal place of residence is built and land used for primary production are generally exempt from land tax. It is usually calculated on the unimproved value of land as determined by municipal council rate notices and this means land tax does not take into account the value of buildings or other works on the land.

The taxes vary significantly from state to state so make sure you discuss it with your accountant before you invest.

Building depreciation allowances

As a property investor you are allowed to deduct from your assessable income an amount equivalent to 2.5% per annum of the original construction cost of a residential building from which you derive income if its construction was commenced on or after the 16 September 1987. This deduction is allowable for a total of 40 years from commencement.

On a residential building commenced between the 18 July 1985 and the 15 September 1987 from which you derive income, the special write-off is 4% p.a. over a total of 25 years from commencement. These depreciation allowances against assessable income also apply to extensions, alterations and improvements to income-producing residential buildings (which includes strata title properties).

Depreciation of furniture and fittings

If you are the landlord of furnished premises that contain large household items which have a limited life, you can depreciate these and claim them as a deduction against the property's taxable income. Typical annual depreciation values are 30% for curtains, 25% for carpets, 25% for TV sets and 30% for washing machines. You can only depreciate these items for a certain period, that is until their theoretical value has hit $0, which will take three to five years from the date of purchase. Smaller items, such as cutlery, glassware, bedding and so on are not depreciable.

What you are doing with depreciation is effectively claiming as a genuine business cost the loss in value, over time, of material goods used in conducting the business. There's no doubt in the case of furnished premises that wear and tear on furniture is a genuine business cost.

Depreciation allowances can make the difference between running a profit or running a loss on your property investment in any given year which, of course, has income tax implications. A discussion of the accounting procedures for depreciation is not appropriate here but it can be important for property investors, and I recommend you also discuss this with your accountant.

Provisional tax

Provisional tax is the tax payable on your anticipated income for the next financial year. The assessment of future income on which this advance tax is payable is calculated by the Tax Office, and the assessment is based on your tax returns for the current financial year.

Provisional tax is payable on anticipated non-salary earnings in excess of $1,000. Rental income is a non-salary earning. So, if your property starts making a profit, not only will you have to pay income tax on this profit, you'll also have to pay provisional tax on it for next year (assuming the profit is anticipated to be greater than $1,000).

Beware of the impact this will have on your cash flow because the first year in which you are charged provisional tax, you will be effectively paying two years worth of tax (income tax and provisional tax) in one go. Make sure you've got the funds to cope with this slug!

Capital gains tax

The impact of capital gains tax (CGT) on your overall property investment returns can be very significant so it's vital you understand the effect and operation of CGT before you invest. CGT is complicated and is looked at more closely in Chapter Ten, 'Tax'.

Briefly, if you hold an asset for more than 12 months, and you bought it after 19 September, 1985, you will be liable for CGT when you sell it if you have made a capital gain on it. A capital gain is regarded by the Tax Office as the difference between the cost of an asset and the amount you receive when you sell it (assuming the selling price is *higher* than the asset's cost).

The cost of the asset includes the original purchase price, the incidental expenses incurred in buying and selling it, and any capital improvements made in between, *all adjusted for inflation during the period to present-day dollars using a CPI-based formula*. This inflation adjustment is an important feature of CGT. It has the effect of reducing, in dollar terms, the amount on which CGT is levied.

In addition to the difference between the selling price and the cost of your asset being the main determinant of how much capital gain is eaten up by tax, the other important influences that determine the final CGT slug are your other level of income in the year the asset was sold, your marginal income tax rate, and the size of the tax-free allowance for past inflation.

I stress again how important CGT is for property investors and, I know how much confusion it causes. I would, therefore, once again commend to all property investors the wisdom of discussing this and other taxes fully with your accountant before you buy.

What enhances and diminishes returns

These will reduce your property investment returns:
- buying a property in a poor position
- buying a property in an area showing below average growth

- buying a property in poor structural condition with high maintenance costs
- buying a property with no aesthetic appeal or no potential to have it
- buying at the top of the market
- paying too much
- selling at the bottom of the market
- overcapitalising
- inadequate maintenance
- bad tenants
- excessive vacancy
- being a bad landlord
- inadequate planning for capital gains, land and provisional tax
- relatively high land value proportional to building value generating high land tax
- rising interest rates
- general economic malaise
- nearby construction of a major road or factory
- inadequate insurance to cover any property damage such as fire, or to cover any claims for damages brought by tenants or neighbours for which you may be legally liable (such as an injury caused to your tenant by him falling through your rotting balcony)
- ineligibility for depreciation allowances
- poor record keeping, poor bookkeeping and poor overall control of costs
- not employing an accountant.

These will increase your returns:
- buying a property with good position in a strongly performing area (in general closer to the centre of a city)
- buying an aesthetically pleasing property or with potential to be so
- buying a property with appeal to aging baby boomers
- buying a property that has a positively unique feature
- buying a property in good structural order
- buying at the bottom of the market
- paying a fair price
- selling at the top of the market
- a property rezoning in your favour, for example, permission to

subdivide a large block of land into two separate blocks, or to convert an old block of flats to strata title units
- low maintenance and other running costs
- relatively low land value porportional to building value for lower land tax
- good tenants on long-term leases
- low vacancy
- being a good landlord
- an appropriate degree of sympathetic renovation
- low interest rates
- a healthy economy
- proper maintenance
- adequate insurance cover
- sufficient planning for taxes
- eligibility for depreciation allowances
- good records, good bookkeeping, good accountancy and good overall control of costs.

> ### ⚷— Key thought
> Residential property investment has been and is a viable investment area but it's no longer as easy as it was in the past. Being diligent and being astute will increasingly become the determining characteristics of the successful residential property investor in the 1990s and beyond.

Commercial property investment

Now, some of you may be wondering why this chapter has dealt solely with residential property. What about commercial property?

Well, okay, this is a major investment sector and has been the source of extraordinary wealth for some people but it is not a traditional area of direct investment for the average small investor. That's not because it's a second-rate investment – far from it. It's because commercial property is too specialised, too expensive and just too difficult an area of investment for most people. If you thought residential property investment sounded involved it's nothing compared to commercial.

I would recommend anyone contemplating direct property investment to start at the easiest end of the spectrum – residential. If this works for you – and if you do it properly there is no reason why it shouldn't – after a few years think about a small commercial property investment, such as buying a shop. By this stage you will have developed a feel for property. You'll know all about the value of good tenants, you'll understand leases, you'll understand property management, you'll have discovered how time-consuming and frustrating dealing with councils and government departments is, you'll know how much time and expense is involved in renovations, and so on. In other words you won't be so green, which is something you cannot afford to be in commercial property investment. There are so many ways you can go wrong in commercial property and being a novice is one of the main ones.

There is another way to invest in commercial property other than directly and this is through becoming a unit holder in a listed or unlisted property trust. I won't go into the details here because you'll find them in Chapter Fifteen, 'Managed Funds', but briefly, when you invest in a property trust you effectively become a part-owner of the underlying assets held by the trust. These typically include shopping centres, office blocks, industrial properties and residential estates.

A minimum investment in a property trust is around $1,000. It's a lot less money and a lot less risk than a minimum direct investment in commercial property which could easily run into hundreds of thousands of dollars.

CHAPTER THIRTEEN

Investing in Shares

If you start asking people in the street what they think about shares, you'll probably find the majority will fit into either the 'I don't think about them at all' or the 'they're not much good' camps. Some of the images that spring to people's minds when you mention shares are those associated with sharemarket calamities, like stockbrokers in top hats leaping out of windows clutching the latest bad market news or desperate shareholders, eyes and veins bulging, ties askew, yelling into the telephone, 'Sell! Sell! Sell!'

These are comic book conceptions that fortunately bear no resemblance to the sharemarket experience of most shareholders – assuming they are long-term shareholders, that is. Like the other main asset classes of property, cash, and fixed interest, over time shares have produced very healthy returns – despite occasional market reversals and even free falls!

Share returns

Many studies have been done on the Australian and overseas share markets which illustrate just how attractive an investment shares can be. Briefly, here are some findings:

Average annual returns from Australian shares

- 5% to 8% after inflation over rolling ten-year periods since 1945. (*Source*: IPAC Securities.)
- 13.6% before inflation and tax; 12.3% after inflation and tax at the *top* marginal tax rate, 14% after inflation and tax at the *lowest* marginal tax rate, in the 10 years to 28 February 1995. Inflation during this period averaged 5.3%. (Note that these figures are *not* misprints. The reason the *after-tax* return for a low marginal rate tax payer is *higher* than the *pre-tax* return

is due to the tax credits from dividend imputation being greater than the tax liabilities on the gross return. (See page 204 for more on dividend imputation.) (*Source*: Towers Perrin and Australian Stock Exchange.)

Average annual returns from international shares

- 6% to 9% after inflation over rolling ten-year periods. (*Source*: IPAC Securities.)
- 20.29% before inflation in the calendar years 1982 to 1994. Inflation averaged 5.81% during the period. (*Source*: IPAC Securities, based on the Morgan Stanley Capital International (MSCI) World Accumulation Index.)
- 10.7% before inflation (US shares only) 1954 to 1994, assuming you bought a parcel of shares once a year only on the annual market peak (the worst day of the year to buy). (*Source*: *Money* (US magazine) April 1994.)

Annualised long-term returns like these for both domestic and international shares ought to satisfy most investors. I reckon the returns are impressive, particularly when you realise they take into account the major losses caused by the global sharemarket crash of October 1987.

In light of these figures it's a shame that there aren't more than the present 21% of Australians who invest directly in shares. The popular image of leaping-out-of-the-window share investors simply isn't justified by these sort of healthy returns. The only time you might feel like jumping out of a window after investing in shares is if you took a big dollar, short-term punt on speculative stock that went wrong. But then again, backing the wrong horse at the track for a lot of money – and it's the same approach to investing – could lead to the same urge.

The reality is, though, that a lot more than 21% of Australians actually do invest in shares, many without being aware of it. Anyone with superannuation – and that's most employees – is an indirect investor in the sharemarket. All superannuation funds invest in a wide range of asset classes comprised of property, cash, fixed interest and shares.

Now, the people managing your superannuation are not going to be investing in shares if they think shares are a good way to lose money. In fact, superannuation managers are a very conservative lot – as indeed they should be, given their responsibilities. They are not the type of people to jeopardise your money by investing it in what they see as risky assets.

Of course, there are shares and there are shares. The type that I recommend and the type your superannuation fund manager would consider investing in are shares in established, solid and well-managed companies that have a good operational track record and good profitability over the years – 'blue chip' companies – like BHP, National Australia Bank and Woolworths. I also like to invest in smaller companies, but choosing these is not easy. Therefore, I prefer to use a specialist managed fund such as Rothschild's Smaller Companies Fund for this purpose.

I certainly don't recommend investing in the shares of what could only be called 'speculative ventures', that is, companies which are small and new and which will need more than their fair share of good luck to be successful. There are a swag of small mining companies on the sharemarket that fit this description. They are the ones that will only go into profit if they strike gold, oil, diamonds, iron, nickel, copper or whatever. Regard these sort of companies as the outsiders in any horse race. If they hit their target they'll make a fortune and so will you, but the odds are slim. There's a better chance they'll go broke and you'll lose your money.

Look, investment in any sorts of shares carries some risk but, if you buy a basket of good quality shares and hang on to them for the long-term, you should generate more than satisfactory returns with minimal risk.

What are shares?

A share is a part-ownership of a company listed on the sharemarket. When you buy shares in a company you become a part owner of that company. You take equity in it which is why shares are also known as 'equities'. Sometimes shares are also referred to as 'stock' but this is a broader term which can encompass other types of securities.

Companies offer shares to the public to raise funds to finance, say, an expansion of an existing business, a new venture, or a company takeover. When shares in a company are being offered

202

to the public for the first time it is known as a share 'float'. Subsequent share offerings from the same company are generally called share 'issues'.

In the case of smaller floats and share offerings, those who have a sharebroker may be invited to invest first before the wider public is given the chance to buy. In this case the shares being offered for sale by the company may be fully taken up ('fully subscribed') by those invited to buy. Having a sharebroker, therefore, can be very useful in getting you in on the ground floor of some (particularly smaller) share offerings.

With very large floats – such as the Woolworths, Commonwealth Bank and Qantas floats – where many millions of shares are being offered, there are usually enough shares for sale for everyone to get at least some. In large-scale floats the opportunity to buy is widely advertised and prospectuses are freely available through all sharebrokers and from the companies themselves.

To illustrate, let's say you are invited to invest in the float of XYZ Investments Ltd, where the minimum investment is a parcel of 2,000 shares with each share priced at $1.50. This means your minimum investment is $3,000.

Now, these are new shares which are not yet being traded on the open sharemarket. Their price of $1.50 is an issue price set by the company, reflecting its view of its shares' worth. The market, however, may see things differently. This means that when your $1.50 shares actually start open trading on the sharemarket (the day the float closes) the price may move, sometimes immediately, to a higher or lower level than the issue price. Over subsequent weeks, months, and years the trading price may move to the point where it bears virtually no resemblance at all to the issue price. The trading price depends on the market's perceptions of the company's past and present performance, and most importantly, its future potential.

How do you make money from shares?

How you make money from shares is twofold. You make it from an income stream (dividends), and also from capital growth, that is, from increases in the share price, from occasional receipt of free bonus shares, and the purchase of discounted 'rights issues' shares.

Making Money

Let's look at share income first. If the listed company in which you own shares makes a profit, as a part-owner of the company you are entitled to share in those profits. You receive your share of the profits by means of a dividend, normally paid to you every 6 or 12 months.

The size of the dividend depends on how many shares you hold and what proportion of the company's profits the directors choose to distribute to shareholders. As a general rule the typical dividend paid per annum by a company listed on the Australian Stock Exchange is around 5% of the share's trading price.

Dividend imputation

Dividend income is taxable but income from shares can be very tax effective compared to income from other investments. In the case of 'fully franked' dividends, the dividend you receive has been distributed from company profits after they have been taxed at the full company rate of 36%. Now, because tax is paid by the company before you receive a dividend, this dividend is deemed to be after (36%) tax income to you. This means that if your effective tax rate is 36%, fully franked dividends are free of tax in your hands. Indeed, if your effective tax rate is lower than 36%, you actually get a tax credit from your franked dividends which can lower the tax on your other assessable income! (Note the after-tax returns to shareholders on the lowest marginal tax rate in the 10 years to 28 February 1995 detailed on page 200.)

This method of taxing dividends is a relatively recent breakthrough. Before 1 July 1987, when the system was changed your dividends were effectively taxed twice. Firstly, the company distributed its dividends from its profits, after it had already paid tax on these profits. Secondly, the shareholder receiving the dividends paid personal tax on them as these monies were considered to be income by the Tax Office. Under this arrangement the tax man was basically getting two bites at the cherry, and the take on the one stream of income could have been as high as a 78% tax rate.

On 1 July 1987 the dividend imputation scheme was introduced, designed to eliminate this double taxation. This is how it works:

- Firstly, the company pays tax on its profits, and 'imputes' (credits) this tax to the shareholders of the company. This means that, as far as the Tax Office is concerned, the tax paid by the company in Australia is deemed to have been paid by the shareholders in the company.
- Secondly, the company distributes dividends out of its profits which have already been taxed. These are called 'franked' (exempt from charges) dividends and are tax paid (normally at 36%) in the hands of the investor.
- Thirdly, when the shareholder fills out her taxation return she includes details of any dividends received and the amount of company tax that has been paid on them. She then receives a tax credit for this amount of tax which can be offset against any other assessable income.

To illustrate, let's say a shareholder receives franked dividends over a year worth $6,400. The company advises the shareholder that it is a fully franked dividend with an imputation tax credit of $3,600 (meaning that the company has already paid $3,600 in tax on the shareholder's behalf). The total to be shown as taxable dividend income is, therefore, $10,000. ($6,400 + $3,600 = $10,000.)

This shareholder earns $15,000 from other sources. Adding the dividend income to this gives her a total taxable income of $25,000. Ordinarily, the tax liability on $25,000 would be $4,522 but the company providing the dividend has already paid $3,600 in tax on it. So the amount of tax owed is reduced to $922 ($4,522 – $3,600 = $922). This is $998 less than the tax the shareholder would have had to pay ($1,920) on just the $15,000 alone, assuming she had no other income. It's not a bad result!

Note that company dividends can be 'fully franked' (tax paid at 36%), 'partly franked' (tax paid at anything up to 36%) and 'unfranked' which have had no tax paid against them. Also note that if your marginal tax rate is higher than the franked rate, you will still have some tax to pay on these dividends. For example, if your rate is 48.5% and the franked rate is 36% then you would still have to pay 12.5% tax. ·

Let's compare the after-tax position of an investor receiving 1) fully franked dividends and 2) interest income.

Making Money

Sharemarket investor		Fixed interest investor	
1) Low marginal tax rate investor			
Dividend payment	$1000.00	Interest payment	$1000.00
Add franking credit	562.60		
Taxable income	1562.50	Taxable income	1000.00
Tax at marginal rate of 21.5%	335.94	Tax at marginal rate of 21.5%	215.00
Less franking credit	562.50		
Tax payable	0.00*	Tax payable	215.00
After tax income	1000.00	After tax income	785.00

The low marginal tax rate share investor is 27.4% better off than the low marginal rate fixed interest investor after tax.

* An excess franking credit of $226.56 exists here ($562.50 – $335.94 = $226.56). This amount can be offset against the tax payable on any other assessable income that the share investor may have, which means his real after-tax share return may be actually better than shown here.

2) High marginal tax rate investor			
Dividend payment	$1000.00	Interest payment	$1000.00
Add franking credit	562.50		
Taxable income	1562.50	Taxable income	1000.00
Tax at marginal rate of 48.5%	757.81	Tax at marginal rate of 48.5%	485.00
Less franking credit	562.50		
Tax payable	195.31	Tax payable	485.00
After tax income	804.69	After tax income	515.00

The high marginal tax rate share investor is 56.3% better off than the high marginal rate fixed interest investor after tax.

Capital growth

Now, let's look at capital growth. This occurs when the traded price of shares in a given company rises, reflecting the company's positive performance, a favourable economic environment and a good outlook. If you buy a parcel of shares at $2 per share and their traded price rises to $4 per share you have doubled the value of your holding and if the share price falls to $1, you have halved your money. It's that simple.

Some degree of capital growth can also occur through taking up 'rights issues', although this sort of growth involves you investing more money. A 'rights issue' is where a company, in attempting to raise more capital, invites its existing shareholders to buy new shares *at a discount to the current market price*. (If there was no discount there would be no incentive for existing shareholders to take up the offer.) The amount of new shares the shareholder is invited to buy is proportional to the number of shares he already holds. As an example, Boral made a rights issue offering one new share for every 10 existing ordinary shares held at 10 March 1994. The rights' price was $3.60 compared to the 10 March trading price of $4.28.

When you are a shareholder you participate in the good fortunes of the company you hold shares in. If the company performs well, you benefit from a strong share price and healthy dividends and, if the company and/or the economy falters you also suffer its misfortunes. But one thing you don't participate in as a shareholder, fortunately, is a company's indebtedness. This means that if a company collapses leaving behind debts, as a shareholder you are not liable. I doubt the modern sharemarket would exist if you were!

The sharemarket

We now know how shares have performed over time, what a share is, how you buy shares during a float and how you make money from shares. But what about the sharemarket itself? How does it operate and how do you use it? Well, let's start with a little history.

The first Australian stockmarket, carried on through the pages of the *Sydney Morning Herald*, was established in Sydney in 1837. In 1859 the first regular stockmarket came into existence in Melbourne and over the next 30 years stock exchanges were established in all state capitals.

In 1987 all six state stock exchanges were amalgamated into the Australian Stock Exchange (ASX). The pre-ASX state stock exchanges still exist in each capital – it's just that now they are completely interlinked by computer and effectively operate as one marketplace.

Today there are some 1,100 companies listed on the ASX, ranging in size from BHP valued at around $35 billion to small, speculative mining exploration companies valued at less than $2 million. In 1993-4 the ASX turned over $128,426 million in shares and $392 million in fixed interest securities (government bonds and company debentures etc).

The ASX is a company made up of member companies, mainly stockbroking firms. All stockbrokers must be members of the ASX. All companies in Australia have to be registered with the Australian Securities Commission but they don't have to be listed on the stock exchange. Rather, companies have to apply to be listed on the stock exchange and, at a certain point in their development, many companies take this route. The reason they want to be listed is that it enables them to raise funds through the sale of shares and other financial instruments.

In order to be listed on the ASX, a company has to be of a certain size (net tangible assets worth at least $2 million and pre-tax profits of at least $1 million for each of the preceding three years); its shares have to be freely available for trading; and the company has to agree to meet ASX requirements for financial reporting and disclosure of key information. (All this is designed to keep shonky operators out of the sharemarket.)

What the ASX deals in

What is traded through the ASX? Well, it handles a range of financial instruments, not just shares. The ASX also deals in fixed interest securities such as bonds, debentures and convertible notes. All of these can be lumped under the general term of 'stock' (which is why I prefer to call shares 'shares' – it's more specific).

The ASX also handles 'derivatives' (options and warrants) which are derived from the standard products above.

Now, let's have a closer look at these 'financial instruments'.

Ordinary shares

Ordinary shares are the most common type of shares traded on the ASX. They entitle you to any dividends that may be paid and to participate in rights and bonus issues. As an ordinary shareholder you are also entitled to vote at any company meetings (not that the average individual shareholder wields much influence).

Technically, a share is a unit of a company's capital which has a 'par' value, also known as the share's 'face' or 'nominal' value. Common par values are 50 cents and $1. The par value is unrelated and normally different to the share's market value or price at which it is trading.

As an individual investor in ordinary shares, par values are of little significance. (It's just useful to be familiar with the term as you will encounter it from time to time.) What is significant to you as a share investor is the share's market value because that's what determines your fortunes.

Preference shares

Preference shares differ to ordinary shares in that they normally pay a fixed rate of return (still called a dividend). This fixed dividend rate is expressed as a percentage of the par value of the share.

Preference shares have certain privileges – for example, dividends are payable against them before being payable against ordinary shares and, in the event of the company folding, any capital left over from other claimants is distributed amongst preference shareholders before ordinary shareholders.

Although preference shares may seem to be more attractive than ordinary shares because of these privileges, this is not necessarily the case. They can be restrictive. Having a fixed dividend, for example, can be an enormous disadvantage if a company is performing well because the dividends paid on ordinary shares would be higher. On the other hand, a fixed dividend is advantageous to the investor when the company is performing poorly and may be paying little or no dividends on its ordinary shares.

There are various types of preference shares which include 'converting', 'cumulative', 'participating' and 'redeemable' preference shares. Your sharebroker can explain the details of these to you, however, because of their *relative* sophistication I don't think you should invest in preference shares until you have invested in ordinary shares and developed a feel for the sharemarket.

Company options

A company option is an option to take up a new, ordinary share from the company by a nominated future date at a fixed price or 'exercise price'. You don't have to take up the new share by the given date but if you don't your option lapses and becomes worthless. (This is a method of raising capital often used by mining companies.)

Listed company options are traded on the ASX in the same way as ordinary shares. The option's price is less than the company's ordinary share price, and the theoretical difference between the option price and share price is the same as the exercise price.

Again, I recommend first-time share investors stay away from company options, perhaps contemplating them once you have developed a better sense of the way the sharemarket operates.

Contributing shares

Contributing shares are ones which you have only paid a part or a proportion of their par value on, the remainder being due when the company requires it in the future. Contributing shares are also known as 'partly paid' shares. They are rare beasts and again, because they are not absolutely straightforward, I don't recommend them to newcomers.

Fixed interest securities

Debentures
Debentures are a way that industrial and finance companies borrow money. A debenture is effectively a loan from you to a company for a fixed term. You are paid interest on this loan at

specified times at a fixed interest rate. At the end of the term the debenture matures and the original amount of the loan is repaid to the holder in full. Typically, debenture terms range from three months to five years with a minimum investment normally being $5,000.

Debentures are issued like shares during a share float – through a prospectus – and you buy them by filling in the application form and sending it directly to the company. Should you wish to sell your debentures before the maturity date (or buy others) you do so through a stockbroker at the going market rate. The market rate will reflect the interest rate for new debentures being issued at the time you wish to sell (or buy) – if new debentures are paying a higher interest rate you will be offered less for yours, if new debentures are paying a lower interest rate you will be offered more.

It may be easier to find a buyer for the debentures of some companies than it is for others and should a company be wound up, the remaining capital will be distributed to debenture holders before shareholders.

Remember, the security of your capital depends upon the company issuing the debenture, so make sure the company is sound before you invest.

Bonds

Bonds are basically the same as debentures, except they are not issued by private companies but rather by government and semi-government authorities. They also come with government guarantees of repayment. Consequently bonds are safer than other fixed interest securities and, therefore, generally provide lower returns.

Some private companies issue what they call 'bonds' but this is a misnomer – they should really be called 'debentures'.

Unsecured notes

Unsecured notes are similar to debentures in that they are loans from you to a company for a specific period at a specific interest rate, but without the same degree of security as debentures. Holders of unsecured notes are on a lower pecking order in the event the company collapses and there is any capital left over to distribute. Staff, the Tax Office and debenture holders will be amongst those paid before unsecured note holders – but unsecured note holders will be paid before shareholders.

The reason these instruments are called 'unsecured notes' is because they have no guaranteed security over the company's assets, which may make you wonder why anyone would want to bother with them. Well, firstly, bear in mind that shareholders have an even less secure stake in a company, and secondly, unsecured notes normally offer a higher interest rate than debentures and many other fixed interest securities. Also, the type of companies that issue unsecured notes are generally big and secure themselves. Obviously, for there to be any market for unsecured notes the companies issuing them have to be seen to be safe, but it is fair to say that unsecured notes are not common.

Convertible notes

A convertible note is an unsecured note which can be converted at a specified date into shares in the company issuing it. It is really a mixture of a fixed interest security and a share, in that, for the first few years, the holder of the note receives a regular interest payment from the issuer and then, at a certain time, the holder has the choice to convert the note into shares in the company at a predetermined price. The date at which the note can be converted into shares is spelt out at the time it's issued. If the holder does not want to convert the note to shares prior to its maturity date, the issuing company will repay the value of the convertible note (the value of the original loan) to the holder at maturity.

Issuing convertible notes allows a company to raise money but to defer the payment of dividends. It's therefore seen as a relatively cheap way of raising funds. Convertible notes can be traded before maturity through stockbrokers at the current market rate, in the same way that debentures and unsecured notes are.

Buying and selling shares

There are two ways of buying shares directly, as distinct from buying them indirectly through a managed fund or through superannuation.

One is from the issuing company via a prospectus. This happens when a company 'floats' or 'goes public', meaning it's offering new shares to the public at a set price per share in specific share parcel sizes. To buy the shares on offer you simply fill in the application form in the prospectus and send it with your cheque, either to the company direct or to a stockbroker.

When a company you have shares in has a rights or bonus issue the same process applies – you fill out an application form for the number of shares you are entitled to and send it back to the company or a stockbroker with a cheque. It's all very straightforward.

Buying shares direct from the issuing company is known as buying on the primary market. The secondary market is the trading of existing shares between shareholders. When you want to buy shares that have already been issued and are trading on the sharemarket, you only have one way of doing it – you must deal through a stockbroker. When you go to sell those shares it's the same story – again, you cannot do it yourself, you must go through a stockbroker.

Finding a stockbroker

Finding yourself a stockbroker isn't hard. In the absence of any that are recommended to you, just phone the ASX. They will give you the names of three brokers to talk to. Alternatively, look in the *Yellow Pages* under Stock and Share Brokers.

It's a good idea to have a chat with a few stockbrokers at different firms before you decide where to open an account or accounts. Brokers have very different personalities and views on investment and it's important to deal with people you feel comfortable with. Also, some brokers aren't interested in small investors, others are.

You can have more than one stockbroker if you wish. In fact, some argue it can be beneficial to be a client of two or three firms (including a larger one) to give you more access to new share issues. Some companies only distribute their prospectuses through a small number of stockbrokers, and many floats are only accessible through one stockbroker. So the more stockbrokers you deal with, the more prospectuses you'll receive – providing, of course, you are a regular investor with each of these brokers.

Once you've picked one or more brokers you'll probably have

to make your first transaction in person. After that you can place orders over the phone. You'll probably be asked to pay for the first buy order in full (or at least pay a deposit) at the time you make the order.

Fees and minimum investment size

To invest directly in the sharemarket the range of the minimum transaction values that most stockbrokers will handle is from $1,000 to $3,000. In addition to there being a minimum transaction or trade value, shares have to be purchased in 'marketable parcels'. A marketable parcel is made up of a set number of shares and this number varies depending on the share price. It sounds confusing, but this table should make it clear.

Share price range	Marketable parcels
0.5 cents to 25 cents	2,000 shares
26 cents to 50 cents	1,000 shares
51 cents to $1	500 shares
$1.01 to $10	100 shares
$10.01 to $50	50 shares
over $50	10 shares

A share costing 30 cents, for instance, can only be bought in parcels of 1,000 shares. So, if your broker has a minimum transaction size of $3,000, your minimum buy order would be for 10,000 shares. You could also order 11,000 shares, 15,000 shares and so on, but not 15,300 shares.

Stockbrokers charge a brokerage fee which varies with the size of the order. For 'small' orders up to around $10,000, the fee is about 2% to 2.5% of the value of the order, dropping down to a negotiable 0.5% to 0.75% for orders over, say, $100,000 (which is normally the domain of corporate clients). Most brokers charge minimum fees per transaction and these vary from $60 to $120. State government stamp duties also apply at the rate of 15 cents per $100 transaction value.

Placing a share order

When you instruct your stockbroker to buy or sell shares on your behalf, you can get him to act in one of two ways. One is where you nominate your price levels. This means you set the highest price you are prepared to buy at and the lowest price you are prepared to sell at. Under these instructions your broker will only act within your limits.

Alternatively you can tell your broker to buy or sell 'at best' or 'at market' which means he will get you the best price he can under the prevailing market conditions.

Once you have given your buying or selling instructions to your broker, he enters your order into a computer terminal. This is linked to the ASX's centralised computer transaction system and he can generally give you an immediate confirmation that the order has been carried out. (There can be delays if there is a rush on particular shares or a lack of interest in others but generally there will be ready buyers and sellers for most shares.)

After the transaction has taken place a contract note is sent to you confirming the trade. If you were buying shares, payment would then be due. When the stockbroker gets your cheque, details of the transaction are sent to the company's share register to finalise the share transfer.

If you were selling shares you would need to send your share certificate or 'scrip' (assuming you were issued scrip in the first place) to the stockbroker after you received the contract note. The broker then sends you payment for the shares minus brokerage fees.

Computer trading at the ASX

Buying and selling shares wasn't always done by a few keystrokes on a computer keyboard. Up until 1990 the six state stock exchanges each had brokers exchanging shares on their trading floors, back-up staff recording the orders and doing the paper-work, and young men called 'chalkies' running up and down in front of enormous blackboards marked with all the locally listed companies, chalking in the latest share prices.

In 1990 the ASX swapped floor trading for its new computer

trading system known as SEATS (Stock Exchange Electronic Trading System). With SEATS, an order for the buying or selling of shares is entered into a computer terminal at any sharebroking office in Australia. The buy or sell order joins a queue in the central computer system which is arranged in order of price and time of lodging.

As soon as a buying bid matches a selling order SEATS executes a trade automatically. Trades at any given price are executed in the sequential order that bids or selling orders have been lodged in the system, whether placed by a large institutional fund or a small private investor. This is designed to give players of all sizes equal access to the market.

In the financial year 1993-4 SEATS handled an average of around 15,500 trades a day, up from 7,500 when the system was first installed. This translated into an annual total of 65.46 billion shares traded, valued at $128.4 billion.

Other important innovations at the ASX were the introduction in 1989 of the FAST (Flexible Accelerated Securities Transfer) computer system, followed by the 1994 introduction of CHESS (Clearing House Electronic Sub-register System). Both of these computerised systems are designed to process and speed up the transfer and settlement of stocks traded on the ASX.

Previously, when you bought shares in a company you received a share certificate known as scrip from the company as proof of share ownership. (Some companies still issue scrip but it is becoming rare.) You kept your scrip in a safe place and when you wanted to sell, you gave it to your broker. This certificate was then forwarded to the company in which you had been a shareholder so that your sale could be entered into its share register. This paper processing could drag on and, until it was finalised, you weren't paid.

The introduction of computerised share transfer and registration processes has done away with the need to physically send share certificates from one broker to another in order to effect an exchange of ownership. Now shareholders have their ownership of shares electronically stored in the ASX's computer system and evidenced by a monthly holding statement, similar to a bank statement. Computerisation has also done away with the need for shareholders to physically sign share transfer forms – which could be very time consuming – by permitting stockbrokers to sign transfers on their behalf. The result is a largely paperless system where share transfers are similar to electronic funds transfers.

These innovations have enabled the introduction of a fixed settlement or payment day five days after a trade is made. And to put this in perspective, prior to the computerisation of the ASX, settlement could take as long as six weeks after trade!

These productivity improvements have been designed to consolidate the ASX as one of the leading sharemarkets in the Asia Pacific region. Certainly, making the ASX more efficient through computerisation has been very welcome to investors, but have these productivity gains made your stockbroker any cheaper to deal with? Not really. Despite the 1984 deregulation of brokerage commissions on sharemarket transactions, many stockbroking organisations still charge the old pre-deregulation scale of 2% to 2.5% for private client transactions of less than $10,000.

Understanding the daily share tables

The daily trading on the ASX is reported in the business section of most Australian metropolitan newspapers. These published share trading tables contain a wealth of information, most of which is relevant to building your share portfolio. But how do you interpret it all?

Let's look at the sharemarket trading tables as they appear in the *Australian Financial Review*.

52 week High	Low	Day's High	Low	ASX code	Company Name and par value	Mrkt Call code	Last sale	+ or –	Vol 100's	Quote Buy	Sell	Dividend ¢ per Share	Times cov	Net asset back	Div yield %	Earn share ¢	P/E ratio
1.77	1.20	–	–	HSH	HowardFin20c	2484	1.50	–	–	–	1.50	5.00	.89	.51	3.33	4.45	33.7
1.03	.62	–	–	HCD	Huadu50c	3166	.65	–	–	.60	.65	–	–	–	–	–	–
12.70	6.70	12.30	12.20	HCO	HudsonCwy$1	2459	12.20	–10	38	10.80	12.20	–	–	7.64	–	62.77	19.4
1.03	.61	.83	.81	HTH	Hudsn T&H50c	2486	.82	–1	575	.81	.83	5.00	4.10‡	.95	6.10	20.50	4.0
.39	.31	.35	.35	HIC	Huntley20c	2463	.35	–	200	.35	.36	–	–	.46	–	–	–
.07½	.01	–	–	HICO	Huntley opt96	2464	.02	–	–	.01½	.02	–	–	–	–	–	–
.65	.30	.31	.31	HPA	HyalPharm25c	2476	.31	–	100	.31	.34	–	–	.17	–	–	–
2.20	.62	.63	.62	HMC	Hydromet20c	2471	.62	–	2025	.62	.63	2.25	2.43	.47	3.63	5.47	11.3
–	–	–	–	HMCE	Hydromet defx20c	3353	–	–	–	.55	–	–	–	–	–	–	–
.86	.40	–	–	IDT	I Drug Tc20c	2496	.51	–	–	.51	.55	1.60	1.53	.28	3.14	2.45	20.8
.99	.76	.91	.91	IPY	I.P.T.A. units$1	2514	.91	–	759	.90	.91	10.00	1.00	.95	10.99	10.00	9.1
11.60	8.70	10.26	10.20	ICI	ICI$1	2492	10.16	–4	347	10.00	10.16	42.00	1.74*	3.98	4.11	72.90	14.0
.90	.80	–	–	ICIPA	ICI cpref$1	2493	.85	–	–	.77	.85	5.00	–	6.17	–	–	–
1.97	.60	1.57	1.52	ISR	ISR Group20c	2515	1.55	–	686	1.52	1.55	–	–	.17	–	–	–
.30	.14	.29	.29	IMD	Imdex20c	4311	.29	–	1270	.29	.30	–	–	–	–	–	–
5.00	3.50	4.90	4.88	ICT	Incitec$1	2494	4.90	–	357	4.85	4.90	20.00	1.38	1.67	4.08	27.60	17.8
.12	.06	.08	.08	IIV	Ind Inv25c	2501	.08	+2	680	.06	.08	–	–	.07	–	.14	57.1
.05½	.02	–	–	IIVO	Ind Inv opt99	2502	.03½	–	–	.02½	.03½	–	–	–	–	–	–
.50	.00½	–	–	INS	Ind Sec25c	2506	–	–	–	.04½	–	–	–	–	–	–	–
.05	.02	–	–	INSPA	Ind Sec crdpf25c	2507	–	–	–	.04½	–	–	–	–	–	–	–
1.25	.75	.85	.85	IHN	I'hadden50c	2500	.80	–	7	.80	.85	25.00	.26*	1.37	29.41	6.50	13.1
.95	.47½	.90	.90	INR	Inprint50c	2505	.90	–1	20	.90	.95	1.00	14.60	.87	1.11	14.60	6.2
.40	.30	–	–	IDH	IntDisti50c	2495	.35	–	–	.25	.33	–	–	.51	–	7.10	4.6
.55	.10	.41	.40	IMM	Int.Media20c	2504	.40	–	310	.40	.44	–	–	–	–	1.01	39.6
1.00†	.30	.37	.37	ITN	Intag50c	2517	.37	–	290	.35	.37	–	–	–	–	–	–
1.21	.69	.83	.80	IHG	Intellect10c	2499	.80	–3	160	.80	.81	–	–	–	–	.67	119.4
.16	.06	–	–	IEG	Inter Eq20c	2497	.08	–	–	.07	.15	–	–	.14	–	–	–
.06	.01	–	–	IEQO	Inter Eq opt96	2498	.01	–	–	.00½	.02	–	–	–	–	–	–
.53	.21	–	–	IPI	Inter Pac50c	2512	.33	–	–	.34	.35	3.00	–	.51	8.82	–	–
.98	.68	–	–	IAL	Inv Aust50c	2491	.74	–	–	.80	.74	1.45	–	.96	1.96	–	–
1.30	.90	1.30	1.30	IPH	Ipoh$1	2510	1.30	+8	58	1.18	1.30	20.00	1.15*	2.16	15.38	23.05	5.6
1.16	1.05	–	–	IPHG	Ipoh cvn99	2511	1.16	–	–	1.16	1.30	10.00	–	8.62	–	–	–

For the shares in any listed company you can discover the following:

52 week high and low: the highest and the lowest price the share has traded between on the ASX in the year to date.

Day's high and low: the range of prices the share traded between on the latest ASX business (trading) day.

ASX code: the code given by the ASX to every type of share on issue.

Company name and par value: the 'par value' of the shares is the nominal or face value of these traded shares. It is of little interest or relevance to share investors, being more for accounting purposes.

Last sale: the price at which the company's shares traded on the last sale of the previous business day. This is the figure used to most accurately measure the value of the company's shares when calculating the value of a share portfolio.

+ or − : the difference (in cents) in the share's last sale price over the last sale price the day before. This shows, on a daily basis, if the share has risen or fallen in price.

Vol 100's: the total volume of shares (in hundreds) traded in the company on the previous trading day. This indicates the level of market interest in a particular stock.

Quote (Buy): the highest price at which a buyer is prepared to buy shares in the listed company. It is also known as the 'bid' or 'buying price'. Shares may not always have been transacted at this price.

Quote (Sell): the lowest price at which a seller is prepared to sell shares, also known as the 'offer price' or 'selling price'. Shares may not always have been transacted at this price.

Dividend c per share: the size of the latest annual dividend distributed by the company per share (in cents and fractions of cents). The 'f' that follows some entries indicates the dividend was franked.

Dividend times cov: stands for dividend times cover which is the number of times the dividend per share (DPS) is covered by the earnings per share (EPS). Dividend times cover is calculated by dividing the EPS figure by the DPS figure. The relevance of the dividend times cover is to show what proportion of the company's net earnings are distributed as dividends.

Net asset back: stands for net asset backing (per share) which is designed to give you an idea of what each share would be worth (in dollars and cents) if all assets were liquidated and all debts paid, with the residual then being distributed amongst all ordinary shareholders on a per share basis.

This figure is arrived at by dividing the value of shareholders' funds as reported in the company's balance sheet by the number of issued shares. Now, if you aren't familiar with company accounting principles (and very few people are) the net asset backing figure will not tell you much. Don't worry, you can easily get by without it.

Div yield %: the dividend return to the shareholder in relation to the last quoted sale price. It is calculated by dividing dividends per share by the last sale price, expressed as a percentage. This method of calculation means the yield changes as the sale price changes. Indeed, if the share price crashed the yield would soar – until the next (invariably lower) dividend was declared.

Like net asset backing, the dividend yield is an interesting figure but due to the vagaries of share prices and accounting practices it isn't enormously revealing. It is also a measure of past performance and says nothing about the future. As a general rule of thumb, the higher the dividend yield, the healthier the company is perceived to be and the happier its shareholders are likely to be.

Earn share c: stands for earnings per share (EPS) expressed in cents. It shows the amount of profit earned for every ordinary issued share. EPS is calculated by dividing the company's net profit by the total number of ordinary issued shares.

P/E ratio: stands for price earnings ratio. It is calculated by dividing the last sale price by the earnings per share. The P/E ratio therefore measures the share price in relation to (as a multiple of) the company's profits.

This ratio provides a means of measuring investors' expectations of the company's performance. If a company has a low P/E compared to other companies *working in the same or similar industries*, this indicates the market anticipates a poor profit performance from the company in the future. A relatively high P/E on the other hand indicates the opposite view. A high P/E ratio could also indicate a company is being valued for its asset backing and not for its earnings potential.

The interpretive ratios are all very well but because they are based on historical data, and because this data is so open to mathematical and accounting manipulation, the insights they bring to present and likely *future* performances have to be viewed with some caution. This warning particularly applies to the P/E ratio to which many investment commentators give far more significance than it deserves.

Studying and understanding sharemarket performance ratios is certainly useful but it will not magically reveal which shares you should buy and which to avoid. These ratios simply provide a way of comparing one share's historical performance to that of another. By all means use them as a guide but don't rely on them when selecting your shares.

Share indices

When reading or talking about the sharemarket you will come across the term 'All Ordinaries Index' or 'All Ordinaries Accumulation Index'. But what are these indices, and what is their purpose?

Well, stock exchanges all around the world develop indices as a quick way of keeping an eye on what's happening in particular markets. An index reflects a change in the value of a sample selection of shares in a single market or in a sample selection of markets. An index may measure changes in the market's capital value based on share prices alone, or it may also take into account the value of dividends paid (and assumed to be reinvested). The shares and markets chosen for inclusion in the sample are those of the greatest interest and relevance to investors.

When an index is created, a particular day is given a base value (say 1,000) and then changes in market direction are measured in relation to that value. Let's say market activity was strong over a period and this example index rose to 1,024. This would mean the value of the market (or more accurately, the value of the sampled shares in this market) had risen by 2.4%

Each stock exchange has a main index that represents the market as a whole and the ones most commonly quoted in the media are: Australia's All Ordinaries (Industrial) Index; New York's Dow Jones Industrial Average; London's FTSE 100 Index; Tokyo's Nikkei Index; and Hong Kong's Hang Seng Index.

In addition to these overall market indices, there are also specific market sector indices such as the Australian All Mining Index, Transport Index, Media Index or the ASX 100 Index which measures the movement of the largest 100 listed companies. You will find all these listed in the share pages of the major dailies. But let's look at some of the more important indices:

- The All Ordinaries Index is the one most frequently quoted in the Australian media and is based on a sample of around 300 actively traded companies listed on the ASX. The companies are chosen to be in the sample based on their market value and between them they represent approximately 93% of the value of the entire Australian sharemarket and 96% of the ASX's share turnover. The base value of the index was set at 500 on 31 December 1979, and the index only measures changes in the market's price.
- The All Ordinaries Accumulation Index is basically the same as the All Ordinaries Index except it assumes a 100% reinvestment of all dividends paid by the sample companies. It therefore presents a more complete picture of the market's performance. There are accumulation indices to complement most price-only indices.
- New York's Dow Jones Industrial Average is the oldest and most widely quoted indicator of share market change. It is not really an index (which is a value relative to an earlier established value) but rather indicates the average share price of a group of 30 blue chip companies actively traded on the New York Stock Exchange (NYSE). This group (which includes American Express and AT&T) accounts for 15% to 20% of the market value of NYSE listed stocks (and the NYSE is the largest in the world). Like other indices, the Dow Jones is quoted in points not dollars.
- London's FTSE 100 is the UK equivalent of our All Ordinaries or New York's Dow Jones. It's commonly called the 'footsie' and it stands for the Financial Times Stock Exchange (Index). The index is based on the weighted average share price of 100 leading UK listed companies.
- Standard and Poor's 500 (S&P 500) is based on US shares mostly listed on the New York Stock Exchange. It tends to be used by professional investors more than the Dow Jones

which is used more in the media. The S&P 500 is a weighted share price index of 400 industrial, 60 transportation and utilities, and 40 financial US listed companies. This index accounts for around 80% of the value of the shares listed on the NYSE.

- The Nikkei is the market index for the Tokyo Stock Exchange. Once called the Nikkei-Dow Jones, it reflects the average price changes of 225 of Japan's leading listed companies.
- The Morgan Stanley Capital International World Index (MSCI World Index) indicates the average change in share prices in a sample of international sharemarkets. The share prices of approximately 1,375 companies in 19 different countries comprise the sample, and this sample accounts for 60% of the value of the world's shares. There is also an MSCI World Accumulation Index which takes into account the value of (reinvested) dividends as well as price.

There are countless other indices in existence and more being developed all the time. So long as you know what they are measuring they are a very useful tool for indicating at a glance the direction in which a market or market sector is travelling and how it has performed over a given time. And when you come across an index you're not familiar with, ring your stockbroker, your funds manager, or the ASX who should have no trouble telling you how the index is constructed, what it measures, and what it can mean to you.

Selecting the right shares

Unless you are very enthusiastic about researching companies I suggest that you let your broker make some recommendations. Having said that, if you are making your first share investment, I'd go for a major blue chip company such as BHP, Coles Myer or a bank such as National Australia Bank or Commonwealth Bank.

Ideally you should end up with a number of shares in different sectors. By 'sectors' I mean mining, banking, media, retail, building and so on. This spreads your risk. If you think this all sounds a bit hard, a managed share fund will take care of diversification for you – and I deal with these in Chapter Fifteen.

When is the right time to buy?

The answer to this question is very simple – when you have the money to do so. If you wait for the market or a particular share to bottom (the optimum time to buy) you could be waiting forever because there is no way of knowing when a share or the market has bottomed!

There is no doubt you can make tons of money by good market timing, but, there is also no doubt that good market timing involves a lot of skill and probably an even greater amount of luck.

When is the right time to sell?

The answer to this question is also very simple – when you need the money. If you don't need the money, don't sell. It's not a good strategy to turn your shares over too often. If you do you will only rack up unncessarily high brokerage fees, you may miss out on the payment of dividends, you may be classified as a share trader by the Tax Office and taxed accordingly (where all profits are taxed as income – but also where any losses are deductible), and you may be out of the market during the 'hot' periods.

Trying to pick the optimum times to buy and sell shares is no different to trying to pick winners at the races. It makes you a punter and we all know how most punters fare – poorly.

Trying to pick market timing

Many financial commentators and investors place great emphasis on making sure you time your entry into and out of the markets correctly. 'Correct' timing means buying when the market or a particular share is at its lowest point and selling when the market or a particular share is at its highest point.

You don't have to be Einstein to see why people urge you to get your market timing right – anyone who can *consistently* pick share movements will end up very rich, in just the same way as anyone who can consistently pick the winning horse or the right number at roulette will do very well. But, like picking the winning horse, getting your timing right with sharemarkets is much easier said than done.

One of the most thorough and sobering studies on 'active trading' (moving in and out of the markets at the supposed right time) was conducted in 1972 by Professor William Sharpe of Stanford University. This study assumed an investor would shift assets between shares and cash on an annual basis depending on his perceptions of the state of the market.

His findings were startling – namely, that an active trader would have to be right as much as 80% of the time before increasing the value of his portfolio. These findings still hold, so let's look at the logic behind Professor Sharpe's study.

Suppose you make two predictions: firstly, that the sharemarket will go up; and secondly, that it will stay up. So you invest $100. Say you're right about the market going up, and the rise is by 50%. Your shares are now worth $150.

But then the market falls, again by 50%. Now your shares are only worth $75. A 50% gain followed by a 50% loss has not returned you to your original level; you are in fact down by 25% on your starting point.

This illustrates how the penalty for getting it wrong with market timing is greater than the reward for getting it right. The penalty is the risk of permanent capital loss and the reward is magnified returns. However, the potential for greater rewards are not in proportion to the risks.

If you trade actively you will theoretically need to get your timing right about 66% of the time to break even – before costs. When you add brokerage fees, and the tax disadvantages you will incur if the Tax Office classifies you as a share trader due to your active trading strategy, you can see why your timing must be right closer to 80% of the time just to break even.

The price of investments can be affected by a huge array of factors including economic, political and social influences, and markets have an unnerving habit of moving in sudden jolts in reaction to unpredictable causes. This makes it impossible to forecast price movements accurately over short periods of time. Therefore, the prospective gain from correctly timing your entry into or out of a market should be balanced against the risk of either being out of the market completely during a rally, or in the market too long during a sudden downturn.

·Consider a study by the University of Michigan covering the bull market period in US shares from 1982 to 1987. The return over this period based on the S&P 500 Index was 26.3% p.a. But missing only the 30 biggest days (out of the full 1,276 trading days) would have reduced an investor's return to 8.5%, only marginally better than the no-risk Treasury Bill return of 7.9% over the same period. (The biggest days are those which experienced the highest daily growth in market prices.)

Between 1980 and 1993 returns from the US sharemarket for a full-time investor averaged 15% p.a. But look at the graph below which shows the average annual returns an investor would have received if they missed out on just the 10, 20, 30 and 40 biggest days of the period.

Time *not* Timing
Annual returns on the US sharemarket 1980 to 1993

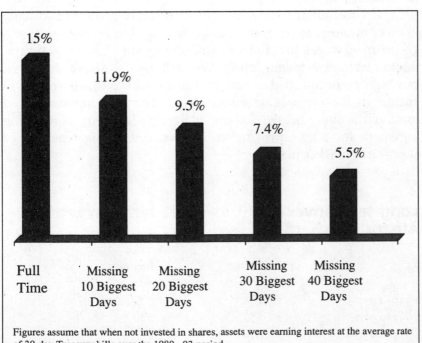

Full Time	15%
Missing 10 Biggest Days	11.9%
Missing 20 Biggest Days	9.5%
Missing 30 Biggest Days	7.4%
Missing 40 Biggest Days	5.5%

Figures assume that when not invested in shares, assets were earning interest at the average rate of 30-day Treasury bills over the 1980 - 93 period

An IPAC study has found similar results for the Australian sharemarket. In the first four months of 1991 the Australian sharemarket rose by roughly 20%. Just ten days trading contributed almost all of that gain, but only once was a 'good' day followed by another 'good' day so you either had to be very sharp indeed with your timing, or else invested in the market at all times.

There are no prizes for guessing which strategy I recommend. Clearly, you should avoid trying to time your entry into and exit out of the sharemarket in the hope of gaining that illusive short-term win. The way to win with shares (or any other mainstream investment) is to hang on for the long-term.

Look, there's no denying the sharemarket has its bad days, weeks and years, and that anyone who has invested just as it goes into a tailspin can really hurt at the time. Some reversals have been terrible – the last great stinker occurred on 20 October, 1987 when the market crashed in average price by 44.7% in one day! Yet, the Australian sharemarket grew in value by 45.4% in 1993, (then fell by 8.7% in 1994).

So, if your initial timing isn't good, don't despair. Try to hang in there because, in time, the market is bound to recover and even go on to new heights. Indeed, since 1875 the Australian sharemarket has never failed, following a fall, to rise above the previous high point and there is no reason to believe this pattern will change in the foreseeable future. If you are still not convinced look at the table below. I think it presents a pretty compelling argument for long-term market involvement and a rejection of short-term market plays.

Long-term investment *vs* short-term investment– Australian shares

	Worst 1 Year performance	Average annual performance
1930–1950	−23.1%	9.7%
1951–1970	−27.8%	10.0%
1971–1990	−29.0%	13.6%

(*Source*: IPAC Securities)

Dollar cost averaging

I mentioned dollar cost averaging in my investment tips, but it's worth thinking about again. Dollar cost averaging is a buying strategy that stands in complete opposition to the active trading strategy of entering and exiting the market in an effort to catch its highs and lows.

It involves investing a fixed amount in the sharemarket (or other investment markets) at regular, fixed intervals. A typical example would be investing, say, $2,000 in the sharemarket on the first business day of every fourth month. (I acknowledge $2,000 is a pretty hefty figure if invested regularly, but this would be an average 'minimum investment size' for shares).

Assuming you can afford it, the logic behind this strategy is pretty simple and compelling. Firstly, it is a disciplined investment regimen. Secondly, it acts to average out the cost of the shares you buy even though the value of the underlying assets and hence the share price have fluctuated. This process frees you up from having to worry about getting your market timing right.

How does it do this? Well, when the market is declining your money buys you more shares than under normal trading conditions, and when the market is climbing it buys you less. You just keep on buying regardless of the state of the market and effectively build your share portfolio at an average market price. This averaging process ultimately means you might not get any bargains, but you should not pay too much for your shares either. You simply keep adding to your share portfolio come rain, hail or shine.

The easiest way and most affordable way of putting this 'get rich slow' technique into effect is by contributing regularly towards a professionally managed share fund or some other type of managed fund. Not only are the minimum ongoing investment sizes (around $300 to $500) much smaller than the minimum size of a direct investment into shares but a managed fund takes the effort out of trying to decide which shares to buy.

International shares

So far we've concentrated on Australian shares and the Australian sharemarket but there's a whole world of shares out there trading on sharemarkets from Jakarta to Paris to New York to Tokyo. Indeed, the range of share investment opportunities laid out before you is staggering when you start thinking globally.

The Australian sharemarket accounts for less than 2% of the volume of the world's sharemarkets. So if you only invest in companies listed on the local sharemarket you reduce your opportunity to participate in the high growth of regions such as China, South-East Asia and Latin America, and miss out altogether on the opportunity to invest in some of the world's best known companies, such as Boeing, Michelin, Thorn-EMI and Minolta which are not represented on the ASX.

The following table shows the Australian sharemarket as a percentage of the world's total sharemarkets as at June 1995.

Australia	1.5%
Malaysia/Singapore and Hong Kong	3.9%
United Kingdom	9.7%
Other Europe	18.8%
Japan	23.7%
USA	39.8%
Other	2.6%

(*Source*: IPAC Securities)

When you look at the historical performance of the world's sharemarkets on a regional basis, the notion of having at least some of your share portfolio invested overseas starts looking very sensible. Compare the level of capital appreciation (price only, excluding dividends) of the following regional sharemarkets between 1970 and (June) 1994:

Asia Pacific	3687%
Europe	811%
USA	537%
World average	845%
Australia	315%

(*Source*: Morgan Stanley Capital International)

Note the relative underperformance of the Australian sharemarket, particularly compared to the stunning performance of the combined Asian Pacific sharemarkets which bettered ours by more than ten times! Indeed, the Australian sharemarket's price-only performance was significantly less than half the world's average during this period.

In the 10 years to 31 December, 1993 Australian shares returned an average of 15.7% p.a. based on the All Ordinaries Accumulation Index. Over the same period, international shares as measured by the MSCI World Accumulation Index, returned an average of 18.8% p.a. This means a $10,000 investment made in the Australian sharemarket on 31 December, 1983 would have grown in 10 years to $42,973, whereas the same investment in international sharemarkets would have returned $56,069 – a bettering of $13,096. (*Source*: Frank Russell Co.)

Now, not all sharemarkets perform similarly at the same time. Some may record losses and others record gains in the same year. In 1984 for instance, the Australian sharemarket lost 2.3% and the Japanese market grew by 27.6%. In 1988, the Australian sharemarket grew by 17.9% and the British market lost 10.4%.

So, given that the world's sharemarkets do not all perform in the same way at the same time, international share investment therefore presents a very good avenue of diversification – which is a foundation stone of effective personal investment. Diversification is all about reducing portfolio risk while at the same time maintaining an acceptable level of return.

The commonly held wisdom is that investing in overseas sharemarkets is riskier than investing in the Australian sharemarket. This is not necessarily the case. The level of risk entailed in international investment depends on *which* overseas sharemarkets you invest in. Some are more risky (more volatile and more variable) than ours, others aren't.

In general, the sharemarkets of the developing world, the so-called 'emerging markets'* are the most risky. They have the potential for the wildest swings which means they may be more prone to plunging, as well as tending to generate the highest levels of growth of any markets. Between 1988 and 1992, for example,

---

* 'Emerging markets' include: in Latin America – Argentina, Brazil, Chile, Colombia, Mexico, Venezuela; in Asia – India, Indonesia, Korea, Malaysia, Philippines, Thailand, Taiwan; and in Europe – Greece, Portugal, Turkey.

returns from the sharemarkets of emerging economies exceeded 25% p.a. The world sharemarket returned just over 5% p.a. during the same period (*Source*: IPAC/Capital International.)

The 'mainstream' markets of Western Europe, North America and Japan tend to have lower rates of growth but also less likelihood of dramatic downturns than emerging markets. And, importantly, investing in mainstream markets is really no riskier than investing in ours. Indeed, investing in certain overseas markets can be less risky than investing in the ASX.

Look at the chart below comparing the returns from the Australian sharemarket as measured by the All Ordinaries Index to the returns from the international markets as measured by the MSCI World Index, between 1985 and 1994.

Comparison of the annual returns for the MSCI and the All Ordinaries Index, 1985 to 1994

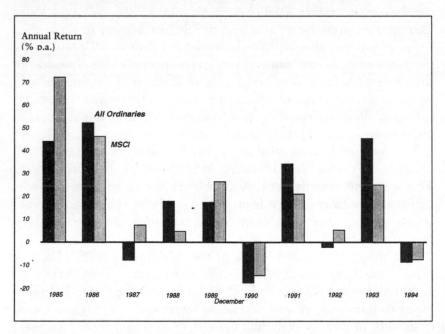

(*Source*: FPG Research)

Note how the incidence of negative returns is less for the MSCI than it is for the All Ordinaries. Over this period the returns from the international sharemarkets measured by the MSCI were less volatile and less risky than the returns from Australian shares – while at the same time producing a higher average annual return! This goes against the normally accepted principle that the higher the return, the higher the risk.

The relationship that existed between risk and return for local and international shares during the 10 years to 31 December, 1993 is plotted in the graph below.

The relationship between risk and return for Australian and international shares, 1984 to 1993

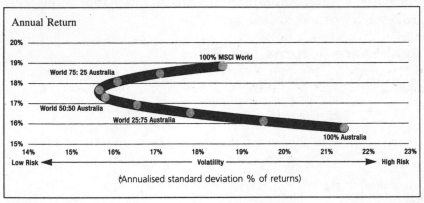

(*Source*: GT Management based on MSCI World Index and All Ordinaries Accum. Index)

Note how the risk level (as determined by the annualised standard deviation percentage of returns) for Australian shares was more than 21%, with a return of 15.7%. Now at the other end of the curve, the risk level of the international sharemarkets measured by the MSCI world index was lower than the Australian sharemarket at around 19%, but with a higher average annual return of 18.8%.

At any given point on the curve you can see what the levels of risk and returns were during this period for any combination of Australian and international shares. For instance, if you had invested 75% in international shares and 25% in Australian, and your average annual return would have been around 18% with your risk level around 16%.

The apex or turning point of the curve – giving the optimum combination of risk and return – occurred at a mix of around

60% international and 40% Australian shares. This illustrates why professional managers hold a mix of local and international assets. It simultaneously achieves the normally mutually incompatible goal of improving returns *as well as* lowering risk.

Don't lose sight of the fact that we have been looking here at historical figures over a single 10-year period. However, IPAC research has shown that in most 10-year periods international shares do slightly outperform Australian shares with a slightly lower degree of risk. So, assuming the pattern is replicated in the future – and there is no reason to think otherwise – diversification into certain international markets makes a lot of sense.

Real Share Returns and Risks

Investment	Long term historic after-inflation return	Risk of a negative return (loss)				
	% pa	1 year	2 years	5 years	10 years	20 years
Shares (Australian)	5–8%	28.2%	15.9%	9.9%	3.4%	0.5%
Shares (International)	6–9%	26.6%	13.9%	8.1%	2.4%	0.0%

(*Source*: IPAC)

Which overseas markets?

By now I suspect you are wondering *which* overseas markets to invest in, *what proportion* of your share portfolio to place into international markets, and how to go about it?

As far as international markets selection is concerned, you need to consider their risk and return characteristics. For convenience we have already classified the world's sharemarkets into mainstream or established markets, and emerging markets. We know that emerging markets are more volatile than mainstream markets. The ratio of emerging to mainstream markets that you should hold, therefore, becomes a factor of how much risk you feel comfortable with. Personally, I believe a ratio of 20% to 30%

emerging markets to 80% to 70% mainstream markets is a sensible mix that should generate good growth with an acceptable level of risk. Remember though, that investment risk depends entirely on your general attitude to risks, your age, income, dependants and so on.

Interestingly, in just the same way that a portfolio comprised of a mix of international (non-emerging markets) and Australian shares actually *reduced risk and increased returns* compared to an all-Australian portfolio in the 10 years to December 1993, adding some emerging markets shares to a mainstream international portfolio also enhanced that portfolio's return while decreasing its risk in the five years to the end of December 1992. The graph below illustrates the result.

Risk/return ratio for international shares and emerging markets 1988 to 1992

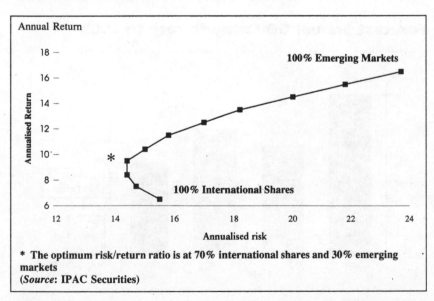

* The optimum risk/return ratio is at 70% international shares and 30% emerging markets
(*Source*: IPAC Securities)

Now at the risk of really labouring the point, I want to stress again just how important it is to treat all share investments and especially international emerging markets share investments as a long-term proposition. By this I mean holding on to them for at least five years, preferably ten. All share markets have good and bad years and if you are only invested for one, two or three years you may just catch the bad ones.

> **⊖─╼ Key thought**
> The point not to lose sight of with shares – whether Australian, mainstream international or emerging markets – is that over time they have generated good to very good returns and there is no reason to believe this pattern will change in the foreseeable future.

As far as economic forecasts are concerned, and despite my general recommendation to take all economic forecasts with a grain of salt, the graph below presents an interesting picture of anticipated regional growth rates up to the year 2003.

Forecast annual GDP growth rate to 2003

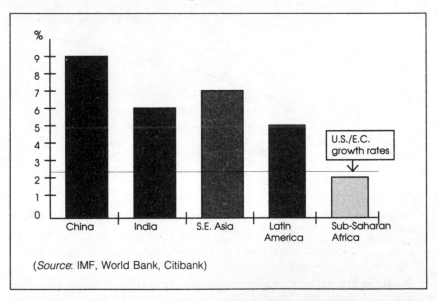

(*Source*: IMF, World Bank, Citibank)

What's the significance of these predicted growth rates? Well, generally speaking, there has been a positive historical relationship between higher rates of economic growth and greater sharemarket returns and there is every reason to believe this relationship between growth rates and share prices will continue.

How many international shares?

To answer the question, what proportion of your share portfolio should be allocated to international shares and what should be allocated to Australian shares, I generally recommend a ratio of around 30% international to 70% local. But given that international shares appear such strong performers, why not more?

Well, firstly, when you invest in the Australian sharemarket you can invest solely in companies that pay fully franked dividends and this benefit does not apply to international shares. Secondly, when you invest in shares listed on the ASX you are investing to a significant extent in Australia. Companies that operate here (even if foreign owned) provide employment, reinvest in Australia, pay local taxes and generate wealth which benefits all of us. There's room for a bit of nationalism here even if, strictly speaking, it's not a normally accepted personal investment criterion. Thirdly, you can keep track of your Australian shares far more easily than you can your offshore ones. Indeed, knowing what companies to invest in overseas and keeping tabs on these investments is very hard for the average individual investor. Finally, you should keep a reasonable percentage of your assets in the community you live in – unless it's a complete basket case!

How to invest overseas

Direct investment in overseas sharemarkets fits into the 'too hard' basket for most people. You would need to appoint overseas sharebrokers and subscribe to overseas publications to keep track of your investments. You would also need to make a large budget allocation for international phone calls.

The simplest way to go about it is to invest in a managed international share fund. A number of these are available to individual Australian investors including those offered by funds managers Jardine Fleming, Thorntons, GT, Fidelity, Bankers Trust (BT) and MLC. Any financial adviser can give you full information about these as well as other managed international share funds products.

The details of managed funds are looked at in Chapter Fifteen, but, briefly, managed international share funds can give you access to a large range of investment options. Some funds concentrate on Asian markets, others on the US market, some on a mix of mainstream international markets and others solely on emerging markets. The choice is very wide.

Managed funds have entry, exit and ongoing management fees – which you wouldn't have to contend with as a direct investor – but going through a funds manager is a very easy form of investing. The funds manager selects all the assets to invest in (within the parameters that you choose) and monitors their progress for you. A typical minimum investment would be $1,000, with minimum additions of around $500.

It's probably fair to say that if you choose to invest in international shares via a managed share fund (and this is the method I recommend), you would indirectly become an investor in literally hundreds of overseas companies. This is because a typical managed fund invests directly in between 50 and 100 companies, which in turn invest in a myriad of other companies, and so on. It follows, therefore, that managed funds provide very good diversification.

Capital gains tax and provisional tax

I may have given you the impression that share dividends are the only things taxable in share investment. Not so. Like other assets, most notably property, when you sell your shares (and assuming you bought them after 19 September 1985), you are required to pay capital gains tax on any after-inflation capital gain (increase in trading price) they have made.

Also, if you earn more than $1,000 a year in unearned income (from dividends and interest payments), you will have to pay provisional tax. I won't go into detail here, because these taxes are looked at in Chapter Ten. Needless to say, I think it's important to draw your attention to their existence and possible impact.

The world's most successful share investor

Have you ever heard of Warren Buffet? No? Don't worry, you're not alone. Most people outside the investment industry haven't either – and I suspect that's the way he likes it.

The fact is, Buffet, who was born in 1931, is the world's richest professional investor and America's second richest man. In 1995, *Forbes* magazine estimated his worth at $US10.7 billion.

Interestingly, he has made his billions on Wall Street yet lives in the same house in Omaha, Nebraska he bought for $31,000 in 1958 and drives a modest car. He runs his investment company Berkshire Hathaway from his headquarters above an Omaha furniture store.

Buffet's investment success is an investment morality tale. He shuns the flashy life and conspicuous consumption that typified his high-flying, Gordon Gekko-like contemporaries of the 1980s – most of whom are now either bankrupt or doing time. Buffet has succeeded when many failed by sticking to his frugal instincts and by eschewing short-term investment gains. He has made billions for himself and for his investors by taking long-term positions in shares in companies often shunned by others.

Buffet likens his search for solid investments to 'bagging rare and fast moving elephants'. By this he means the secret is not so much picking the so-called 'sunrise industries', as identifying the right opportunities in any industry regardless of its glamour quotient and what the rest of the investment industry thinks.

Buffet says, 'We [Berkshire Hathaway] get excited about shares only when we find businesses that:

1. we understand
2. have favourable long term prospects
3. are operated by honest, competent people, and
4. are priced attractively.'

He says, 'We can usually identify a small number of investments meeting requirements 1, 2 and 3, but meeting 4 often prevents action.'

So, what are some of Buffet's investment coups? Is his company big on biotechnology outfits and rocket technology shares? Not at all. In 1994, Berkshire Hathaway owned 11% of Gillette, 15% of the *Washington Post*, 7% of Coca-Cola, 48% of Greco Corp (a large insurance company), 18% of the media conglomerate that owns the (US) ABC network and 12% of the Wells Fargo Bank.

Buffet's key skill has been his ability to recognise good quality, undervalued stock. Arguably, his perceptions (based on strong analysis) are second to none. Now, I can't tell you exactly how he so consistently picks the right companies (he would keep that a well-guarded trade secret) but I can tell you this much – his methods include the use of 'quality filters' to assess the attractiveness of a share's price. This entails analysing factors like level of company debt and strength of cash flow. He also looks for shares that are neglected and hence, possibly underpriced by the market. (I didn't say it was easy – if it was we would all be billionaires!)

I doubt Buffet would recommend (and I certainly don't) that you try to rival his clairvoyant ability to consistently pick under-valued stock. This is an astoundingly difficult job which even the best-trained investment professionals struggle to get right. So, what are you supposed to do? Well, if you have a slim chance of emulating his share selection style one thing you can emulate is his holding style – which is for the very long-term.

Once Buffet has bought stock, he hangs on to it. He summarises his company's shareholding philosophy as, 'our favourite holding period is forever'. He also doesn't like too much turnover on his own company's share register. He has told his investors, 'our goal is to attract long-term shareholders who, at the time of purchase, have no time frame or price target for sale but instead plan to stay with us indefinitely'.

Without any doubt this is an uncompromising endorsement for the long-term, and while it's perhaps too strong for some, it is a strategy that's proved very beneficial for Buffet and his shareholders.

Buffet also adheres to the view that a diversified portfolio of shares is preferable to a limited range of shares. And, in choosing your shares, Buffet advises you ignore the sentiments of the crowd as this is likely to lead to some bad investment decisions.

Finally, timing. Against the background of a general recommendation that you don't let your opinion of the market's future overly influence your share buying (because your opinion could well be wrong), Buffet says a bad time to buy shares is when there is a universal mood of investor optimism. This means the sharemarket is bound to be overpriced. Rather, buy when the mood is gloomy and prices are lower. Then, whatever the market does, hang on to your shares for as long as possible.

Warren Buffet's investment strategy

These are the key points which have helped make Buffet the world's richest share investor:

- thrift and prudence, combined with a relatively frugal lifestyle
- thorough analysis and a strict investment criteria leading to the selection of quality, undervalued stock
- a diversified portfolio across all market sectors
- a very long-term approach to share investment, a rejection of market timing strategies and an indifference to popular market sentiment.

CHAPTER FOURTEEN
Interest-bearing Investments

Anyone with a mortgage, a personal loan or a credit card knows all about the rigours of being in debt. It's no fun paying debts off, or paying all that interest into someone else's pocket. So what about putting the boot on the other foot? Why don't *you* be the lender and have someone pay *you* interest for a change? Sounds good? Well, that's what interest-bearing investments (interest-bearing securities or debt investments) are all about.

Whether you put your money in a bank term deposit, invest in government bonds, or buy finance company debentures, you are basically doing the same thing. You are lending your money to another party on the understanding that interest will be paid to you for the privilege of that money's use. And, as with any loan, at the end of its term, you get your original amount (or 'principal') back.

The beauty of interest-bearing investments is that they are generally safe – they're liquid and they provide a sure return. They are particularly suited to those who need a *regular and dependable income* such as retirees. They are not as well suited, under normal circumstances, to those looking for long-term capital growth – which is usually the domain of shares and property.

Interest-bearing investments can be broken down into two camps or 'asset classes' which are fixed interest and, cash.

Fixed interest

A fixed interest investment is one where you effectively lend a company (like TNT or Custom Credit), a semi-government authority (like Telstra or the Australian Industry Development Corporation), or the federal or state government an amount of money for a fixed period of time at a fixed rate of interest. The

240

interest due on it is paid to you in fixed amounts on a regular, fixed schedule, say, once every month, or every three, six or 12 months and generally the more frequent the interest payments to the investor, the lower the effective interest rate you receive. (This is because of the higher costs involved in more frequent income distributions.) The original amount is repaid to you in one lump sum at the end of the term, at 'maturity'.

Let me illustrate the way fixed interest investments operate by looking at the classic example of bonds. If you buy, say, a three-year bond for $10,000 which promises to pay 11% p.a., what you are effectively doing is lending the issuer $10,000 for three years on the understanding that you will be repaid in full at the end of the term and receive regular interest payments in the meantime.

If regular interest payments (known as 'coupons') are due twice yearly on this bond you will receive a cheque for $550 every six months ($10,000 at 11% p.a. = $1,100 p.a. = $550 per 6 months). At the end of the third year you would also get your original $10,000 (the 'maturity value' or 'principal amount') back.

In Australia the word 'bond' is usually taken to mean a fixed interest-bearing security issued by the Commonwealth Government, however, it can also be applied to fixed interest securities issued by semi-government authorities. And because bonds come with a government guarantee of repayment, when you hear the word 'bond' you think 'safety and security'.

You can buy Australian bonds for terms ranging typically from one year to ten years, with one to five year terms being the more popular. Commonwealth Bonds are available in either three year or 10 year terms. At the other extreme you can buy US Government Bonds that mature in 30 years (though individual Australian investors rarely get involved in these because they entail a minimum investment of $50,000).

The bonds we are talking about here should not be confused with insurance bonds which are a form of life insurance policy based on managed funds and which are distinctly different.

Other fixed interest-bearing investments include:

Making Money

Term deposits

Term deposits with banks, building societies and credit unions are for terms ranging from three months to five years. With these, you deposit a lump sum with the institution on the understanding you don't have access to the money until the end of the agreed term. At that time you get your money back plus interest which is paid to you at set times. To compensate you for tying up your money in this way, term deposits pay a higher rate of interest than normal bank accounts.

Note that your money isn't totally locked away. If an emergency crops up and you need to get your hands on it before the term expires you can. But you'll probably be charged a penalty fee for breaking the arrangement and have your interest recalculated at a lower rate that's more in line with the normal savings account rate.

Debentures, unsecured notes and convertible notes

Debentures, unsecured notes and convertible notes are dealt with in some detail in Chapter Thirteen, 'Investing in Shares' but briefly:
- Debentures are basically the same as bonds except they are loans to companies, typically industrial and finance companies, rather than being loans to government or semi-government bodies. Debentures don't come with government guarantees so they are riskier than bonds and consequently they normally pay a higher rate of interest.
- Unsecured notes are similar to debentures in that they are a fixed term, fixed rate loan to a company, however, these loans are not secured against the company's assets. This puts them on a higher risk level than debentures but, in compensation, they tend to pay higher returns.
- Convertible notes are fixed term, fixed interest loans to companies, like debentures. Where they differ is that at a set date and at a set price the note can be converted into shares in the issuing company if the note holder so wishes. Up until the time the note is converted into shares the holder receives regular, fixed interest payments from the issuer. If the holder of the note

chooses not to convert the note to shares, the issuing company repays the principal value of the note to the investor on the note's maturity.

Cash investments

A 'cash' investment can be as straightforward as putting your money into a bank savings account or as sophisticated as investing in a cash management trust – which is a managed fund investing in a diversified range of short-term, interest-bearing securities. 'Cash' also covers investments in the short-term money market or in bank bills with terms of usually no more than 180 days.

The returns from cash investments are based on short-term market interest rates and, because these rates are variable, you can't be sure exactly what your income will be. This puts cash into direct contrast with fixed interest investments.

Cash is an ideal short-term investment. It's a great place to park funds while you organise a more appropriate long-term use for them. Of course, you can keep your funds in cash forever if you wish but don't expect high or tax effective returns.

Performance

Research by IPAC shows that *over the long term*, traditional after-inflation annual returns for cash and fixed interest investments have been:

- Australian cash   0% to 1%
- International cash   0% to 2%
- Australian fixed interest 0% to 3%
- International fixed interest 1% to 2%

In certain periods however, after-inflation returns have been far better than these, for example:

Calendar year	Australian fixed interest %	International fixed interest %	Cash %	Inflation (CPI) %
1982	22.57	38.31	15.50	10.87
1983	14.33	14.93	11.93	8.70

1984	12.02	15.15	11.24	2.49
1985	8.07	60.82	14.02	8.31
1986	18.92	29.52	12.38	9.76
1987	18.60	6.29	12.23	7.07
1988	9.39	-10.58	12.88	7.64
1989	14.41	14.59	18.43	7.83
1990	18.24	13.36	16.13	6.85
1991	24.43	20.12	11.20	1.51
1992	10.16	18.24	6.92	0.28
1993	16.58	19.41	5.39	1.95
1994	-6.76	-14.18	5.36	2.55
Annualised return	14.87	17.39	12.79	6.27

Liquidity

Of all the investment classes cash is the most liquid. This means you can get your hands on the money you have invested immediately in the case of a bank deposit, or within 24 hours in the case of a cash management trust. This liquidity is one of cash's great attributes – the money is there when you need it.

While not quite as liquid as having cash in the bank, fixed interest securities are, nevertheless, liquid enough. This is because they are tradeable, primarily through the stock exchange and, in some cases, by selling them back to the issuer.

Under normal circumstances there should be a buyer for any fixed interest security you wish to sell. The exception to this would be if the security was issued by a company whose financial integrity had come into question, in which case finding a buyer could be very difficult. (In the USA these types of securities are called 'junk bonds'.)

Also be aware that the price you get for fixed interest securities if sold before maturity will depend on interest rates at the time of sale, which means you may get less than you paid for them.

Risk

Cash is extremely safe. When you deposit it in a bank, or invest in bank bills and Treasury notes via a cash management trust there is virtually no likelihood of losing any of your money except under the most extreme and bizarre circumstances, such as the failure of the bank or the collapse of the entire financial system. And in keeping with the time-honoured relationship between risk and return, the returns from cash are designed to be the lowest of all investments. That's the price you pay for safety. (Of course cash may not always generate the lowest returns – it can do better than a poorly performing shares, property, or fixed interest sector).

Fixed interest investments normally have a higher risk profile than cash investments and, as a result, are designed to generate higher returns under normal market conditions. However, there are some exceptions and provisos to this generalisation. Arguably, nothing is safer than Commonwealth Government bonds with their government guarantee of repayment. This makes them 'gilt-edged' securities – with the proviso being that you hold them until maturity.

I'll show you how you can lose money on bonds in the next two pages.

Fixed interest securities and variable market value

When you hold bonds, debentures and other fixed interest-bearing investments to maturity you know exactly how much you will receive in interest payments, when you will receive the interest, and you also know you will get your principal back at the end of the term (unless the issuer or the financial system collapses in the meantime). But with many interest-bearing securities it's possible to trade them on the open market before their maturity date. This means they have a 'capital value' or market price, and this capital value fluctuates in line with changing expectations of future interest rates.

The important thing to realise is that the changing capital value of an interest-bearing security is quite separate from its fixed income value, and that the capital value, regardless of whether it has risen or fallen, is *only realised if and when the security is traded*. So, if you choose to hang on to your interest-bearing investment until maturity, the fact that its capital value fluctuates throughout its term is immaterial.

Bear in mind the usual reason individual investors buy bonds, debentures and so on is for the regular, dependable income they provide. They are not normally bought by small investors for their capital growth potential. Usually it is only the big players like banks, insurance companies, funds managers and governments who trade in interest-bearing securities with an eye to making a capital gain and, at this level they are traded in enormous dollar volumes (millions) – well and truly beyond the financial scope of individual investors like you and me.

While you might not have any intention of trading your bonds, it's useful to know how their capital value is arrived at. One day you may need the money that's stored up in them or their value could have increased to the point where, by selling them, you'll realise a tidy profit on their purchase price.

Let's say you bought a two-year bond for $1,000 paying (or 'yielding') an annual interest rate of 12% ($120 p.a.). Now, if interest rates were expected to rise to 14% for the next two years, who then would want to pay $1,000 for your bond yielding only a fixed 12% when they could buy brand new bonds for the same price yielding a fixed 14% ($140 p.a.)? The answer isn't 'no one' – people *will* be prepared to buy your relatively lacklustre bond – *but only at a discount*.

So, what's the bond you paid $1,000 for worth now? Well, its new price needs to be set at a value which will give the new buyer a return *equivalent* to an interest rate yield of 14%. In other words, your bond needs to be discounted to the point where it will make no difference to an investor's return whether he buys your old, lower rate bond at a discount or a new, higher rate bond at the full (face) value. And using 'present value' arithmetic the discounted amount works out to be around $966 (I won't explain how this value is calculated – please just trust me!), representing a capital loss on the $1,000 bond of around $34 or 3.4%.

This valuing system works in reverse, too. Let's say interest rates were expected to fall from 12% to 8% for the next two years. People would now have to pay a premium for your 12% bond because it would be returning more than newly issued bonds rated at only 8%. The new price would be around $1,073 and, at that level, it would give the buyer a return equivalent to 8%. It would also give you a capital gain of about 7.3% on the bond you paid $1,000 for.

Added to this is a further factor, namely, the longer the security has to maturity the more pronounced the change in value as interest rate expectations change. For example, if interest rates were expected to rise, the value of a bond with 10 years to maturity would fall further than one with two years to maturity, and vice versa.

When expected interest rates rose from 12% to 14%, in the example above, the bond with two years to maturity fell in value by 3.4%. However, a bond with ten years to maturity under the same set of circumstances would fall in value by 10.6%. Again, I won't go into the mathematics involved in calculating the size of this fall because it is based on 'present value' calculations and is quite involved. Let a broker do it for you. I am simply illustrating the higher volatility or risk of longer term fixed interest securities compared to shorter term ones.

The process of fixed interest valuing

We can sum up fixed interest valuing like this:

- As expected interest rates rise the capital value (the market price) of a fixed interest security falls, and as expected interest rates fall the value of a fixed interest security rises.
- The longer the term to maturity the greater the rise (or fall) in the value of the security as expected interest rates rise (or fall). (This means securities with longer terms to maturity are more volatile or more risky than those with shorter terms to maturity.)

Now you may be able to better understand why bond markets everywhere suffered big capital losses in 1994. The world was emerging from the early '90s recession and, with growing prosperity, the expectations about future interest rate levels also rose, and quite sharply. Consequently bond values tumbled, particularly longer term bonds, and many investors and financial institutions were caught holding too many of them. This is why so-called 'capital stable' managed funds had such a bad year in 1994 – capital stable funds normally hold around 50% of their assets in fixed interest securities.

Let me just add to this my usual remark – the short-term performance of any asset class can be bad, but *over time*, all the mainstream asset classes have performed well. And interestingly, the bond crash of 1994 was preceded by five years of fabulous returns from the fixed interest sector.

Unfortunately, guess when most smaller investors raced into bonds? Yes, you guessed it, at the end of the 5-year bond 'boom' to see losses on their investments. Many then rushed out of this investment to miss out on the recovery in the first half of 1995! This is typical human behaviour, and a lesson worth remembering.

Buying and selling fixed interest securities

Buying fixed interest securities is pretty straightforward. There are two basic ways to do it. Firstly, you can buy securities direct from the issuer through an application form found in the prospectus, or you can buy already existing securities from another investor via a stockbroker.

Selling is not quite as straightforward. You can sell some fixed interest securities which have not yet matured to another investor on the open market via a stockbroker, some you can sell back to the issuer, some you cannot sell back to the issuer, and some you may have trouble finding any buyer for at all, obliging you to hang on to them until maturity. It's important, therefore, that you understand how tradeable any particular fixed interest security might be before you buy it and this is specific information you can get from a security's issuer, a broker or a financial adviser. In general however, government bonds are more easily tradeable than debentures and, indeed, debentures may not be tradeable at all if the issuing company gets into financial strife.

Note that you will be charged brokerage should you buy or sell securities through a stockbroker. Again, you could simply invest via a fixed interest fund run by a professional manager and you will find more on this in Chapter Fifteen, Managed Funds.

Nominal and effective interest rates and yields

When you see bonds and debentures advertised in the newspapers you will often see the terms 'nominal' and 'effective' interest rates and yields. The nominal interest rate is the simple annual interest rate. It's the amount you would earn if you were paid interest in one lump sum at the end of the year. For example, let's say you invested $20,000 for 12 months at a nominal interest rate of 5%. At the end of the year your nominal return or yield would be $1,000 ($20,000 x 5% = $1,000).

Now, if the interest was paid monthly, and this was then added to the principle for reinvestment, and this process went on for 12 months, at the end of the year you would have earned $1,024 in interest, representing an effective return of 5.12% (The effective return of 5.12% is generated in this case through the compounding of interest, which is where interest is paid upon interest.)

The difference between the effective and nominal returns might seem pretty insignificant here, but with larger sums and more time it can really add up. Just make sure when you invest in a fixed interest product you clarify which type of return you're getting.

Tax

While tax relief can be found in shares through dividend imputation and in property through a wide range of tax deductible costs and depreciation allowances, there is no tax relief to be had with cash or fixed interest investments. All interest payments you receive are classified as income and are taxed at your highest marginal rate.

To show you how significantly this can affect your real investment earnings, let's look at the Towers Perrin/ASX study measuring Australian investment performance by asset class in the 10 years to 28 February 1995. Unlike most studies this has a 'before' and 'after' tax component:

	Before tax	After tax[1]	After tax[2]
	%	%	%
Shares	13.6	14.0	12.3
Property	12.8	11.5	9.8

Fixed Interest	12.8	10.1	6.5
Cash	10.8	8.5	5.1

1) These figures are after tax payable on an annual income of $15,000 p.a. The marginal rate of tax on $15,000 in February 1995 was 21.4%, including Medicare levy.

2) These figures are after tax paid at the highest marginal rate during the survey period, including Medicare levy. Be aware a top marginal tax rate of 60% or more applied during much of the 1980s. The top marginal tax rate in February 1995 was 48.4%, including Medicare levy.
(*Source*: Towers Perrin)

It's clear from these figures that tax is a real problem with fixed interest and cash investments. While the before-tax returns for the four asset classes above are very similar, the after-tax return for shares (at the top marginal tax rate) is 142% greater than the after-tax return for cash and 89% greater than the after-tax return for fixed interest. Before tax shares beat cash by only 26% and bettered fixed interest by only 6%.

Income investments *vs* growth investments

With long-term investment studies normally ranking the gross returns from cash and fixed interest last and second last, and this after-tax study doing the same, you might ask why invest in fixed interest and cash at all?

Well, remember that they do have their place, which is providing relative safety, liquidity, and a *dependable source of income*. Cash and fixed interest also provide good diversification benefits as the asset performance table on page 148 shows. In this period, (1982 to 1994) interest-bearing deposits were the best performers out of all the main asset classes in five of the 13 years.

However, you need to shift your portfolio's mix of assets away from interest-bearing income investments and more towards growth investments of shares and property, both Australian and international, if:
■ liquidity and regular, dependable income are not high priorities

- you are prepared to take a bit more risk than that involved in cash and fixed interest investment
- you're a tax payer
- your focus is more towards longer term capital growth

In the graph below look at the final value of an initial $10,000 investment across the four different asset classes in the 15-year period 1979 to 1995. This dramatically shows how growth-producing investments outperform income-producing investments over the long term.

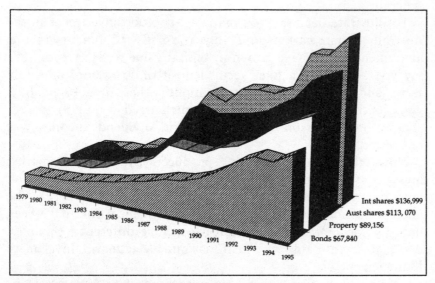

1979 1980 1981 1982 1983 1984 1985 1986 1987 1988 1989 1990 1991 1992 1993 1994 1995

Int shares $136,999
Aust shares $113, 070
Property $89,156
Bonds $67,840

(*Source*: Macquarie Investment Management)

Now, let's compare the performance of bonds and Australian shares over a 62-year period, from 1933 to 1995:
- over a one-year period shares outperformed bonds 56% of the time
- over five-year periods shares outperformed bonds 71% of the time
- over 10-year periods shares outperformed bonds 91% of the time
- over 20-year periods shares outperformed bonds 100% of the time.

Between 1933 and 1995 there were 62 one-year periods, 58

five-year periods, 53 10-year periods and 43 20-year periods.

Finally, while income from a fixed interest term deposit is definitely more reliable on a short-term basis than the dividend income from a sharemarket investment (and may even be higher in some years, such as in 1994), over the longer term the share investment is almost certain to produce greater income. Why? Well, the capital value of a term deposit does not change over time, whereas the capital value of a portfolio of quality shares can increase (and indeed ought to). And, as the capital value of your shareholdings increases, so does the amount of income it generates.

To illustrate, let's say you made a $100,000 investment in the Australian sharemarket on 1 July 1979. By 30 June 1995 this investment would have grown in capital value to $583,090. Let's say you also made a fixed term deposit of $100,000 on 1 July 1979, and rolled it over every 12 months thereafter. By 30 June 1995 its capital value would still be unchanged at only $100,000. (These figures assume *no* interest or dividend income was reinvested.)

Now, the dividend income produced by this sharemarket investment in the financial year 1994-5 would have been $28,265 (and partly tax-free due to dividend imputation), whereas the interest income from the fixed term investment would have been only $5,500 (and fully taxable). It's a huge difference. (*Sources*: ASX, Reserve Bank of Australia and Macquarie Investment Management.)

This all looks like a fairly big put down of 'income assets' at the expense of 'growth assets', particularly shares. Let me make it clear that this is not my intention. What I am trying to show is the strengths and weaknesses of the two broad groupings and where one is more appropriate than the other, depending on your circumstances and goals. Generally speaking, shares and property better serve your need for longer term, tax-effective capital growth leading to a strong future income. Cash and fixed interest, on the other hand, better serve your need for security, liquidity, and a reliable source of income right now. There is probably a valid place in most investors' portfolios for both.

⚬━ Key thoughts

The following list sums up the characteristics of cash and fixed interest securities:

Cash:

- low risk, low return
- income returns fluctuate in line with current market interest rates
- very low likelihood of capital loss
- high liquidity
- open to erosion through inflation
- suitable for short-term investing
- inappropriate for long-term growth
- returns fully taxed.

Fixed interest:

- a suitable investment over a wide range of periods, from relatively short term to long term
- predictable income – returns are fixed until the investment or security matures
- potential for capital gains or losses due to changes in market interest rates if the security is sold before maturity
- less liquid than cash
- generally higher returns than cash
- varying risk profiles, from the safest available investment through to riskier than cash (but less risky than property or shares)
- not suited to long-term growth
- returns fully taxed.

CHAPTER FIFTEEN
Managed Funds

Having read through the preceding sections on property, shares and fixed interest you'll know that each of these asset classes satisfy certain investment objectives, and that your short-, medium- and long-term needs and goals ought to determine what proportion of each you hold in your portfolio.

If long-term capital growth is your goal you should bias or 'weight' your portfolio towards shares and property. If you need regular income and security you should weight your portfolio towards cash and fixed interest. If you want both growth and income then you should have an even spread of investments across all these assets.

So far, so good, but how are you going to do all this? How do you know what proportion of each class you should hold and how will you know which specific investments to select within each class? What about monitoring your investments' progress? Do you have access to all the raw information you'll need to keep up-to-date with the markets and will you be able to make sense of it when you get it anyway? And what about the time involved – how much have you got to spare?

If it all sounds like too much hard work, don't worry. There is an easy way around the difficulties, namely, investing in professionally managed investment funds.

The idea behind managed funds is very simple. You let investment professionals do some or all of the work involved in creating and managing an investment portfolio for you. They charge a fee for this service but, in return, they save you the time and effort involved in selecting stock and monitoring its performance. Theoretically, they should also be able to generate better returns than you can because they're the professionals with their fingers on the pulse. (The theory's good – but it doesn't always hold up in practice.)

Whether managed investments are right for you depends on:
- to what extent you want to control the investment selection process yourself

■ how much you want to be involved in your portfolio's ongoing management.

If you have the confidence and the time to manage your own investments and are reluctant to delegate this responsibility to another party, albeit a professional one, fine – that's a perfectly acceptable way of managing your affairs and one I recommend to many investors, particularly those with some market experience. But for those of you with limited time, limited investment experience, and limited confidence in your ability to pick the right assets, investing through managed funds is a sensible way to go.

Other people would seem to think so too. Managed funds are a very popular investment in many parts of the world and Australians have around $260 billion invested in them, which includes around $190 billion invested in superannuation funds and Approved Deposit Funds.

What are managed funds?

The term 'managed (investment) fund' is a generic one that covers a range of related investment products including balanced funds, listed or unlisted property trusts, pooled superannuation trusts, insurance company savings bonds and some annuities. Although all are structured differently and may have varying taxation treatments, they share basic similarities. Sometimes managed funds are also referred to as 'managed trusts', 'pooled funds', 'investment trusts' or 'unit trusts'.

A managed fund is a vehicle where the investments of a large number of smaller investors are pooled together and managed as one large investment portfolio by a professional investment manager. Managed funds can invest in either shares, cash, property or fixed interest securities, or can invest in some or all of them. They can also invest in these assets directly, or indirectly by investing in them through other managed funds.

Managed funds can specialise in all sorts of assets – whether Australian, international, Asian or from any other region or mix of regions. They can also invest in fish farms, pine plantations and feature films. In fact, the mix and type of assets and ventures you can invest in through a managed fund is limited only by the imagination of those offering them.

Making Money

Investors in a managed fund are effectively part-owners of the assets held by the fund. Earnings generated by the fund's assets can be distributed as income to investors on a regular basis (monthly, quarterly or six monthly) or, alternatively, its earnings can go towards increasing the capital value of the investors' units. This capital appreciation (designated by an increase in unit price) is realised when the units are sold by the investor.

Most managed funds stipulate minimum initial investments in the fund, minimum additional deposits and minimum balances. As a general guide, an average minimum investment would be around $1,000, a minimum additional investment would be around $300, and a minimum balance would be around $500.

Fund managers and the trustees

A fund's investment manager is usually an experienced and reputable investment organisation such as AMP, ANZ Funds Management, BT or Rothschild. (You need to select well but more on this later.) The fund may also have a professional trustee. Both the fund manager and the trustee charge fund investors a fee for their respective services.

Working within defined investment parameters for the fund, the fund manager's job is to invest the pooled monies in a range of assets. The manager has the right and the responsibility to shift the fund's monies in and out of assets as they see fit and as changing market conditions dictate. The manager's objective is to achieve as high a sustainable return on the investors' pooled monies as possible within certain (usually conservative) risk limits.

The trustee's responsibility is to supervise or oversee the management of the fund on behalf of the investors, and ensure the fund manager follows the spirit of the Trust Deed which sets out how the fund's income is to be distributed and, in general terms, where the fund's monies are to be invested. The key details of the Trust Deed are included in any managed fund's prospectus. The trustee does not get involved in the day-to-day management of the fund or select the specific assets that the fund invests in – that is the responsibility of the fund manager.

Put simply, if a managed fund is offered to you with a prospectus, it will have a trustee. Insurance products, such as insurance bonds, do not have a prospectus or a trustee as the financial services industry has two regulators. The Australian Securities Commission (ASC) looks after prospectus products, while the Insurance and Superannuation Commission (ISC) looks after insurance companies. Given an insurance bond or super fund is a managed investment, having two regulators makes little sense, but that's the way it is!

Units

Managed funds are divided up into 'units' of equal value. Like an ordinary share, they give you a part ownership of assets. Although shares and units are technically quite different, the concept is the same and some units – those of 'listed trusts' – are traded on the Australian Stock Exchange.

The number of units issued for sale in some funds is fixed, whereas in others funds new units are always available to anyone who wants to buy them. In general, listed unit trusts are 'closed', meaning the fund has a fixed number of issued units. This number of units can only be increased later by a separate offering of new units taking the form of a rights issue.

Unlisted trusts (those not listed on the Australian Stock Exchange) can be either open or closed. An 'open' unlisted unit trust which wants to continue issuing units to the public simply does so by updating its prospectus every six months or so. Managed funds such as superannuation and insurance or friendly society bonds are nearly always open – you can increase your stakeholding in them by as much as you like at any time.

Valuing units

With the exception of listed trusts' units which are valued (or priced) on the stockmarket, other managed funds value their units (put a price on them) daily or, at least, weekly. The method of valuation must be done strictly in accordance with the rules laid out in the Trust Deed (where one exists). Actually, two values per unit are calculated – a value for buying units and another for selling them.

257

Making Money

The buying price of a unit is determined by taking the current valuation of the fund's total assets, adding a loading to cover purchase costs like stamp duties and brokerage, and then dividing this amount by the number of issued units. The selling price is calculated similarly – by taking the current valuation of the fund's total assets, adding a loading to cover selling costs, and then dividing this amount by the number of units on issue. The difference between the two prices can be as high as 6%, which reflects these costs as well as commissions payable to a licensed adviser.

Let's look at a very simple illustration of how changes in a unit's value affects you. You invest $10,000 in an unlisted managed trust with units selling for $1; this buys you 10,000 units.

Now, remembering the value of units fluctuate in line with the value of the fund's underlying assets, if you later wished to redeem 2,000 of these units and the unit price had risen to $1.10 (because the value of the fund's assets had risen), you'd get back $2,200, representing a profit of 10%.

Liquidity

Managed fund units vary significantly in their liquidity. You can get your money out of cash management funds more or less immediately. Converting your units in an insurance bond to cash may take a few days, and redeeming share trust units may take up to two weeks – which is about the maximum it should take under normal circumstances to cash any type of units. Having said this, real problems with liquidity have occurred with property trusts in the past due to the relative lack of liquidity of their underlying property assets in tough market times.

There are potentially two ways of buying units and two ways of redeeming them. When a managed fund is listed its units can be bought and sold through a stockbroker at a price set by the market, just like shares. The mood of the market will determine just how quickly a buyer or seller is found for a particular fund's units but, under normal circumstances, a transaction should take place almost instantly.

If the managed fund is unlisted you can only buy and redeem units directly from the fund manager. There is no other method of trading units in an unlisted fund, and more to the point, there is no other simple method of cashing them. This is why you need to ensure the fund manager or managers you invest with are reputable and competent and therefore likely to keep their doors open.

Safety

Let me make this clear – the vast majority of mainstream managed funds are managed by competent investment professionals who take their jobs seriously and act in good faith. They are aware of their enormous responsibilities and manage accordingly – in a conservative manner. Fund managers are not cowboys by nature or by training.

A disaster like the collapse of the Estate Mortgage unlisted mortgage trust in 1990 was a rarity. The investors in Estate Mortgage were very unlucky – the probability of everything going off the rails in a mainstream managed fund at the same time is very low. Collapses of this kind can happen but they should remain freak events. However, remember, if everything being said about a particular fund sounds too good to be true, it usually is.

There are thousands of managed funds in which Australians have invested and can invest. The proportion that fail is far less than the proportion of listed companies on the ASX that fizzle out taking their shareholders' funds with them. And the proportion of those who have lost money in managed funds would certainly be nowhere near as great as the proportion of direct property investors who have been burnt by buying the wrong property; paying too much; over-capitalising; buying on a market downturn; losing control of costs; poor rentals; bad tenants or interminable delays with the approval of development plans, and so on.

Having said this, different managed funds have different risk profiles. The ones with the lowest risk of management failure are those mainstream ones managed by established organisations like banks, major insurance companies and reputable financial houses. The funds with the lowest risk of major asset devaluation are those investing in (in increasing order of risk):

- cash
- fixed interest
- property and shares.

259

Following these come more speculative managed investments in areas like feature films, horticultural plantations and even racehorses. Usually these are ventures being established from scratch, where the sale of investment units is the way the promoter raises the necessary capital to get the scheme off the ground.

The failure rate of non-mainstream managed investments like these is high and I generally advise you against them. They are unacceptably risky because:

- *all* new ventures are riskier than established ones
- the fund manager is often the operator of the business venture and may lack the requisite managerial and operational skill and experience
- the underlying area of investment is often very risky by nature, where even having the best managerial and operational team in the world is no guarantee of financial success, such as in movie making.

What to look for in managed funds

From a safety – and performance – point of view you should look for a managed fund with these characteristics:

- investments in diversified, mainstream asset classes
- management by an established and reputable financial organisation, preferably recommended to you by a credible third party
- a track record of sustained investment performance
- a high level of security
- a clear, comprehensive and easily understood prospectus detailing all authorised investments of the fund.

If you don't feel confident about judging these things for yourself, don't hesitate to seek the assistance of an accountant or a financial adviser. Another option is to contact the Investment Funds Association of Australia on (02) 262 3599.

The pros of managed funds

- Managed funds take the hard work out of selecting which assets to invest in and having to monitor their performance. They are, therefore, a very easy and time effective means of investing.
- When you invest in a managed fund you effectively employ a

team of investment professionals whose combined experience, knowledge of the markets, investment research capability and exposure to the latest information would be hard to match as an independent investor.

■ Investing in managed funds provides a level of diversification well beyond the reach of most independent investors. A single investment, for instance, in a share fund ('share trust' or 'equity trust') could make you an indirect shareholder in hundreds of companies in which the fund has invested.

■ Some investments can only be purchased as expensive single items (such as city buildings) or in minimum sized parcels with high ticket prices beyond the reach of small, independent investors. However, these investments are not beyond the reach of many managed funds with their large, pooled financial resources.

■ Managed funds can be an effective and relatively painless savings vehicle. Many have a direct debit facility where say, $300 per month or quarter can be automatically transferred into the fund direct from your cheque or savings account.

■ Managed funds can be a regular source of income. Certain funds provide a monthly, quarterly or half-yearly income distribution to unit-holders which reflects the level of income earned by the fund's investments. Unit-holders can take the regular distributions in cash or have them reinvested as additional units in the fund.

The cons of managed funds

■ Managed funds charge fees. Normally there are entry, exit and ongoing management fees. Some funds charge no entry fee but have a higher than average exit fee, or vice versa. Some funds only charge an exit fee if you leave the fund within a certain time of first investing. Some funds have no entry and/or exit fees so long as you maintain your investment for a minimum number of years. It varies tremendously and the level of fees is an area of competition between the funds.

As a guide, entry fees range from 0% to 5% of the value of your deposit. Ongoing annual fees, primarily going to the fund manager and trustee (often referred to as the Management

Expense Ratio or MER) range from 0.5% to 3% of the value of your balance, and exit fees usually range from 0% to 2% of the value of your withdrawal.

- Managed funds dilute the degree of control you have over your asset selection. For instance, when you invest in say, a share fund, you invest in the shares of companies that the manager, not you, selects.
- Of course, managed funds (like any other investment) can generate losses. In this case the capital value of your investment declines.
- Should the fund experience a major devaluation of its underlying assets, or the manager is thought to be or found to be dishonest, a 'run' may be made on it. This is where a number of investors try to bail out and cash their units at the same time. If the fund does not have ample liquid reserves to cope with this rush of redemptions it could be faced with the prospect of a major asset fire-sale in order to raise the necessary cash. This would probably trigger the trustee to step in and 'freeze' the fund, temporarily preventing any further redemptions until the fund could be put in order.

Let me illustrate what can happen. During the 1980s when property prices were booming, unlisted property trusts had no difficulty meeting unit redemptions – the coffers were full of cash because the inflow of investor capital far outweighed the demand for redemptions. This also meant the trusts could offer short redemption times. However, by 1990, when the commercial property market had collapsed and we were having 'the recession we had to have', the demand for unit redemptions increased as investors bailed out of what were, then, very poorly performing investments. The result was that some (unlisted) property trusts found they didn't have enough cash to meet the redemption demand.

To prevent fire-sales of property into a depressed market (in an attempt to raise the necessary cash to meet the level of redemptions) many property trusts indefinitely suspended redemptions altogether or substantially increased the redemption period to 12 months or more.

If fire-sales had been conducted to meet redemption demand, the value of the trusts' units would have been decimated, severely hurting those who were prepared to hang onto their units and ride the recession. It also would have caused the overall property market to decline even further and there would have been enormous realised losses all round.

The approval to extend unit redemption times, or suspend redemptions altogether, would normally be granted to the trustee by investors at an extraordinary general meeting. However, the trustee generally has the right to impose changes to redemption policy in order to protect the assets of the fund. Under severe circumstances of mismanagement and/or lack of integrity the fund manager and/or trustee can be sacked and replaced.

For the record, I should point out that institutions as safe as banks can, like managed funds, also experience mass investor desertion and a consequent run on funds – however, such events are very rare.

Types of managed funds

Let's take a look at some of the forms that managed investment funds can take.

Share or 'equity' trusts

You can select from a range of unit share trusts. Some, for instance, invest solely in:
- shares on the Australian stockmarket
- shares on major international stockmarkets
- shares in companies in 'emerging' or developing world markets
- shares in gold, mining or energy companies.

You can also buy into share trusts that invest in a mix of these areas, or that say, only invest in fully franked Australian shares for particularly tax-effective returns. There is probably a share trust for almost every conceivable market and sector mix, each with its own different risk and return profile.

Property trusts

Assets owned by property trusts can include major city office blocks, suburban shopping centres, industrial properties, hotels and residential holdings and can be unlisted or listed on the Australian Stock Exchange.

Many property trusts offer investors a choice between income units and growth units. Holders of income units receive most of the rentals from the properties invested in by the fund, and growth unit holders are allocated most of the capital growth generated by the fund's properties. You can also invest in split property trusts where you hold some income units and some growth units in a ratio that best suits your needs.

Income derived from property trusts may be tax free or tax reduced in the hands of investors due to the passed-on benefits of property depreciation and investment allowances.

Fixed interest or bond funds

Bond funds – not surprisingly – invest in bonds. Most bond funds hold a mix of Commonwealth Government bonds, State Government bonds and semi-government bonds. They may also hold some cash and bank bills.

You can invest in funds which only hold international bonds, or invest in funds holding a mix of Australian and overseas bonds for greater diversity. Investing in bonds through a pooled bond fund also gives you access to the big ticket bonds which are beyond the financial reach of most independent investors.

Cash management trusts

Cash management trusts invest in bank bills, treasury notes, cash, and other money market instruments guaranteed or supported by governments, banks or companies. Cash management trusts or funds are very safe and very liquid and some may even have cheque book facilities. These trusts normally earn more interest than bank deposits and a minimum balance generally needs to be maintained.

Diversified funds

All managed funds are diversified to the extent that very few of them simply hold one asset. A share trust, for instance, may invest in the shares of literally hundreds of companies.

You can invest in managed funds that don't just hold a diversity of assets in *one* asset class (such as all international shares or all Australian fixed interest), but rather, hold a diversity of assets across *a number* of asset classes. These funds are commonly known as 'diversified funds'.

Diversified funds can be broken down into three broad categories generally known as 'capital stable', 'balanced' and 'growth' funds. Exactly how these three terms are defined is open to wide interpretation within the managed funds industry, but basically:

- *capital stable funds* invest primarily in a range of cash and fixed interest securities, with a small percentage of share and property assets usually thrown in too. They're designed for investors looking for a regular and reasonably secure source of income over a relatively short term, say one to three years minimum. These funds are characterised by: low risk; low capital growth; strong income; short-term horizon; and few, if any, tax breaks.
- *balanced funds* are for investors looking for medium to longer term capital growth accompanied by some regular income during the term of the investment. An appropriate investment in a balanced fund would be three to five years minimum. These funds should have a ratio in the vicinity of 75% growth assets (shares and property) to 25% income assets (cash and fixed interest). Balanced funds can be characterised by: low to moderate risk; moderate to good capital growth; low income; medium-term horizon; and reasonable tax breaks (due to share dividend imputation and property allowances or depreciation).
- *growth funds* have a higher proportion of growth assets and a lower proportion of income assets than balanced funds. They are characterised by: moderate to higher risk; strong capital growth; low income; long-term horizon (five years minimum); and better tax breaks than balanced funds.

To give you a better idea of how capital stable, balanced and growth funds can be structured, look at the pie charts. This is the actual asset allocation used in IPAC's Strategic Investment Trusts' diversified funds.

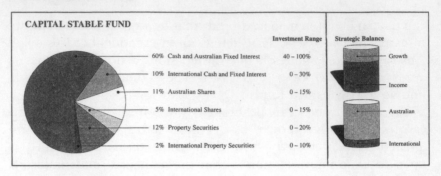

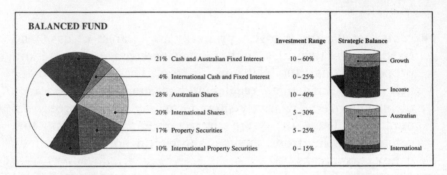

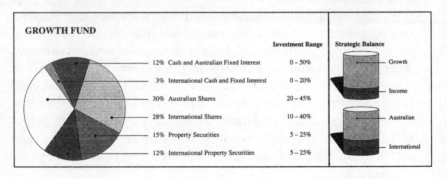

The actual level of investment (falling somewhere within the 'investment range') in each of the asset classes in each of the three funds is designed to produce the highest probability of achieving the risk and return objectives considered appropriate (by IPAC) for each fund.

The table below shows the risk and return relationship for these funds.

	Capital stable	Balanced	Growth
Minimum term	1 Year	3 Years	5 Years
Income/growth assets	70%/30%	25%/75%	15%/85%
Range of expected returns in every 2 years out of 3	1.8%–12.4%	0.2%–20.0%	0.3%–22.1%
Likelihood of negative return	1 year in 12	1 year in 7	1 year in 6

(*Source*: IPAC Securities)

Remember, the particular asset allocation used in any diversified fund will depend on the risk and return objectives of the manager. For example, the objective of IPAC's capital stable fund is to provide a significantly better return than the average return from cash funds over rolling or consecutive three-year periods, with a low probability of a loss over any 12-month period. IPAC research indicates its present capital stable asset allocation should produce the highest probability of achieving this objective. Specifically, with this asset allocation this fund should be expected to outperform a cash fund by around 2% p.a. on average, and to provide a positive return in 91.5% of one-year periods.

The objectives other managers have for their capital stable funds (or any other managed fund for that matter) may be quite different to IPAC's and this will be reflected in them having different asset allocations. Just make sure you find out before you invest what the objectives of any given fund are, and that these objectives match yours.

Mortgage funds

Mortgage funds invest primarily in residential, industrial and commercial property mortgages. For added security and liquidity they may also have large holdings in cash and fixed interest investments.

267

Making Money

Mortgage funds are designed to provide the investor with a dependable income flow which will fluctuate in line with interest rate movements. The security of an investment in mortgage funds is largely underpinned by property values.

Insurance bonds

Insurance bonds are managed investment products offered by life insurance companies and are nothing like the fixed interest securities offered by governments and semi-government authorities. (In fact, labelling these investments 'bonds' is really a misnomer.)

Another source of confusion arises from insurance bonds being officially classified as 'life insurance policies'. They bear no resemblance to classic term or whole-of-life insurance policies at all, or any other form of insurance for that matter. The only conceivable life insurance component in these investments is simply that if the investor, referred to as the 'life insured' dies before the 'bond' matures, the investment is closed, valued (based on the total of all contributions and investment earnings to that point), and then paid out to a beneficiary. There is no typical insurance component in the sense that if you die while insured your beneficiaries will be paid a set amount determined by a premium.

So, insurance bonds are managed funds which may be balanced, may invest primarily in growth assets, may invest primarily in industrial shares, may invest primarily in fixed interest securities or may be capital guaranteed (where the asset allocation is so conservative that the unit value is guaranteed never to fall in value). The choice of underlying assets is wide, and, as with all managed funds, the higher the ratio of growth to income assets in the fund, the greater the potential long-term returns – but the higher the risk of an occasional loss.

With insurance bonds, the earnings generated by the fund are accumulated or reinvested back into the fund – there are no regular earnings distributions – causing the capital value of the fund's units to grow over time. These investments are designed to be held for 10 years at which point they 'mature' and your (hopefully much more valuable) units are paid out in cash. The important thing about these 'bonds' is their treatment of tax. Tax on an insurance bond's investment earnings is paid by the manager

268

each year and after 10 years all the bond's earnings are tax-free in your hands, regardless of your marginal tax rate.

Now, if you wish to close the investment and get your hands on the cash before the 10 years have expired, you can. Your investment earnings, however, will be taxed at your highest marginal rate but you are entitled to a 39% tax rebate against these (taxed) earnings. This applies at any time throughout the 10 years but this doesn't mean a short-term investment in these funds is a good idea. It means that if your marginal tax rate is less than 39% you will get all the tax back that's been paid on these earnings. Indeed, if your tax rate is less than 39%, the rebate will actually generate a tax credit (being the difference between your tax rate and the 39% tax rate) which can help reduce the amount of tax you are obliged to pay on your other assessable income.

With insurance bonds you can make just one investment and wait 10 years for it to mature, or, you can add more money to it annually. However, there are stipulations about when and how much you can add which, if you ignore, can reduce the long-term tax effectiveness of the investment. I won't go into the specific details here but it's important that you understand them. They will be spelt out in the bond's promotional literature.

Friendly society bonds

These are basically the same as insurance company bonds in that they are managed funds designed to be held for 10 years at which point they mature tax-free in your hands. They simply happen to be offered by friendly societies rather than insurance companies.

If you cash a friendly society bond before it matures you will be taxed at your highest marginal rate on its earnings, however, like insurance bonds, you also get a tax rebate which could actually mean you get all the paid tax back. You may even end up with a tax credit to be offset against other assessable income.

The size of this tax rebate is effectively equivalent to the rate of tax that has already been paid on your investment by the friendly society. In the 1980s this rate was 20%. On 1 July 1994 it rose to 30%, then rose to 33% on 1 July 1995. It will remain at 33% until at least 30 June 1997 (when the rate may change, depending on the findings of a government review underway at the time of writing.)

Performance of managed funds

The managed funds industry is mushrooming. In 1994 there were 1300 and in early 1995 there were about 1900 managed funds for Australian investors to chose from. With so many funds, and with none of them holding exactly the same mix of assets, it's inevitable that a large range of returns will be generated – far too varied to be detailed here.

In general, managed funds comprised primarily of one asset class such as all shares, all property or all bonds, perform similarly to the main market indices for those asset classes. Real, after-inflation, long-term average performance figures for the main asset classes are looked at quite closely in Chapter Eleven, but to recap, they have traditionally been:

Australian cash	0% to 1% p.a.
International cash	0% to 2% p.a.
Australian fixed interest	0% to 3% p.a.
International fixed interest	1% to 2% p.a.
Residential property	1% to 3% p.a.
Australian property securities	3% to 5% p.a.
International property securities	3% to 7% p.a.
Australian shares	5% to 8% p.a.
International shares	6% to 9% p.a.

Hopefully, the single sector fund you've invested in will do better than the average market returns for that asset class, though there is no guarantee of this. Indeed, it is a great and understandable source of consternation when, say, your fund investing primarily in Australian industrial shares underperforms the All Ordinaries Index. It raises the obvious, ugly question of why are you paying a team of investment professionals if they can't do better than the market average, or worse still, if they can't do as well? My answer to this is:

- make sure you clearly understand what the fund manager's risk and return objectives are (they may take a very conservative or a very high-risk line)
- determine whether these objectives suit yours or not – ideally you should make this decision *before* you invest
- if these objectives don't really suit you, consider leaving the fund (but be aware of the costs involved in doing so, such as

exit fees, the loss of benefits, potential capital gains tax, and the cost of entering into other managed funds or other investments)

- if you are satisfied with the fund's objectives but it fails to achieve them over the longer term I suggest you take your business elsewhere, despite the costs.

Now, let's say your money was not in single sector funds but in diversified funds. Because of the sheer variety of domestic and international assets they can invest in, in whatever proportion they wish, and at whatever risk level they wish, diversified funds generate a very wide range of returns. That said, in the five years to the end of 1994, *average* annual returns for diversified capital stable funds were in the order of 4% to 6% after tax and fees; balanced funds averaged in the order of 6% to 8% after tax and fees; growth funds were in the order of 8% to 10% after tax and fees. (*Source*: IPAC Securities)

As a comparison to these five-year average returns ANZ Funds Management's Investment Monitor quoted managed funds returning 13.37% p.a. after tax in the 10 years to 31 December 1994. This figure was derived from a range of diversified, balanced, pooled superannuation funds investing across the main asset classes.

Over the long term you should expect real average annual returns of 2% to 4% for diversified capital stable funds, 3% to 5% for balanced funds and 5% to 8% for growth funds. These returns are after fees, tax and inflation.

The spectre of 1994

Any discussion about fund performance is bound to raise the year 1994. As those of you holding managed fund investments will remember (and this includes anyone with superannuation) it was a shocker. It was a year in which most asset classes generated a loss. Indeed, in 1994 only direct property and cash produced positive returns (9.2% and 5.36% respectively).

It saw 10-year bonds take an absolute pounding as interest rates rose, saw the sharemarket drift relentlessly downwards, and saw property securities languish below the waterline. It really was unusual for so many asset classes to generate losses in the one year, and it was this very range of losses that caused diversified funds (in particular) to turn in such poor results. They averaged (after fees):

- -4% to -6% for capital stable funds
- -6% to -8% for balanced funds
- -10% to -11% for growth funds.

IPAC's research has concluded that a year like 1994, where almost every sector goes wrong, has a probability of occurring only once every 25 years. Certainly no comparable year has occurred since IPAC began keeping records. In this light, I advise you not to let it sour your view of investments in general and of diversified funds in particular. Remember, all investments have their good and bad years – it's the nature of the game. So let's just keep 1994 where it belongs – in perspective, and behind us – and take heart that such a year is unlikely to recur again for some time (although one day it will).

Buying into retail and wholesale funds

There are two kinds of managed funds you can invest in – retail and wholesale. In essence, retail funds are those you effectively buy into direct 'off the shelf' or, in the case of listed trusts, through the stockmarket. Wholesale funds are those you can only invest in indirectly through another managed fund.

Retail funds are the ones you see advertised in the press and on television. You can buy into them for a minimum, say, of $1,000, by approaching the fund manager direct or by going through a financial adviser, securities dealer or stockbroker.

On listed units purchased through the ASX you pay brokerage on top of the units' trading price as you would for shares, and at the same brokerage rates as for shares. With unlisted products you will pay the same entry fee (anything from 0% to 5%) regardless of who you buy through, be it the fund manager or a financial adviser. However, if you deal through a financial adviser who charges on an hourly fee-for-service basis you'll probably find he'll rebate some, if not all, of the entry commission fee to you. Also, so-called 'discount brokers' will rebate up to 95% of the entry commission fee, however, they provide no investment advice as the trade-off.

Discount brokers advertise regularly in the business section of the main newspapers and are an inexpensive way to buy into a managed fund if you know exactly what you want and what you're doing. If you don't, I recommend you deal through (an advice-giving) financial adviser. I also recommend you shop around for a financial adviser who does rebate managed fund entry commission fees.

Wholesale managed funds have lower fees attached to them but are essentially unavailable to the average independent investor for direct investment. The reason is simply the minimum investment parcel may be as high as $50,000, $100,000 or more. Specialty funds such as emerging markets' funds are often structured this way.

You can only access wholesale funds indirectly by investing in a retail managed fund which in turn invests in them (many managed funds invest very heavily in other managed funds), or through a 'mastertrust'.

Mastertrusts

A mastertrust (or 'masterfund') is an investment fund that invests in *other* investment funds but may also invest directly in assets such as shares, cash and bonds. When you invest through a mastertrust your money goes into a selection of its own funds which, in turn, invest primarily in other managed funds – many of which are wholesale funds beyond the financial reach of most independent investors. It sounds confusing but it's not really.

There are two types of mastertrusts – 'fund-of-funds' and 'discretionary'. The major difference between the two is the amount of choice you have in selecting which assets the mastertrust invests in.

With a fund-of-funds mastertrust you (together with an adviser) select the appropriate broad asset area or areas to invest in (in terms of risk *vs* return, income *vs* growth). You might decide, for instance, to invest in the mastertrust's Australian bond fund (for income) as well as its international shares fund (for long-term capital growth). These two funds will, in turn, invest in a wide range of assets appropriate to their investment parameters.

Now, while you have been free to select the mastertrust's funds

273

which invest in certain *broad* asset areas, you are *not* free to select the *specific* assets (mostly other wholesale managed funds) that these funds invest in. The choice of specific assets is left to the mastertrust's manager who over time may increase the funds' exposure to some investments and withdraw from others as changing market conditions and performances dictate.

In a discretionary mastertrust you *can* select the managed funds from a menu. Discretionary mastertrusts are targeted at those investors who prefer a greater degree of control over their own asset selection.

The cost of investing in managed funds through a mastertrust structure is around the same as investing at a direct level through a retail fund manager. So why deal through a mastertrust? Well, firstly, you normally get a wider choice of managed funds to invest in than through a single retail fund manager. Secondly, mastertrusts claim to provide a generally higher level of client service than that provided by most retail managed funds. This service takes the form of periodic meetings with an adviser to monitor your investments and adjust them if necessary (most mastertrusts allow you to switch between their own funds at no charge). More importantly perhaps, this service also takes the form of the provision of regular reports detailing where your money has been placed, how your investments have performed, what tax (if any) has been paid on them, and a tax statement, all being very useful and convenient documents.

Managed funds are convenient

Managed funds are a modern way of achieving your investment goals. I do own some direct property and direct shares, but I use managed funds for the majority of my Australian investments, all my international investments and specialised Australian investments such as in small companies.

It really is an issue of attitude and personality. For me, they are the way to go. I'm busy and I know that most of my investment returns will come from the asset mix that I select. In other words, it is more important to me whether I have 30% or 50% of my investment in shares rather than whether I buy BHP or Coles Myer.

Ο—ᴨ Key thought

Work out your risk tolerance first. Then plan your investment mix. Finally choose between direct investment (buying your own investments) or indirect investment (using managed funds).

Unless you have the time and the knowledge, I think managed funds will work the best for you.

CHAPTER SIXTEEN

Your Own Business

You may be wondering why I've put this chapter at the end of the investment chapters. Well, it's done quite deliberately, because there is another debate we need to consider – is owning a business the best way to make money?

This was definitely a belief that I held in my early twenties – that to create real wealth you had to own a business. I'm not sure if I was influenced by my family, friends or things I read, but I always wanted to start a business of my own.

Now I know I was wrong about this. Wealth can be created by anyone who consistently spends less than they earn and who invests their savings on a regular basis. In fact, the more I look at business failure statistics, the more I wonder about the wisdom of starting any business, despite certainly understanding why people want to.

Once again, we get back to risk and return. Starting or buying a business is risky, but if the business goes well the rewards are high. The business in which I am a shareholder (my four partners and I each own 20% of the business) was started by us in 1984. We put in $20,000 each and rented a very small, serviced office. Today, we employ well over 100 staff in our Australian and New Zealand offices and, by any measure, IPAC Securities has been a great success.

Funnily enough the 'academic' theory about starting a business is correct. You do need a vision of what you want your business to be and a well-formulated business plan. You must control your cash flow and, in the good years, you must leave money in the company to build up its strength. I feel fortunate that we took the risk in 1984 to quit our quite well paid jobs, because today business ownership makes me proud, gives me an unbeatable sense of job security and the benefits of controlling my own destiny.

How quickly, though, we forget the reality of starting a business from scratch. In my case, this meant earning next to nothing for five years, working outrageous hours – my partners and I used to laugh about our 35 hours of work. Thirty-five hours on Monday, Tuesday and part of Wednesday; another 35 hours on the other part of Wednesday, Thursday and Friday; and just to top things up, working on Saturday as well. Sometimes we didn't work on Sunday, holidays were a few days off at Christmas and, as for sick leave, well, we just couldn't afford to get sick!

If you do want to create significant wealth, building a successful business is certainly one way to get there. Look at people in the '500 most wealthy' lists. Some inherit the money, but most create it by building a business.

Few small businesses will ever grow into a BHP or a Lend Lease and not too many will ever be worth a lot of money, but running a business has benefits beyond purely the financial side. This really struck me when I was sitting on Avoca Beach (about one hour north of Sydney). While my kids and some friends were paddling around on a hired aqua bike, I started chatting to the owner of the aqua bike business who was originally from Sydney. He explained that the business was no world beater but it was pretty good and, living on a beautiful lagoon, next to a beach, hiring boats to generally pleasant tourists was somewhat better than working in a factory in Sydney's industrial suburbs. He has a point. For him, his business provides lifestyle and a reasonable cash flow. He may have earned more working in Sydney but tinkering with boats on Avoca lagoon seems much better.

For every success story like this, though, I know of dozens of failures. Buying or setting up a business for lifestyle is a dangerous thing – you may act on emotion, not logic. If you do plan to start up or buy a business for whatever reason, please be careful.

Look, there's no denying owning a business sounds good, and, assuming it works, it is. However, as I found, you'll probably end up working an awful lot harder for a lot longer than in the job you leave and for the short term at least, not earning as much.

You'll also miss out on the benefits that full-time employees are entitled to and often take for granted, such as: employer-funded super; worker's compensation cover; paid sick leave; four weeks paid annual leave; holiday loadings; long service leave; and maternity (or paternity) leave. You may also have to forgo other goodies which include: discounted goods and services; the full use of a company car; an expense account; paid telephone expenses;

low interest loans; employer funded further education; study leave; holiday expenses; annual bonuses; share options; and the support of a union or industry association. In other words, when you work for yourself there's no safety net – you're on your own.

Don't let me scare the wits out of you, however. While self-employment is not all beer and skittles, the great thing about it is the freedom it gives you to run your own race which I believe outweighs the negatives.

Clearly, I'm not the only one who feels this. Many people are already involved in, or are moving to self-employment, as indicated by recent small business data. In NSW for instance, in 1994 there were 257,000 small businesses which made up 97% of all enterprises in the state and accounted for 50% of non-agricultural private sector employment. (*Source*: NSW Office of Small Business). (Note that a small business is defined by the ABS as having 20 employees or less, or 100 employees or less if in manufacturing.)

ABS data shows that between 1986 and 1992 there was a 10% increase in the number of private sector jobs in small firms. This was the strongest growth of any sized industry sector during the period, and it's in this sector that most self-employed persons are found. The average sized small firm in the survey comprised only 4 persons. (*Source: Where the jobs are 1993*, Institute of Applied Economic and Social Research, University of Melbourne).

Business hazards

What the growth figures for small business don't indicate is the low survival rate, estimated by the NSW Office of Small Business to be only 60% in the first three years of operation. Other estimations put the survival rate even lower.

There are countless factors that can bring a business undone, including: managerial inexperience or ineptitude; inadequate financing; excessive debt; low sales; high costs; high interest rates; market collapse; lack of market knowledge; overwhelming competition; poor product, service or quality; economic downturn; excessive optimism; production inefficiencies; poor planning; poor forecasting and sheer bad luck.

Think the proposed business through

By doing your homework very thoroughly, though, which involves seeking considerable professional advice and preparing a proper business plan, you will address and resolve many of these hazards before you even pass 'Go'.

You may even discover during the research phase that your proposed venture is unlikely to work. As disappointing as this may be, it is infinitely preferable to go back to the drawing board at this point rather than be forced to bail out one or two years into the business. You'd be amazed how many businesses have been set up simply off the back of an idea without any dispassionate research being done. Of course this ad hoc approach can work, sometimes spectacularly, but mostly it doesn't.

O━┳ Key thought

A great sounding business idea does not necessarily translate into a viable business.

Consider the following points because they will help you focus on the issues critical to business success, (and note, this list is far from complete):

- What is the main reason why you want to become self-employed, either by buying an existing business or by setting one up from scratch? If it is basically to 'buy' yourself a job, think again. Working for someone else who is established is generally more secure, easier, and initially better paid than working for yourself. (It is also less exciting!)
- Do you have experience or training in the type of business you wish to establish or buy? If you don't, I strongly recommend you spend some time in paid employment in the area you want to enter in order to discover more about the industry's dynamics and performance, and whether it is really for you. This experience will also help reveal how much sheer physical energy and drive you will need to succeed in the industry.
- What are your people skills like? Success in this vital area calls for integrity, wisdom, leadership, authority, humour, patience,

intelligence, tact, empathy, fairness, and an ability to listen just as much as an ability to get your message across clearly. Do you believe you can judge people well, and could you recognise merit in a potential employee? How would you motivate staff, win their respect and trust, get the best performance from them, and retain them?

- What about the people closest and most important to you – your family? Their support is vital and can't be taken for granted. You must give first priority to this relationship and be sure that it is sound before you embark on self-employment because there are times it will be strained by the demands of the business.
- Do you have the financial know-how to run a business? Do you know what the costs of setting up your proposed business would be? Could you construct a cash flow analysis and predict when the business would generate profits? Having adequate capital to tide you over the early lean times is critical. Where will the money come from? From personal savings, from an equity partnership, or from a bank loan? If a loan, how and when do you intend to pay it back?
- Do you understand marketing? Do you know what competition you will be up against? Can your product or service evolve to meet changing market conditions?

Resolving lack of business experience

At this point you may be thinking self-employment sounds nigh on impossible. You may be wondering how anyone who had never been in business for themselves could possibly know half these things before taking the plunge. Well, the answer to that is many newcomers to self-employment actually don't know much about these things. That is why so many do just jump in – they don't know what they don't know, and if they did they might not do it!

Those newcomers to business who do succeed have to climb a very steep learning curve and invariably need and seek plenty of assistance from outside specialists in key areas like finance, sales, marketing and production. This is an eminently sensible and recommended way of dealing with a lack of business knowledge and experience.

Having said that, I recommend to anyone contemplating self-employment to seek as much information as possible about it yourself before making any commitments. Seriously consider doing a general business course or a specialist course covering the area you wish to work in. At the very least, read extensively on the general principles of running a business, read about your target business or industry, talk to any people running their own businesses, especially in the area you are interested in. At a later point, if you proceed with the business, join the trade association covering your industry to meet other people in it and to keep informed of industry trends and developments.

Both the Commonwealth and state governments have departments that provide excellent support services for those wishing to establish and for those already in their own businesses. Between them they publish numerous pamphlets and booklets on business basics and specific businesses, provide advice, run courses, and help in the preparation of business plans. Much of this is free or very inexpensive and I strongly recommend you take advantage of it.

Organisations to contact

- The Commonwealth Department of Industry, Science and Technology publishes a number of useful booklets of interest to small business and provides information and referrals. The Department is also the base for the National Executive of Small Business Agencies which can give you the phone number and address of the Government Small Business Agency in your state.

  I strongly recommend you contact your state's Small Business Agency. They offer an excellent service including referrals or free advice, publications and small business courses. Phone (06) 276 1000 for the appropriate contacts in your state.
- The Australian Bureau of Statistics is a mine of information for anyone in business with facts and figures on a mind-boggling array of relevant topics.

  The ABS also provides a very useful survey called a '4-Site Report' which is a detailed demographic profile of any specified area within Australia. Costing $195, the reports provide information on the people who live in a specified area, including what they do, what they earn and what language they speak. These reports also provide information on existing businesses and local industry, including the number and type of business in the specified area. This is a very useful marketing tool for targeting the right location for your business – which can be a critical factor in success. The ABS has offices in every capital city.

- The Australian Chamber of Manufacturers and local Chambers of Commerce also provide useful information and assistance to those in business.
- The University of New England publishes 'Business Profiles' providing hard facts on a very wide range of businesses including newsagencies, service stations, hotels-motels, fashion retailing, hardware retailing, delicatessens and restaurants. The Profiles cost $49 each and can be obtained from the Financial Management Research Centre, UNE, Armidale, NSW, 2351.

⚷ Key thought

It's impossible to be an expert in every area of business – no one is. Successful business people are those who have a good overall understanding of the business and know what's needed to make it work. They have no hesitation using specialists to take care of those areas that they can't attend to themselves. They are also willing to broaden their own business education.

The business plan

Preparing a business plan is an enormously important exercise in getting set for self-employment, or, for expanding or diversifying your existing business.

What is a business plan? Well, it is a written statement of all the research and thinking you have done in developing your business idea. It is a blueprint for your business, or, if you prefer, a road map. It is also the vital document you'll need to raise capital for the business, be it a loan or equity partnership.

Of course, like many plans or maps you may find a better

method or route once you get underway, however, you do need to be pointed in the right direction to start with. And this is where the business plan, or more to the point, the act of preparing the business plan is invaluable.

Preparing a business plan will oblige you to address all the factors necessary for running a viable business. This entails finding answers for questions that include (but are not limited to) the following:

- What business and what industry are you in?
- What is your product and who is your market?
- How big is that market?
- Is the market growing?
- What share of the market do you aim for?
- What will the market look like in five years?
- How will you capture that market?
- Where does your business fit into the industry in which you will be operating?
- Who are your competitors?
- What are their strengths and weaknesses? How will you deal with these?
- What will set your business apart from the competitors?
- What is your 'competitive advantage'?
- How will you overcome any perceived weaknesses your business may have and what are the major threats to it and to the industry? How will you overcome these?
- How will you capitalise on the perceived strengths and opportunities your business and industry has?
- What level of sales do you expect to generate?
- What level of sales do you need to break even?
- What will your establishment costs be?
- What will your ongoing costs be?
- When do you expect to go into profit, and what size will the profit be?
- How will the business be funded, and how much capital is needed?
- How and when will any debt be repaid?
- What production techniques will you use?
- Is production obsolescence a likelihood?
- What staff will you need?
- How will you train them?

- What will be the structure of the business? (that is, sole trader, partnership, company or discretionary trust)
- What will happen to the business in the event you become sick or leave?
- How much of the business will you own?
- What will be the return for any investors in the business?
- How and when will they receive their return?

If you have got this far and the business still looks viable, then there's a very good chance it will be! But, if in the process of putting the plan together you discover a fatal flaw in the business idea, you can thank your lucky stars the discovery happened now rather than after opening your doors. And just bear in mind that successful entrepreneurs (a word badly tarnished in the 1980s and one that deserves to have its positive associations restored) have normally discarded numerous business ideas before hitting on one that stands up to the rigorous analysis that producing a business plan calls for.

Putting together a business plan takes a lot of effort and you will very likely need assistance in doing it, particularly in the financial section which calls for cash flow and profit projections. An accountant can help you with these. But try to do as much of the work yourself as possible. This will help you understand what running a business involves in general, and in particular what *your* business will need to succeed.

Buying or establishing a business

So, let's assume you decide your business idea is viable and you are determined to forge ahead with it. Let's also assume your idea is fairly straightforward and that it could be realised either by establishing a new venture from scratch or by buying a similar existing business and adapting it to your particular vision. Now, because both routes have pros and cons, trying to decide whether to buy or establish a business can be a very difficult decision indeed.

Buying a business

Buying a business addresses the problems associated with establishing a business from scratch, namely, tight cash flows and low income during the business's formative period, inordinately long hours, and a high probability of ultimate failure. However, buying a business is no Sunday picnic. It's a serious exercise that requires time, effort, money and great care. Don't lose sight of the fact that there are plenty of sharks out there hawking a swag of awful, fundamentally flawed businesses to budding, bright-eyed entre-preneurs ready to be ripped-off.

Regardless of how appealing a business may look, and how keen you may be to get your hands on it, don't rush into it. Take plenty of time to confirm the details you are given and look for those details which may have been withheld. It is better to miss the opportunity than to act without adequate research.

The three golden rules to follow when buying a business:

- Never decide on the purchase without seeking the advice of someone you trust who has relevant business experience.
- Never commit to the purchase until the figures have been examined by an accountant.
- Never sign the contract until a solicitor has advised you.

If pressure is applied to you to bypass any of these measures, walk away from the deal.

There are specific areas of any business you (and your account-ant) must investigate before deciding whether it's worth buying or not, which are:

- Sales. Is the sales level seasonal or related to a business cycle? Are sales increasing, decreasing or static? Will the business still be able to buy from existing suppliers? Does a new product or new competitor exist – or is imminent – which will pose a threat to the business? Is the level of stock adequate and up-to-date? Also check if a high proportion of sales are dependent on one or two big customers – vulnerability exists where this is the case.
- Costs. Are all costs shown in the records? Will you have the same level of expenses? What effect will increased or decreased sales have on your costs? And take into account your extra cost of interest on the borrowings used to buy the business.
- Profits. Check that records – balance sheets, profit and loss statements, purchases and sales records – have been accurately

kept, and go back for as many years as possible to determine the profit trend. Determine if gross profit levels are in keeping with industry norms, and consider the likely effect on profits from a rising or decreasing level of sales. At this point you can determine whether the existing and likely future profit levels warrant the risk of investment in the business.

■ Assets. Make sure you know exactly what it is you are buying. Get a list of all equipment, fixtures, fittings and check them off, and also check the depreciation schedule on these items. Is the equipment in good order, and current? Have a licensed valuer check the equipment for you if you are in doubt.

■ The seller. Determine why the seller is selling. If he is not being fully co-operative, be wary. Ask to be given a trial period in the business for a few weeks to verify its operations and takings.

If everything about the business at this stage is still looking positive then ask yourself this key question – is it really you? Can you see yourself doing the work and serving the customers the business has? Does the business fit your temperament, interests and personality, and is it really an appropriate vehicle for your business concept?

You will also need to consider whether you could build the business up into something bigger and better than at present; whether the business's clientele and staff will remain loyal to the business under your ownership; whether the asking price of the business and particularly the price put on its 'goodwill' is fair, realistic and good value; and, whether you can really afford to buy it.

Assuming that, after dealing with all these issues, you still wish to proceed with the purchase, when drafting the purchase agreement ensure all assets and liabilities are specified, and include escape clauses should the performance of the business during the trial period not be as claimed. You will definitely need to engage the services of a solicitor at this point.

> 🔑 **Key thought**
> Buying a business is a major move requiring great care and consideration. You will need to cover many angles and seek much advice before choosing that path to self-employment.

Establishing a business

Choosing to establish your own business from scratch will save you the hazards of buying a business that could prove unsatisfactory, unworkable, inappropriate, intolerable or a rip-off. It will also save you what could be a very large purchase price. But establishing your own business will present you with a different set of challenges including summoning up and sustaining the sheer drive and energy required to establish a business; having enough capital to fund the establishment costs of the business and supplement the lean cash flows of the early months (or years); finding the right location; developing the right product for the market; getting your pricing right and your promotion right; finding the right staff; and, building up a loyal clientele.

As a general rule, the more innovative your business concept is, the more appropriate it is to set up a business from scratch. There is little point buying an existing business which needs major adaptation to your vision. But, if you can buy a going, viable business at a fair price that suits your business concept closely, well, it does seem a sensible approach to self-employment.

Franchising

Franchising is another option for anyone seeking self-employment, and is probably more suited to those with limited or no business experience who feel uncomfortable going out into business entirely on their own. Being a franchisee means forgoing some of the freedom of traditional self-employment – that is, the ability to completely call your own shots – in that a franchisee must operate within a strict framework laid down by the franchisor. But in return, the franchisee has the support of a 'big brother' providing a (*supposedly*) proven business formula.

Another attraction of franchising, which is particularly popular in Australia, is that the failure rate for franchises is taken to be significantly less than for those in non-franchised self-employment. The most visible franchises include McDonald's, Pizza Hut, and KFC but many other successful franchises exist in areas as diverse as carpet cleaning, building maintenance, hardware, automotive products and services, lawn-mowing, restaurants, greeting cards and real estate.

The main advantages of franchising for a franchisee are the recourse to assistance and expertise provided by the franchisor, co-operative marketing, bulk buying, and the use of an established concept, name and image. Capable franchisors may also save a failing franchisee by arranging a sale, or by purchasing it themselves, thereby avoiding a major loss by the franchisee and damage to the system's public image.

The purchase price of franchises varies dramatically, from a low of around $20,000 to in excess of $1 million. Clearly, the higher the profile of the franchise and the greater its commercial success, the higher the price. However, obtaining bank finance to buy into an established franchise network is much easier than getting finance for a totally new business.

A major cost in running a franchise is the ongoing payment of royalties and service fees to the franchisor, which need to be clearly understood at the outset by a potential franchisee. Other costs and problems can arise with tied supplies and restricted product ranges, or if the ability or integrity of the franchisor is brought into question.

When assessing a potential franchise, consider the following:

- The franchise's track record and plans for the future.
- The managerial ability and background of key franchise personnel.
- The reasons why the franchisor is seeking expansion.
- Is the franchise operating in a growth industry?
- How co-operative and 'open' are key franchise personnel, particularly in relation to financial records?
- Scrutinise the projected figures of the territory you are being offered. Are they realistic, and do the returns justify your effort and risk?

- What is the demand in the marketplace for the franchise's product?
- How are other franchisees in the network faring? (Get feedback direct from them, not via the franchisor.)
- Fully understand the up front and/or ongoing fees involved.
- What sort of training is provided for franchisees, and how thorough and binding is the franchise operations manual?
- How long does the franchise agreement last for, and where do you stand at the end of it?

Whatever you do don't sign any franchise agreement before you have your solicitor and your accountant check it closely. For more information on franchising I recommend you contact your state government's Small Business Agency.

Working from home

Many people who go into business for themselves choose to work from home, at least to start with. The advantages of doing so include: no commuting; working in a pleasant, familiar environment; no travelling costs; being close to family; no need to wear a suit; no need to pay rent on an office or shop; flexible hours; and the ability to claim a proportion of household costs such as mortgage, rent, home insurance, electricity, rates, maintenance and telephone as tax deductions – because a part your home is now your 'place of business'.

Against this you have to consider the disadvantages which include: a feeling of isolation from the 'real' world of business; limitations placed on running the business by local council ordinances; the need to exercise self discipline in starting and stopping work at sensible times; household distractions such as the needs of a crying baby; limited space; the vaguely unprofessional image of a home-based business; and the potential application of capital gains tax where your home has been used to gain assessable income.

Where it is possible to conduct your business from home, in most circumstances it would make sense to at least start there. It's certainly cheaper than setting up an office or shop somewhere else and, so long as you are not too distracted by other things going on in the house, it can be a lot of fun.

I would recommend anyone contemplating setting up a business at home to talk to as many people as possible who have already done it and also to get hold of a copy of *Home-based business – guidelines for setting up a small business at home*, published by the Australian Government Publishing Service and costing around $5. It's available from the AGPS and from Small Business Agencies in each state.

Business structure

Once you have decided to go into business for yourself one of the more important matters you will have to address is choosing the right business structure.

The most appropriate selection is likely to be one of the three most common small business structures, which are:

- sole trader
- partnership
- proprietary limited company.

Different taxation treatments, different personal financial liabilities, and different establishment and ongoing compliance costs apply to each. The differences are important, however, their significance, couched in legalistic and accounting concepts and terminology, may not be at all apparent, particularly to newcomers to business. Therefore, I strongly recommend you seek professional advice from an accountant and/or a solicitor in making this choice.

That said, these are the most important characteristics of each structure:

Sole trader

You are classified as a sole trader if you conduct a business alone, without a partner – and this definition applies even if you have employees.

The advantages of operating as a sole trader are:

- you are entirely your own boss
- all business profits are yours
- any business losses can be offset against any other present and future income you may have

- it's the cheapest and simplest business structure to establish and maintain
- statutory reporting requirements are less than for other structures.

The disadvantages of operating as a sole trader are:
- you are fully liable for your business's debts. This means your other assets, including your home, can be put at risk
- you pay tax on profits at your marginal tax rate – which may be higher than the company tax rate
- you are fully exposed to provisional tax
- you are solely responsible for the business, which can make taking leave from it difficult.

Partnership

A partnership exists where two or more persons share ownership of a business. Partnerships have the following benefits:
- the responsibility for running the business is shared
- there is a greater potential input of time, talent and money into the business than under sole trading
- taxation benefits may arise if business partners are members of the same family
- partners may be able to take time off from the business without causing undue disruption to it.

Partnerships have the following disadvantages:
- you may be stuck with a bad choice of partners and/or an inadequate partnership agreement
- the retirement or the death of a partner can cause severe capital problems
- liability is unlimited, and it is shared jointly between all partners, even where the liability has arisen from the actions of only one partner (under certain conditions limited liability partnerships can be structured, however).

Proprietary limited company

This is a structure better suited to a more developed business than the average self-employing, start-up venture.

Making Money

A minimum of two persons is required to form a proprietary limited company – because by law a company requires at least two directors, and the ownership of a company lies in the hands of its shareholders.

The advantages of a company structure are:
- the liabilities of a company's shareholders are limited. Shareholders' personal assets cannot be seized to pay company debts
- a company pays tax on profits at the company tax rate (36%), which may be lower than its shareholders' marginal personal tax rates
- shareholders receiving company dividends may obtain tax credits through the company imputation tax system (see 'Dividend imputation' in Chapter Thirteen).

The disadvantages of a company structure are:
- establishment costs are relatively high, normally being between $1,000 and $1,500
- annual fees for preparing accounts and reports are also relatively high, normally being around $1,000
- company losses cannot be offset against shareholders' other income
- greater reporting obligations – to the Tax Office (and to the Australian Securities Commission) – apply to companies than to other business structures
- company directors have strict obligations under company law.

Now, be aware that this list of advantages and disadvantages is far from complete and also note that other business structures exist, such as discretionary trusts and co-operatives. I therefore repeat my recommendation that you must seek professional advice – from your solicitor, accountant or state government Small Business Agency – in making the involved and important choice of most suitable business structure.

And to all of those of you who do make the leap into self-employment – work hard and good luck!

CHAPTER SEVENTEEN
Retirement

In the early 1980s, I started doing the occasional talkback radio segment on Sydney radio station 2BL. Retirement was something many callers wanted to discuss. It seems to me that at that time, people planned to retire at 65. Most financial planning was fairly haphazard and tended to take place after the date of retirement.

Today, barely a decade later, we have changed. People plan to retire much earlier and better health means we are living much longer. It has now got to the point where some Australians will spend more time in retirement than in the workforce.

This makes retirement a serious business. A 55-year-old male will live on average for another 21.6 years. A 55-year-old female, 26.6 years. On top of this, our material expectations for retirement have changed. We do not expect to sit at home minding the grandchildren. We hope to be healthy, active and doing those things that we did not have time to do in our working lives such as travel – and in my case, more golf!

Now the bad news here is that an active lifestyle tends to cost more. Travel can be done cost effectively, but it still requires money. You will want to run a car, be able to eat out occasionally, and not worry about the cost of a meal with friends.

Don't get me wrong. You also don't need to have a fortune to live well. In fact, most Australians don't have a fortune to retire on and today, around 78% of 65-year-olds are on an age pension.

A retired couple I know live on a public service pension, plus an investment portfolio of around $150,000. They own a modest but comfortable home. Sure, they are well set up, but not dissimilar to many other retired Australians. Between the income from their portfolio and the pension, their annual income is around $25,000. Due to a few of the simple tax strategies like income splitting and franked dividends that I talk about in Chapter Ten, they pay very little tax – which helps a lot.

What fascinates me about this couple is that they lead a truly global lifestyle. In retirement they decided they wanted to learn the languages and culture of other countries, so they live four months a year in Australia, four months a year in Italy and the other four months in France – all on $25,000 a year. Sounds ridiculous doesn't it? But they are able to do it, and this is how:

- They rent their home for at least six of the eight months they are away. Yes, this is a hassle because they have to store all their personal possessions with their family, but they rent it out fully furnished for a bit below market rent and do very careful reference checks on the people moving in.
- The eight months they are away each year, in France and Italy, they take a small apartment well away from the tourist haunts and they find that they can live more cheaply than in Australia. Remember, they can now speak both languages fluently so they mix and eat with the locals at local, not tourist, prices.
- They book and pay for their airfares well in advance to get the best deals.

Even if the last thing you want to do is live overseas, my point is that your retirement should be, and can be a time when you reap the rewards of your working life.

Okay, so these days you need to start planning your retirement early. If you are young or middle-aged, just follow my 10 key steps in the opening chapter. If you are getting close to retirement, you need to start thinking about a number of other things as well.

- What are your plans for your retirement. What do you want to do and what will it cost?
- Will your assets provide the income you need to live comfortably? Can you top this up with a pension?
- Where will you live? How will this impact on your lifestyle and your family?
- What are your views on estate planning? Does your will reflect your wishes?
- Investment will become very important. Do you need an adviser, and if so how do you choose one?
- What plan do you have to ensure your retirement is a stimulating time in your life?

My best tip on retirement is, of course, to plan early. For younger readers of this book, or those of you who can influence younger readers, please do think about it and encourage people to plan for retirement from the day they start work. An 18-year-old only needs to put aside about 12% of her salary into super and she can retire on 75% of her final salary, linked to inflation. This would provide quite a decent standard of living. At 35 years of age the requisite contribution increases to around 30%, at 45 around 49% and at 55 you'd need to save 108% of your salary to retire on 75% of your final salary. Now I know some good savers, but putting aside 108% of your salary would not be easy!

Please don't feel depressed if you are retired or close to retirement and have saved very little. After all, the importance of saving has only been made clear in the last few years. Fortunately, we do have a reasonable age pension system. I know it isn't generous, but it does provide a minimum standard of living and is certainly better than nothing. Let's take a look at it.

Who is entitled to the age pension?

The most basic condition of eligibility for the age pension is that you are aged 65 years or over, regardless of whether you are male or female. It wasn't always like this. Prior to 1 July 1995 the age at which women became eligible for the pension was 60 but in these egalitarian times that's all been swept aside. (Raising the female eligibility age also will save the government a lot of money!)

For those women presently nearing the eligibility age, the rise from 60 to 65 is being gradually phased in, as the table below illustrates:

Women born between	Eligible for age pension at age
1/7/35 and 31/12/36	60.5
1/1/37 and 30/6/38	61
1/7/38 and 31/12/39	61.5
1/1/40 and 30/6/41	62
1/7/41 and 31/12/42	62.5
1/1/43 and 30/6/44	63
1/7/44 and 31/12/45	63.5
1/1/46 and 30/6/47	64
1/7/47 and 31/12/48	64.5
1/1/49 and later	65

In addition to having to be 65 (except as specified directly above) to satisfy the basic eligibility for the age pension you must also have been an Australian resident for at least 10 years, with at least five of these years comprising one period of residency. You must be resident in Australia on the day the claim is lodged and on the day it becomes payable.

Your application for the age pension is also subject to an annual means test comprising an appraisal of your assets and income. More on this below, but for now, let's look at what the age pension actually provides.

Age pension benefits

(Note that all the figures below are accurate at 30 June 1995 and that they are revised half yearly in line with changes to the Consumer Price Index).

If you are on the full age pension (and it is possible to be on a part age pension, dependent on the income and assets test) you are entitled to:

- $326.10 per fortnight for a single person
- $544.00 per fortnight for a (married or de facto) couple ($272 each).

Age pensioners renting a private home to live in may also be entitled to receive rent assistance in addition to the age pension, to a maximum of:

- $66.20 per fortnight for a couple (combined)
- $70.20 per fortnight for a single person.

A pharmaceutical benefit of either $5.60 or $2.60 per fortnight is also available to some pensioners. In addition to these monies, as an age pensioner you receive a Pensioner Concession Card which entitles you to a wide range of other benefits. These include either free or concessional access to dental care, eye care, hearing services, pharmaceutical prescriptions, council and water rates, gas and electricity charges, driver's licences, car registration, insurance premiums, adult education courses, entertainment, public transport and interstate rail fares.

All age pensioners are entitled to these benefits, regardless of the size of their pension. Even someone on a part age pension of only $1 will qualify.

Means testing

As I've noted above, any entitlement to the age pension is also subject to means testing, and this is done by separate valuations of both your assets and of your income. The size of the age pension you will be entitled to is based on whichever of the two valuations produces the lower rate of benefits.

The assets test

To June 1995 the total value of the assets you were permitted to hold under the assets test in order to qualify for the age pension were:

Family situation	For full pension*	For part pension
For homeowners		
Single	up to $115,000	less than $225,500
Couple (combined)	up to $163,500	less than $347,000
For non-homeowners		
Single	up to $197,000	less than $307,500
Couple (combined)	up to $245,000	less than $429,000

* For every $1,000 worth of assets above these amounts the pension reduces by $3 per fortnight.

The income test

In order to qualify for the age pension under the income test, to 30 June 1995 you were permitted to earn the following amounts, per fortnight:

Family situation	For full pension†	For part pension‡
Single	up to $90 ($2340 p.a.)	less than $725.60 ($18,865.60 p.a.)
Couple (combined)	up to $156 ($4,056 p.a.)	less than $1,254.40 ($32,614.40 p.a.)

Limits are more generous if dependant children are involved. Being retired is *not* an official prerequisite for age pension eligibility.

† For every dollar of income per fortnight over these limits the pension reduces by 50 cents for singles and by 25 cents (each) for couples.

‡ These limits may be higher if rent assistance is also paid with the pension.

Now, your assets and income are valued by the Department of Social Security (DSS) in an idiosyncratic way. They are not valued the same way as they are by the Australian Tax Office for tax purposes.

The income test and 'deeming'

Under the income test, 'income' includes normal things such as salaries and wages, rent, interest and dividends. But there's more. There's also the income that's 'deemed' to be have been earned from a wide range of financial investments including shares, managed funds, insurance bonds, bank deposits and fixed interest securities.

The concept of deeming was introduced in March 1991 in response to pensioners putting large sums of money into low or zero-interest savings accounts. They were doing this to keep their incomes low in order to qualify for the full pension. To discourage this the government decreed that these low-return investments were 'earning' more interest than they actually were, based on a prescribed interest rate known as the deeming rate. The key point about these deemed, theoretical investment 'earnings' is that they counted as 'income' for the purposes of the income test, whether or not the investments actually produced any real or comparable income at all.

The idea behind deeming was firstly, to cajole pensioners into putting their money into higher yielding investments than say, bank savings accounts – after all, if you are going to be deemed to be earning higher theoretical returns and having your pension entitlement reduced as a result of it, you may as well try to earn those higher returns in reality. Secondly, deeming was designed to reduce the drain on the public purse – through overall pensioner income levels rising and overall eligibility for the age pension consequently falling.

On its introduction the deeming rate was 10%, dropping to 8% in June 1991. In 1994 it was 4%, moving to 5% on 1 July 1995. (The deeming rate was and is supposed to reflect current interest rates and realistic market returns.)

Now, the deeming concept wasn't only applied to low interest savings accounts. A variation of it was and is used to determine the income produced from a wide range of other financial investments including unit trusts, insurance bonds and deferred annuities.

The overall return that these financial investments were deemed to be generating was calculated from the pensioner's applicable portfolio performance over the 12 months prior to the annual pension assessment. But the calculated rate of return on the portfolio may have no longer been a true reflection of the actual current performance of the portfolio (which could have fallen), or of the composition of the pensioner's current portfolio (which could have changed) at the time of assessment.

Most importantly, the assessment ignored the fact that the return on the pensioner's portfolio over the previous year may have been entirely attributable to capital growth and not to income. Yet, for the purposes of the income test this capital growth or gain was deemed to be *income* – even where the capital gain was unrealised!

Clearly, this method of assessment made life unreasonably hard for many pensioners who took a reduction in their age pension entitlement without receiving any actual increase in real income to compensate for it.

By 1995 the deeming system had all become horribly convoluted (much more so than outlined here) and, particularly in the case of shares and managed growth investments, horribly unfair. This was partly addressed in the May 1995 Federal Budget. The system was overhauled, and while now being far from perfect, has been made fairer and much simpler, with the proposed changes (at the time of writing) taking effect from 1 July 1996.

These proposed changes will see a uniform deeming rate applied to most types of financial investments including managed funds, shares, friendly society and insurance bonds, bank accounts and fixed interest securities. Also, unrealised capital gains on these investments will no longer be treated as income in determining pension eligibility.

From 1 July 1996 the DSS will apply a deeming rate to the total value of the pensioner's financial investments to work out assessable income for the pension. A deeming rate of 5% of income earnings will apply to the first $30,000 worth of (most) financial investments for single pensioners and for the first $50,000 worth of (most) financial investments for couples. Above these thresholds, the deeming rate will be 7%. Actual performance of the investments will not be taken into account, whether higher or lower.

To illustrate this, a single pensioner with $100,000 worth of managed share funds will be deemed to be generating $6,400 annual income for the purposes of the income test, calculated thus:

$30,000 x 5% = $1,500
$70,000 x 7% = $4,900
Total deemed income $6,400   ($246.15 per fortnight)

Personal assets like the family home, car, furniture, stamp collection, life insurance policies and investment properties are excluded from the new deeming rules. Additionally, income stream products like allocated pensions, immediate or allocated annuities and superannuation pensions are also excluded from the new deeming rules and will continue to be assessed under their own rules.

Under the proposed parameters the DSS claims the new deeming rules mean pensioners will get a full pension under the income test where their only income is from financial investments worth less than $42,000 for singles or $72,000 for couples (but bear in mind pensioners have to satisfy the assets test too).

The assets test and 'deprivation'

Under the assets test, if you own the home in which you live it is excluded from the calculations, as is superannuation – until it is actually paid out. Things that aren't excluded include shares, bonds, investment property, managed funds and the present surrender value of any life insurance policies.

All assessable assets, also including items like cars and furniture, are valued at their present market value, not the price you paid for them. Additionally, if there is a loan outstanding against an asset, its value is taken to be its present market value less the amount of the debt.

Now, if the thought crosses your mind of giving away some of your assets ('depriving' yourself of them) to say, your family or a charity in order to qualify for the age pension under the assets test, think again. This is because the DSS may treat these gifted assets as still being in your possession and earning income.

Like the rules applying to the income deemed to be earned on certain financial investments, the rules applying to 'deprivation' or 'gifting' are also proposed to change on 1 July 1996. Therefore, for reasons of brevity we will only consider the rules proposed to take effect then.

From 1 July 1996, it is proposed you will be able to give away assets up to the value of $10,000 in any 12-month period without affecting your entitlement to the age pension under the means test.

However, if you give away assets worth more than $10,000 in any 12-month period, the value of the gifted assets in excess of $10,000 will be added on to the value of your other financial investments and will be subject to evaluation under the deeming regulations.

For example, if you gave away assets worth $100,000 in one year, $90,000 of this would be treated as still being in your possession. This $90,000 would then be deemed to be earning annual income at the rate of 5% on the first $30,000 (on the first $50,000 for couples) and at 7% p.a. on the remainder.

In other words, by gifting your assets you can reduce or eliminate your entitlement to the age pension by falling foul of the income test under its deeming provisions. Any gifted assets subject to this treatment will be considered to be in your possession for five years and will be accounted for in every annual means test reassessment for five years following the gifting.

Making Money

Applying for the age pension

Unlike the way your entitlement for the age pension is determined, applying for it is reasonably straightforward. Simply phone or visit the nearest Department of Social Security office to obtain the appropriate forms. These are quite detailed and require a description of your asset and income position, and may need to be accompanied by supporting documentation.

The DSS has a Financial Information Service, and a FIS officer will help you with your application if you require it. Alternatively, your accountant can assist you. The DSS's Financial Information Service will also help you with any enquiries about your eligibility for the age pension and how your assets, your income and your investments affect it. This service is free and I recommend you make full use of it.

Okay, so that's broadly how the age pension works. The thing that most surprises many people I know, is that you can still get a part pension if you are a married couple earning $32,614 and have $347,000 in assets apart from your home. So, if you qualify, apply for it. You theoretically paid for your pension with your taxes (if past governments didn't save to pay for the pension they promised you, then it's not really your problem) and, in retirement, every dollar helps. The fringe benefits, too, are valuable.

Retirement villages

Another big issue to consider is the most suitable place to live in retirement. What do you do when everyday activities – simple things like cooking, cleaning, gardening or climbing stairs – become too much like hard work? What if your health is not 100% and you need easy access to good medical attention? What if you have lost a lifelong partner and are feeling lonely and even a little unsafe?

Well, a growing number of elderly people are hoping the answers to these and similar questions are found by moving into a retirement village. And, if you pick a good one and you're of a suitable temperament, moving into a village may well be the right thing to do. However, from an investment point of view it's likely not to be.

So what is a retirement village? Well for starters, it's *not* a nursing home (which is for the elderly who need regular medical care and who can't properly look after themselves), *nor* is it one of those Dickensian horrors that used to be called 'old men's' or 'old women's' homes, bleak institutions full of old people with nowhere else to go.

A retirement village is a self-contained community for people aged 55 and over. A typical village will have a combination of residences or styles of accommodation for both singles and couples, ranging from independent units with all mod con's and kitchens, to serviced units, to those with a nursing home facility and/or special accommodation for the infirm on site or nearby. Retirement villages provide communal areas for socialising, and may also provide communal dining for those for those who don't wish to cook or who don't have the facilities for doing so.

Typically, retirement villages range from around 20 units to more than 500. They can be very pleasantly set out amidst attractive grounds which might feature bowling greens or tennis courts and the swankiest of them can resemble holiday resorts.

A single person or couple moving into a retirement village can expect to receive at least as much care and support as they would living in their own homes or possibly even with their families. Much of this support comes from being part of a community of people at a similar stage in life with similar outlooks and interests.

Of course the very idea of living in a retirement village fills some people with dread. Many elderly people enjoy the diversity of the larger community – with different age groups and types – and couldn't be dragged off kicking and screaming to a retirement village, no matter how good they may be.

O─ Key thought

Retirement village living must suit your temperament. To fit in happily you need to be quite social and content in a very homogenous environment.

Making Money

Villages are generally poor investments

In most cases buying into a retirement village is a poor investment decision – in one form or another it could be a drain on your funds and/or on the size of your estate. (Of course this won't bother those who are able to afford the costs and who are not interested in leaving behind a large estate anyway.)

Now, whether moving into a retirement village will in real terms cost you (or your estate) a lot, or, whether you end up making a small capital gain on the sale of your unit when you move out – to a hostel, a nursing home, or a grave – depends to a large extent on the type of tenure or 'occupancy right' you have. You may have strata title ownership, you may own it under company title, or you may possess it under a licence or under leasehold.

What profit or loss you or your estate finally do make out of your 'investment' in a retirement village also depends on any special provisions or restrictions the village owners or operators place on your occupancy rights, and these will be stipulated in the contract you sign before taking possession. Make sure you understand them – and for this you will definitely need the help of a solicitor – because retirement village contracts are very complex and very lengthy, commonly running to around 100 pages. Don't even think of signing before you have sought professional legal advice on the contract's meaning and implications.

Your tenure

Let's look at the four main occupancy rights that retirement villages operate under, and which are so important in determining the price you pay on entering and the amount you receive on leaving one.

Strata title

When you buy an ordinary property under strata title you are entitled to sell the property to whoever you like, for whatever you like, whenever you like. This, however, may not be the case with the strata title of a retirement village unit – they can come with restrictive clauses attached.

304

For example, you may only be able to sell the unit to someone 55 or over who is going to live in it, and you will probably be required to sell it if you want to leave the village. In some retirement village strata title contracts it's stipulated the unit must be sold back to the village if the owner moves out or dies, at a price determined by a formula specified in the contract. Alternatively, the owner may be entitled to sell the unit on the open market but will have to pay the developer a 'deferred management fee' (more on this below) and/or a share of the capital gain on the sale.

And, believe it or not, strata title is considered the least restrictive of the available forms of retirement village tenure and consequently strata village units cost more than any other type.

Leasehold

An increasingly common form of occupancy right is leasehold, generally being a 99 or 199 year transferable lease. Under this arrangement you have no ownership rights over the unit – that remains with the village developer. Your lease simply allows you to occupy your unit and to use the village facilities.

When you enter into a lease you pay the developer a 'lease price' which covers the cost of the unit and a proportion of the communal facilities. When you leave, the developer pays you back the original lease price minus a specified percentage, plus a proportion of the unit's capital appreciation (if any).

Leasehold is cheaper than strata title because it is less secure and more restrictive. Your lease, for instance, may not permit you to sub-let your unit to someone else if you intend to vacate it for some time – to take an overseas trip, for example.

Licence

Another form of tenure (similar to leasehold) is a licence agreement under which you usually pay a fairly large, non-returnable entrance fee – possibly up to 25% of the unit's value – as well as making a compulsory interest-free 'loan' to the village owner for an indefinite period. In return for this you are entitled to live in the village and use its facilities.

When you leave a village under this form of tenure the 'loan' is repaid (minus any deferred management fee) with any capital appreciation on the unit going to the village owner.

The advantage of licence agreements is that they tend to give you cheaper access to village life than under say, strata title, but there are trade-offs, particularly in the area of security. For example, under a licence agreement you can be evicted (subject to compliance with the relevant Residential Tenancy Acts and Retirement Village Acts) and, in the event of the owners selling the village or going into liquidation, you have no guaranteed tenancy rights. This is because the licence is with the original owners only.

Under licence tenure there is also no provision for the residents to have any say in the running of the village – which can lead to serious discontent. Licence arrangements are fairly common in (but not isolated to) villages run by non-profit organisations such as churches and charity groups.

Company title

If you purchase a unit under a company title, you effectively buy shares in the company that owns the village and this entitles you to live there. Company title is a fairly uncommon and unpopular form of tenure due to its perceived disadvantages. The main one is that you usually can't sell your unit to whoever you like – instead you are obliged to sell your 'shares' (meaning your unit) back to the company – and it controls the sale.

The company's board of directors make the main decisions relating to the village and also appoint the village managers. If the residents have any problems with the board they have to deal with them as any shareholders would – via a general meeting. The shareholders should have a representative director on the board, but they could be out-voted by directors representing the interests of the village developers, its management company, investors, and so on.

Because of the restrictions placed on the sale of units and the potential for difficulty in resolving problems which can arise between residents and the board, company title units are normally cheaper than comparable strata title units.

Fees and charges

The cost of buying into a retirement village can vary tremendously depending on the calibre of the village, the type of accommodation and the occupancy rights. You generally pay a lump sum to get into a village and then you're up for a range of regular fees which pay for the services and facilities on offer.

In Sydney in early 1995, you could buy into a retirement village for anywhere between $90,000 and around $350,000, with an average two-bedroom unit costing about $240,000. At the time there were around 150 retirement villages in the greater Sydney area. (*Source: Sydney Morning Herald*, 1 February 1995).

On top of the buy-in price you will have a weekly, fortnightly or monthly service or maintenance fee. This is designed to cover regular village expenses like staff salaries, cleaning, grounds maintenance and so on. The service fee varies depending on the size of your unit and how independent you are. For instance, if you are looking after yourself in a small self-care unit the service fee can be as low as $25 per week. If you are in a large serviced unit it can be as high as $250 per week.

If your tenure is under strata title you will also have body corporate levies as well as the usual overheads of council rates, water and electricity. It's also wise to check out the village sinking fund requirements. This is an annual fee paid by each resident towards the long-term maintenance of the village.

In addition to these fees some villages also charge a '*deferred management fee*'. This is a charge that builds up over the term of your tenure, due when you quit the village. It is invariably deducted from the sale price and can be very hefty indeed, usually calculated as a percentage of either the selling price or the purchase price multiplied by the number of years you have lived in the unit. The practice of charging deferred management fees has been widely criticised and is gradually being phased out.

Selling

Leaving your unit and wanting to sell it can cause some of the greatest friction between you and the village owners or operators. Not only could you be presented with the deferred management fee on selling, but you are likely to find the village will retain all or part of the capital gain that your unit has accrued.

You may also find that there are restrictions on the method of selling your unit. In many cases only the village is entitled to handle the sale and this includes setting the price. Now, if the village will only accept top dollar for the unit this can effectively condemn it to staying on the open market for ages. In the meantime, however, you are still being levied service fees and other charges even if you have already moved out. (If you have died your estate will be paying these fees.) It can all get very ugly indeed. My recommendation is not to move into a village where this method of selling is practised.

Do your homework well

All these restrictions and charges can make the idea of moving into a retirement village sound quite frightening but it isn't my intention to put you off the idea. I am just trying to draw your attention to some of the areas that can cause problems and which need investigating before you buy into any village.

Just make sure you never to buy into a village sight unseen (yes, it has been done!) Make a proper inspection, not only noting the available facilities but also noting proximity to outside amenities such as shops, transport, medical centres, clubs, sporting facilities, restaurants, cinemas, libraries, churches etc. Also ask the management about village policies on things like pets, noise, long-term visitors, parking, conducting a business from your unit, alcohol on the premises, the right to continue residence if your health deteriorates, who caries insurance on the buildings and contents, how complaints are dealt with, residents' rights, how policies are arrived at, and the rights of management to change the rules.

In addition, talk to existing residents to get their overall impressions of living in the village, to find out if there are any quirky restrictions that may impact on your enjoyment of village life, and to find out what they think about the management and/or the owners.

Legislation

Retirement villages have sprung up like topsy in recent years and operate in a semi-regulated environment. All states except Tasmania do have Retirement Village Acts, but these pertain more to matters of tenure and the way villages are run, rather than to the financial aspects of village living.

In an effort to protect you from rashly entering into a retirement village contract, the laws in some states stipulate that prospective residents must be given certain key information 21 days before signing a contract. This is to give you time to digest it and investigate further. There would normally be a three-day cooling-off period as well if you wished to pull out of the contract, though you may incur some charges in doing so.

It's a lifestyle decision

You should not try to use investment criteria to determine whether or not to buy into a retirement village. The overriding consideration should be a question of lifestyle.

Put very simply, retirement villages are not good investments for residents. If you want a good return on your money put it into the sharemarket or buy an investment property instead. Private retirement villages are designed to make a decent return for their developers, not for their residents.

The village exists to offer a service to its customers (the residents) for which the customers are obliged to pay – and there is nothing abnormal or wrong with that so long as the price is fair and all conditions are understood and agreed to. Just treat it as a bonus if you manage to leave a retirement village with a small profit – but certainly don't expect it. The most important consideration about whether to move into a retirement village depends on whether you think you will be happy living there.

And also think, before you sign on the dotted line, that if you are looking at paying weekly service fees of say $250 in a serviced retirement village unit, you might just be happier staying at home and paying someone to come in and cook and clean for you for a similar, probably smaller sum.

Making Money

For further information

Working out whether you should move into a retirement village or not, and then trying to find the right one are major decisions. It's likely you'll require some assistance so a good starting point is the Commonwealth Department of Human Services and Health which has a section dealing with residential living requirements for older people. The phone numbers are:

NSW	1800 048 998
VIC	1800 133 374
WA	1800 198 008
QLD	1800 177 099
NORTH QLD	1800 019 030
SA	1800 188 098
TAS	1800 005 119
NT	1800 019 122
ACT	1800 020 102

For more specific information about retirement villages, you can contact:

Retirement Village Residents Association (Inc)
PO Box 1127
Dee Why NSW 2099

WARVRA
Villa 48, Parklands Villas
510 Marmion St
Booragoon WA 6154

ARQRV (Inc)
Unit 5, Sunnybank Green
239 McCullough Rd
Sunnybank Qld 4109

SARVRA
Unit 22
120 States Rd
Morphett Vale SA 5162

The Retirement Village Residents Association in NSW publishes a very useful booklet entitled *Guidelines for People Contemplating Retirement Village Life* which I recommend to you. It has been written by people living in retirement villages and can be obtained by sending $4 to the Association – which is rebated if you join.

The most common questions on retirement

I have had thousands of meetings with retirees and here are the most common questions I am asked.

Lump sum or pension?

The question of whether your employer offers you a lump sum or pension is an extremely important issue and you need to be very careful how you handle it. Unfortunately, too often, investment advisers recommend going for the lump sum for the simple reason that they often make no money if you go for the pension option.

The first step is to analyse your employer's pension scheme. Take a close look at how much it is and whether it is indexed to inflation. Be sure you understand what happens if you die. Is the pension *reversionary*, meaning, does 100% or more commonly, 66%, go to your spouse for their lifetime? Equally, consider what happens if both you and your spouse die or are killed in an accident. Does your estate receive any benefit?

Looking back over the last decade, it seems to me (with hindsight) that many Australians would have been better off with a pension from their employer. With a pension you are usually guaranteed a fixed payment and when paid to public servants, they are effectively government guaranteed.

There can be however some pretty good reasons *not* to take a pension which could include:

- The pension offered is very low, given the lump sum alternative.
- The pension is not linked to inflation.
- It isn't reversionary to your spouse if you die.
- You need a lump sum for a specific (and sensible) purpose.

- You want to be in full control of your own investments.
- Your life expectancy, and that of your spouse is very low.

Most private enterprise schemes, only offer a lump sum at retirement, but believe me, if offered, I'd be very tempted by a guaranteed monthly payment, linked to inflation and reversionary to my spouse. This would provide investment certainty, no hassles and a regular income. I like the sound of that, so don't throw the pension option away too quickly if you have it. And remember, a good 'each-way' bet may be to take a part pension and part lump sum.

Should you buy your own pension?

When your employer only offers you a lump sum you can then buy your own pension if you like. The main options are an annuity or an allocated pension.

Annuities

Annuities are offered by a life insurance company. They come in various types and the best known is probably a lifetime annuity which will pay you a fixed monthly amount depending upon how much money you have and the current interest rates. Interest rates were very high in 1990 and it was a great time to buy a lifetime annuity, conversely 1994 was a very poor year as they were at a cyclical low.

The old lifetime annuity was very unpopular – if you died you got nothing, on the other hand if you lived to 100 you 'won'. Modern annuities are more flexible with 'term certain' annuities where you nominate a minimum payment period say, 10 years. If you died for instance, after one year, your estate would receive payments for the next nine years.

You can also get annuities with payments linked to inflation and with a wide array of options. This flexibility is making annuities more attractive to retirees. A key tip with buying your own annuity is to shop around as rates vary from one life insurance company to another.

Allocated pensions

Due to their greater flexibility, the most popular privately purchased pension has been the allocated pension. Their appeal is
that you can rollover your Eligible Termination Payment (usually
your super money) into an allocated pension and pay no lump
sum tax. Once in the allocated pension, no tax is paid on investment earnings.

You have to take a minimum pension and there is also a
maximum pension. This is calculated by a formula that looks at
the size of your investment in the allocated pension and your life
expectancy. If for instance, you had $100,000 accumulated after
1 July 1983 and were 65, your minimum pension would be
around $5,500 and your maximum would be just under $11,000.

The big advantage of an allocated pension is that not only can
you nominate which investments you want (what percentage of
shares, property and so on), you can also take out a lump sum if
you wish (and pay the normal lump sum tax rates). On the
pension you draw, there is also a 15% tax rebate. This means
that you could be taking a pension of around $18,000 and pay
no tax if this was your only source of income.

It all sounds pretty good, but an allocated pension is not always
the best option. It all depends upon the size of your Eligible Termination Payment, its components, your age, personal situation,
other assets and your tax planning.

Please remember that unlike an employer pension or a lifetime
annuity, your allocated pension can run out of money. If you
draw a higher pension than the earning rate of your investments
over many years, naturally you'll use up your capital. In addition,
because you can make the investment decisions with an allocated
pension if you so choose, poor decisions can also lose you capital.

Should you sell the house?

It's human nature to think the grass is greener elsewhere but only
a few of my clients have successfully and happily moved to
another suburb or more distant location. The key tip here is to
rent where you would you like to live before you sell your home
and rebuy elsewhere. Often the 'lifestyle' advantages of moving

to the beach simply don't happen – or they are overshadowed by living too far from friends and family.

Depending on how emotionally tied you are to the family home, the option of selling and buying something smaller, even in the same area is quite valid. For a number of my clients this has meant a lower maintenance property, but importantly it has also freed up a sizeable amount of money which can provide a better lifestyle.

Do you rollover your money?

Believe me, I have plenty of sympathy with people who tell me that the superannuation rules are too hard, that the system keeps on changing and they want their money out of it. But there are definite benefits of rolling over your Eligible Termination Payment and staying in the super system:

- By rolling over (and remaining rolled over) you pay no lump sum tax on your ETP.
- If you do choose to take your money out of the system, lump sum tax is much lower if you take your money out after age 55. At least consider leaving your money rolled over until then.
- Inside a rollover fund, you will pay a maximum rate of tax of only 15% on investment earnings. In an annuity or allocated pension you will pay no tax on investment earnings.
- Compared to investing in your own name a *maximum* rate of tax of 15% is very attractive to most Australians.

These are the most common reasons for rolling over, however, due to your personal circumstances (involving things like excess benefits) you may actually be better off taking the money out of the superannuation environment. Whatever you do, seek good advice and be sure to weigh up the facts before committing yourself.

How do you invest a large amount?

Apart from a property sale or possibly an inheritance, for many Australians retirement is the first time that they have a large amount of cash to invest – and it can be pretty scary. With retirement money you get no second chances, so you must invest wisely.

I strongly suggest that you go over my 'Ten Keys to Successful Investing' in Chapter Eleven. Following these can't guarantee you success, but they will certainly put you on the right track.

Above all, please remember it's your money. Your future depends upon it, so I really want you to put in the time and effort to invest the money in a way that best suits you. This means doing your planning, budgeting and having a serious think about your attitude to risk. In the long run, the amount of investment risk you take will determine your return.

How should you manage your money?

Unfortunately, we all age and relatively simple money and investment decisions can get harder as we get older. It isn't a sensible option to pretend it won't happen to us so, basically, we have three choices:

- Increasingly pass responsibility over to your spouse, trusted family member or professional adviser.
- Consider purchasing a pension or annuity type product which pays you a regular income.
- Simplify your portfolio by holding a smaller number of investments or use balanced funds provided by professional managers.

Managing your own portfolio in retirement can be fun and providing you are happy to monitor your investments closely and keep detailed records, 'doing it yourself' can work. Just make sure you avoid the temptation to take a punt on speculative shares or property investments. Believe me, full-time investment professionals know that punters lose more often than they win. Set a long-term strategy and have the discipline to stick with it.

Most of you, though, are not budding professional investment managers and will want or need professional help in structuring and managing your investments. Investment alone is complex enough, but add to this tax issues such as capital gains, franked dividends, lump sum tax, excess benefits and so on and it all gets pretty tricky.

While the majority of retirees will seek professional help, it's still really important that you understand the broad strategy, the level of risk and potential long-term returns from the portfolio suggested to you by your adviser.

The choice of money management is very personal, but from my experience as an adviser I find that having a simplified investment portfolio monitored by a competent adviser who has a good client reporting system is usually the best approach in the later part of your life.

What does a typical retiree do?

As you can imagine, different people do different things with their money. Some put it all in the bank, some buy property. My most valuable tip here is to diversify and spread your risk. We all like to think we know the 'best' investment, but why take unnecessary risk with retirement money?

A typical diversified retirement portfolio for a 65-year-old couple who own their own home could look something like this:

Cash	15%
Bonds and Fixed Interest	40%
Property securities	10%
Australian shares	25%
International shares	10%
	100%

Now, your investments are a very personal thing. I know retired clients who have 100% of their money in a Commonwealth Bank account and I also know retirees who keep 80% of their money in shares.

It all depends on how much risk you can sleep with at night, but do remember, the lower the risk you take, the lower your long-term returns.

Why not put your money in the bank?

Well, the advantage of this strategy is that providing you put it all in a strong bank, your chance of losing capital is just about as close as you can get to zero. Unfortunately though, your long-term financial prospects look pretty bleak. Let's say that you can earn 6% on your cash and that you pay a 20% average rate of tax. Let's also assume that inflation averages 4%.

In this example, the 6% you earn is 4.8% after tax. In other words, you are generating an after tax return of 0.8% above inflation. Now, even if you could live off the 4.8% and not touch your capital, inflation still eats away at it.

To illustrate the effects of inflation, let's assume you have $100,000 in the bank and inflation is 4% p.a. Let's look at your nest egg's buying power every year over 20 years:

The buying power of $100,000 over 20 years after 4% inflation

Year	Buying power
1996	100,000
1997	96,000
1998	92,160
1999	88,473
2000	84,934
2001	81,537
2002	78,275
2003	75,144
2004	72,138
2005	69,253
2006	66,483
2007	63,823
2008	61,270
2009	58,820
2010	56,467
2011	54,208
2012	52,040
2013	49,958
2014	47,960
2015	46,041

More depressing than this relentless erosion is the thought that even the interest income you earn each year from your bank deposit buys you increasingly less.

Making Money

This is the main argument for investing in growth assets such as property and shares. Not only will your money grow in value over the long term, but so will the income you receive. Unlike interest returns, both rent and share dividends grow over time.

Sure, property and shares are more risky than cash but funnily enough, over 20 years, cash is a poor investment despite its low risk. Its buying power is ruined by tax and, in particular, inflation.

How much should you leave to the kids?

One of the things that we tend to do very poorly is estate planning. It frustrates me to see so many Australians with a valuable home and other assets living on a very restricted income due to a desire to pass on all the money to the kids.

Your attitude to this issue should be one of your first areas of thought and discussion. Let me put this in perspective. If a couple, both aged 65, own a home and have $300,000 to invest, they can basically set three broad objectives for their money:

- Objective 1. To preserve their capital and to pass it all to their children in today's dollars. (That is, to increase the $300,000 by inflation each year.)
- Objective 2. To preserve their capital and pass $300,000 on to their children without increasing it with inflation.
- Objective 3. To plan to spend all of it by the time they are 90. At that stage they will still own a home and will receive an age pension. At age 90, they doubt that they'll need too much money for gallivanting around the country!

Now, how does this affect our imaginary couple? Well, this is how much they could spend each year after tax under each scenario.

Objective 1	$11,000 per year
Objective 2	$16,250 per year
Objective 3	$19,000 per year*

* These figures assume long-term investment in a conservative balanced portfolio appropriate to a retired couple. The portfolio would be comprised of cash, fixed interest investments, property securities and shares and is assumed to be generating 4% income and 4% growth p.a. Inflation is also assumed to be 4% p.a.

Now, I could top these annual income figures up with an old age part pension, but to keep it simple, let's just focus on the principle of investment and using your capital. Do note, however, that under Objective 3 our couple would get the highest pension over the years, as their capital would be the first to fall under the assets test applied by the Department of Social Security.

The message here is simple. I don't see how most of us can live our lives to the full, have fun along the way and enjoy our family and friends if we aim for Objective 1, or for many of us, Objective 2. You just need to have so much money to do it.

Don't get me wrong, I'm not trying to encourage you to leave your children with nothing. For most of us, after decades of raising our children, we quite sensibly want to give them the best financial advantages we can. What I am saying is that unless you have significant wealth it is difficult to have a decent standard of living and preserve all of the assets that you have built up over a lifetime of work for the children. This is a time when a family conference would be a great idea.

CHAPTER EIGHTEEN

Bankruptcy and Wills

There are many possibilities in life and very few certainties. On a less than cheerful note, one possibility is that you could go broke and one certainty is that you will die. Hopefully you will get through life without experiencing the first but no one can escape the second. At least you may be able to reduce the trauma by being better informed in the case of bankruptcy and by having your estate in order when you die.

Bankruptcy

Bankruptcy is a legal status that can follow on from being insolvent meaning not being able to meet your debts. It is covered under Commonwealth law by the Bankruptcy Act so the provisions are the same in all states.

Bankruptcy is a legal status that applies only to individuals. Companies or businesses don't go bankrupt but rather become 'insolvent' and are put into 'receivership' where a 'receiver' is brought in to take total control of the company's financial affairs.

Now, if you get into real trouble with your debts and bankruptcy is looming on the horizon, there are some basic steps to take which could head it off.

Inform your creditors

The first thing to do is to seek help from an accountant or a consumer advice bureau as soon as you realise you're in trouble. Then, discuss your financial situation with your creditors. This is absolutely critical and ideally should be done before you miss a repayment, because nothing gets a creditor offside so thoroughly.

By revealing your financial problems sooner rather than later, you may be able to come to an agreement with your creditors where they accept a reduction in repayments and an extension of time to repay or, accept a temporary halt to repayments altogether while you get your finances in order. Your creditors may have no problem with 'rescheduling' your debts, particularly if the cause of your insolvency is an unusual occurrence, say, an accident temporarily keeping you off work.

Honesty and good communication are the passwords here. If you don't speak up before missing a repayment it may be too late. Don't wait for the creditors to force the issue such as the bank foreclosing on your mortgage. You will be in a much better position to pay off your debts (and stay out of bankruptcy) if *you* take the first step without delaying.

Becoming bankrupt

Now, if it's apparent there is little chance of you being able to repay the money you owe or if your creditors won't reschedule or restructure the debt in any way, you can either become bankrupt voluntarily or your creditors can petition the courts to declare you bankrupt. And to be declared bankrupt you need to be indebted for more than $1,500 (comprised of one or more debts).

No matter how it happens, once you become bankrupt, an Official Trustee in Bankruptcy takes control of your estate. From the moment the bankruptcy trustee is appointed, all claims for payment by creditors have to be made through the trustee whose responsibility it is to locate all your assets and to make an equitable distribution of them between the creditors.

The appointment of a bankruptcy trustee is designed to protect both the creditors and the bankrupt. Having a trustee take control of a bankrupt's financial affairs theoretically means that the bankrupt will not be able to conceal any saleable assets from the creditors, or that a particularly aggressive creditor will be able to get more than their fair share of the disposable assets.

To become bankrupt voluntarily involves signing a Debtor's Petition at the Office of the Registrar in Bankruptcy and presenting a full statement of your affairs nominating your assets, your debts, any summonses issued and your anticipated income for the next 12 months. Once the Registrar is satisfied your financial predicament is legitimate and your petition is accepted, you officially become bankrupt and a bankruptcy trustee is appointed. There are Registrar and trustee fees involved in this process but none to pay at this point – they are deducted once your estate is wound up – and take priority over any other debts.

Alternatively, a creditor or creditors can force you into bankruptcy. This process is quite involved and expensive:

- The creditors must firstly obtain a judgement on your debt from the Local Court.
- The creditors then apply to the Registrar in Bankruptcy who issues a Bankruptcy Notice instructing you, the debtor, to pay the debt within a specified period (generally 14 days).
- If the debt is not paid by the due date the creditors then must apply to the Federal Court to have you declared bankrupt.

At every stage in this process you have the opportunity to halt proceedings by paying the debts.

Restrictions placed on bankrupts

Once you are bankrupt there are a number of restrictions placed upon you, including:

- You can't be a director, a promoter, or a manager of a company without permission of the Federal Court.
- You aren't allowed to seek credit for more than $3,000 without informing the potential creditor of your bankrupt status.
- You are unable to hold certain types of licences. For example, you can't hold a builder's licence for 10 years after declaring bankruptcy.
- You must hand over your passport to the trustee and cannot leave Australia without the trustee's permission.

But it's not all bad news becoming bankrupt if your finances spin out of control, and this is why some people choose the path voluntarily. By becoming bankrupt:

- Creditors stop pestering you – because all claims are handled by the trustee.
- Interest ceases to be added to debts outstanding once bankruptcy is established.
- Although most property of any value is taken from you as a bankrupt, some property is protected such as household furniture, a car worth less then $3,000 and tools of trade worth up to $2,000. This even applies to goods which might have

been seized earlier by a bailiff – you may get them back.

- You are allowed to retain half of any income you earn over and above a trustee-determined threshold (which can be no less than 3.5 times the basic pension). The other half you are required to hand over to the bankruptcy trustee.
- Under bankruptcy, pensions, superannuation and benefits are usually protected from creditors.
- If you declare yourself bankrupt you can choose your own bankruptcy trustee, generally a private accountant who is registered with the Federal Court. It is probably better to deal with someone you know who is sympathetic to your problems, rather than with a Court appointed trustee who may not be.

Now, please don't let me give you the impression that being bankrupt is no big deal or a rort enabling you to welsh on your responsibilities. It is definitely not something to be casually embraced. Despite legitimately providing you with some protection against further financial ruin, bankruptcy is restrictive, it deprives you of control over your affairs, it's invasive and rightly or wrongly it carries an eyebrow-raising stigma that lingers long after the bankruptcy (which remains on your credit record for seven years) has been discharged – and that's probably its nastiest characteristic.

Discharging bankruptcy

As a bankrupt you can apply to the Federal Court at any time for your bankruptcy to be discharged. The Court will look at how much of your outstanding debts has been paid and whether the creditors are happy for the bankruptcy to be discharged. Bankruptcy is normally discharged automatically after three years but if an objection has been lodged, generally by the trustee, that can be extended to five or even eight years from the date of becoming bankrupt. Occasionally the Court will discharge a bankruptcy on the condition that payments continue to the creditors for up to a further five years.

In special circumstances bankruptcy can last indefinitely, for example where the trustee is not satisfied that all available assets have been disclosed. And, if after a bankruptcy has been discharged, the trustee discovers undisclosed assets that existed during the period of the bankruptcy, the discharged bankrupt can be declared bankrupt again.

> **0— Key thought**
> If you are in financial difficulties don't put your head in the sand – seek help from an accountant, and ask your creditors for their co-operation in your efforts to get your financial house in order. In many cases you will receive it but if you just stop making repayments and wait for them to contact you, bankruptcy may be just around the corner.

Wills

You might not have to go through bankruptcy during your lifetime, but there's no avoiding death. And while there's also no way of avoiding the anguish it causes, it's cruel to exacerbate the suffering by not leaving behind a clear, current and valid will.

Around 30% of Australians who die every year do so without leaving a valid will – a remarkable figure when you think how simple and inexpensive it is to prepare, and how much consternation is caused by dying without one.

What a will does

Simply, a will is a document stating what you want done with your possessions and property after your death. Anyone over the age of 18 is legally entitled to have a will and married people aged under 18 can have one too.

Broadly, a will should:

- provide primary directions for the distribution of your property following your death
- provide secondary directions in the event a beneficiary or beneficiaries dies before you
- nominate guardians for any children under 18 or for any other dependants

- make provision for all people who are dependent on you – such as your partner, your children and elderly relatives
- revoke previous wills
- appoint an executor, as well as an alternative one in the event the first one can't or doesn't wish to do the job, or dies before you.

Dying intestate

If you die without a valid will, known as dying 'intestate', the probate division of the Supreme Court will appoint an administrator to distribute your estate to your next of kin according to statutory priority laid down by the relevant state laws. To illustrate, let's look at the intestacy rules that apply in NSW where, if you die without a will, your estate will be divided (in descending priority), thus:

- Where there is a spouse and no children, the entire estate goes to the spouse.
- Where there is a spouse and children:
  if the estate is worth less than $150,000, the entire estate goes to the spouse
  if the estate is worth more than $150,000, (including the value of the matrimonial home), the spouse gets the first $150,000 plus all household effects, and the remainder of the estate is split 50/50 between the spouse and the children.
- Where there are children and no spouse the estate is split equally between the children.
- Where there are no children and no spouse the parents of the deceased share the estate equally.
- Following this comes other relatives. (There is a pecking order amongst them too.)
- If no relatives can be located the estate goes to the State of NSW.

Note that in all the cases above, a de facto partner has the same rights as a spouse if the relationship has been in existence for at least two years.

If a married or de facto couple die at the same time and both are intestate, the older person is deemed for probate purposes to have died first. This means that before the younger person's estate is passed on to its beneficiaries, the younger person's estate firstly becomes the recipient of its statutory share of the older person's estate.

Bearing this in mind, let's look at an example of how dying without a will can really direct your assets to the wrong recipients and be nothing short of disastrous. We'll assume a 45-year-old divorced male – with three children – is killed with his 35-year-old female de facto partner in the same car crash. We will also assume he has assets worth $250,000, that both persons are intestate, and that probate is under NSW law.

Because the male is older he is presumed to have died first and, therefore, the first $150,000 of his estate plus half of the remainder goes to her estate. This amount totals $200,000, leaving only $50,000 left for his children. Because the female is intestate her estate, including the $200,000 from his estate, will go to her next of kin which could be her children (by another partner), parents, siblings, aunt or uncle. If she has no relatives her estate will go to the government. None of these are very likely to be the recipients that he would have wished 80% of his estate to go to – particularly as he has three children of his own! The 15 minutes it would have taken him to organise a will would have prevented such a travesty.

Who needs a will?

Anyone with an estate, a spouse or partner, children, a family and a desire for some, if not all, of the estate to go a certain party or parties needs a will. And if there is no one in the family or no friend you wish to leave your estate to, you can always leave it to a charity, a foundation or an institution.

Clearly, as circumstances change, your will needs revising. If you have separated, divorced, remarried or entered into a de facto relationship you need to change your will, stating your new instructions. You may also need to change it if you have children, if any of your beneficiaries die or change their marital status, or if your executor dies.

Also be aware that divorce may automatically revoke part or all of your will. It ranges from total revocation in Tasmania (where you would die intestate if you hadn't written another one) to partial revocation in some states to no affect at all in others. This is something you need to check.

Preparing a will

You can write your own will using a do-it-yourself kit. These are available from stationers, and cost up to $15. Make sure you get one with instructions on how to fill them out and ensure you do it correctly – a badly written will may cause more grief for your beneficiaries than no will at all.

For your will to be valid there are two formal requirements you must meet, namely, it must be in writing, and it must be signed by you and by two witnesses on every page. The witnesses (and their spouses) cannot be beneficiaries.

You can also have a solicitor draw up your will, which if your affairs are simple should cost you no more than $100. What you get for this is a document that's properly worded and better able to withstand legal challenge from a party or parties who believe you may have short-changed them.

While drawing up your own will is certainly inexpensive, I recommend that you employ a solicitor to do it. This should ensure that all the legal requirements are complied with, that it is unambiguous, that it is free of technically incorrect terms, and that it is most likely to achieve the results you wish.

A solicitor can also advise you on the establishment of discretionary family trusts for certain beneficiaries, particularly for those who are especially dependent, vulnerable or hopeless with money. These trusts are not considered part of your estate and carry on independently after your death providing income to the nominated recipients. They are managed by a trustee and cannot be touched by other claimants against your estate.

The executor

In your will you need to appoint an executor, and *it's a choice you must make with care*. This is because it's the executor's job to administer your estate and to see your will is carried out as you intended. Your executor is responsible for ensuring that all legal requirements relating to the estate are properly dealt with, and that the funeral is carried out as wished. Most importantly, your executor has the final say in any dispute over the will, short of a legal challenge.

You can also give discretionary powers to your executor

enabling him or her to use their best judgement as to how parts of your estate are divided up. This saves you, for instance, having to list every single knick-knack you own and everyone you would like something to go to.

Anyone can be an executor, including a beneficiary, a solicitor or a professional trustee. So, who do you nominate? Well, clearly, given the responsibilities and powers an executor has, it's vital your executor be competent and above all, trustworthy. An executor doesn't need prior experience and certainly not legal qualifications. What they do need is integrity and a genuine desire to see your last wishes properly fulfilled. My advice is to pick someone you know well and trust implicitly, preferably your spouse or partner, a close family member or friend. The person you nominate as executor doesn't have to accept the position, so it's best to ask first. You can also specify a fee in your will for executorial efforts if you wish.

In the event there is no one you consider suitable to be your executor you can nominate a professional to do the job, either a private trustee or the Public Trustee. A professional trustee will help you prepare your will for little or no charge, but in return for administering your estate will take a percentage of its worth following your death.

Trustee's fees are usually determined on a sliding scale, normally beginning at around 4% on the first $100,000 of the estate. This can be expensive, particularly if you are leaving a large estate, but where trustees are of most benefit is when the estate is complicated and involves the long-term administration of a trust fund for your beneficiaries. Professional trustees are also very useful if there are some sharks amongst the beneficiaries.

⚬━ Key thought

Death is never easy for those left behind. Don't make it any harder on them by not having a valid, well-considered will. It's such a simple, inexpensive document to prepare and it's such a simple way to ensure your estate goes to the people you want it to. And if you don't have a will, you owe it to your family to get right on to it, today!

Two things you should know about estate planning

1. **Power of Attorney.** When doing your estate planning, I strongly advise you to think about having a power of attorney. This gives someone you trust the ability to act on your behalf. Now, a power of attorney can be a dangerous thing but the kind I recommend can only be used by the person or persons you nominate if you are incapacitated by an accident or illness. Remember, if you can't sign, your assets can't even be used to help you. Sure, your relatives could get a court order but having a specific power of attorney is worth discussing with your solicitor.

2. **Testamentary Trusts.** Ask your lawyer about a testamentary trust. If something happens to you, this type of trust can mean that your children will receive income from your assets and earn up to the normal adult tax free threshold of $5,400 each. This could make a huge difference to your family so it's worth checking!

CHAPTER NINETEEN

Choosing an Adviser

A question I am often asked is 'How do I find an honest adviser who will work for me, and not for themselves?' Sadly, the investment and insurance industry has built up a reputation as being full of shonks flogging product to people for commission. The problem with this is that commission varies dramatically from product to product and if your adviser is paid on this basis, there is always an uncertainty about whether the product he recommends is based on the fact that it is the best product for you – or pays the most commission to him.

Let's look at an older style life insurance company savings plan for example. After five years, it's likely to have a cash value of less than your total contributions. These plans usually take 10 years just to get back what you have put in, let alone getting in front. If the plan called for a $10 per week contribution, and instead you put that $10 per week into your mortgage you'd be much better off.

So, why didn't the adviser recommend this course of action? The answer is painfully simple. By putting $10 a week into your mortgage the adviser earns nothing. By selling you a long-term savings plan, the adviser would have made around $500. In this instance, the way the adviser is paid makes it very hard for him to give you the advice that's best for you.

So, what's the solution? Well, your money is really important to you, and a good adviser can really help but you have to be tough and up front with your concerns and questions.

My advice, if you need an adviser, is to do the obvious things. Ask family, friends and work colleagues for a referral. Keep an eye on the money sections of newspapers and see who the journalists talk to. Get a 'Registry of Financial Planners' from the Financial Planning Association by ringing 1800 337 301.

Once you have a name, make an initial appointment. At the meeting, I want you to ask the following questions:
■ How long have you been giving advice ?

This is most important. You can't beat experience. Also remember to ask how long they have been working for their current employer. You don't want someone who switches jobs every few years!

- What are your qualifications?
A degree in economics or business is a good start, but especially keep your eye out for ASIA (Associate of the Securities Institute of Australia) or DFP (Diploma of Financial Planning). The best advisers are likely to have the letters CFP (Certified Financial Planner) after their name.

- Tell me about your company? Do you own part of it and who are the shareholders?
You need to know how long the company has been around and its background. I am always a keen student of who the company directors are – a solid group of directors makes me more comfortable. Also, if your adviser owns all or part of the company they are not likely to leave too quickly.

- What type of client do you specialise in?
Some advisers tend to deal with smaller clients, others with larger clients. If you are not the type of client the adviser wants, you won't get looked after well.

- What resources does your company have in terms of investment research?
Investment is complicated. Your adviser will need technical support so find out how strong this support is.

- Do you give independent advice?
The company may be owned by a big institution but still give independent advice, meaning they don't flog only their own products.

- How do you charge?
I prefer 'fee for advice' advisers, meaning they charge you for their time and either don't take commission or brokerage, or give it back to you. If they do charge commission, make sure that they disclose this to you and the amount they get.

- Do you hold a licence?
To give broad investment advice the adviser will need to hold an authority to operate under his or her company's licence. Have a look at the authority and also the company licence. You are looking for restrictions on the type of advice they can give. For example, many companies cannot give advice on direct

share investments. While this should not be a major drama, you should know about it.

- Do I get my advice in writing?

  If you don't, leave straight away! Getting your advice in writing is essential because this will help to protect you if things go wrong.

- Describe your ongoing service. What does it cost?

  You'll need ongoing advice. Find out how the adviser does this. I'd be very concerned if it's free. Free ongoing advice is usually worth what you pay for it – absolutely nothing!

- Are you a member of the Financial Planning Association (FPA)?

  In my admittedly biased opinion (I am a member and was its President in 1993-4), the FPA is the premier body for financial planners. Its Code of Ethics, Commission Disclosure Rules and Disputes Resolution system help to protect you.

Now, I know it's a pain asking these questions, but you must. Invest 20 minutes in getting satisfactory answers and while I can't promise that everything will be perfect, at least you'll be on the right track.

Also, while you are talking to the adviser, please be aware of the environment. Is it a professional workplace? Files lying everywhere always worry me. Does it feel efficient and comfortable? Were you greeted by the receptionist in an appropriate fashion? Did your adviser take phone calls during your meeting, or race out to get a cup of coffee – these are bad signs.

Also, be fair to the adviser; at the end of the meeting ask, 'Am I the sort of client you want? Please be honest about this or I'm sure we'll both be disappointed.' No point starting this important professional relationship if it does not suit both of you.

To finish on a positive note, there are now many good advisers, but in the final analysis, your money is your responsibility. Treat it seriously.

Conclusion

There are more than 100,000 words in this book, and in writing this conclusion, I've been thinking about which are the most important in terms of helping you be financially successful. And, you know, I reckon the important stuff – the things that really make a difference – are pretty much commonsense.

If all you remember are the following words, I think you'll do well.

- Think about what you want your life to be like. Set yourself simple, achievable financial goals in the short-, medium- and long-term. Plan to consistently spend less than you earn and to put these savings into buying and paying off your home and building superannuation. Once your home is paid off, put your normal mortgage repayments into investments such as shares and property.
- Always remember that risk equals return and never make an investment without really understanding it. Avoid 'get rich' schemes. Plan to minimise your tax, but stay away from tax schemes of dubious merit. Think about your retirement plans early in your life, and when you do retire, plan to make the most of your money. Remember, your estate planning will impact on the life you lead in retirement.
- Above all, never forget that your money is no good to you if you forget to enjoy it. Money is important, but health, family and friends are more important. Money only provides choice about how you lead your life.

Money preoccupies much of our lives, and I'd love to see every Australian with a plan to become *financially* independent. No, we won't all get there, but those with a plan will have a much better chance. I hope this book helps you to build that plan and puts you firmly on the road to financial security, independence and wealth.

Index